Eva Gore-Booth: An image of such politics

Eva Gore-Booth: An image of such politics

Sonja Tiernan

Manchester University Press
Manchester and New York
Distributed in the United States exclusively by Palgrave Macmillan

Published by Manchester University Press
Oxford Road, Manchester M13 9NR, UK
and Room 400, 175 Fifth Avenue, New York, NY 10010, USA
www.manchesteruniversitypress.co.uk

Distributed in the United States exclusively by
Palgrave Macmillan, 175 Fifth Avenue, New York,
NY 10010, USA

Distributed in Canada exclusively by
UBC Press, University of British Columbia, 2029 West Mall,
Vancouver, BC, Canada V6T 1Z2

British Library Cataloguing-in-Publication Data
A catalogue record for this book is available from the British Library

Library of Congress Cataloging-in-Publication Data applied for

ISBN 978 0 7190 82313 hardback
ISBN 978 0 7190 82320 paperback

First published 2012

Typeset
by Action Publishing Technology Ltd, Gloucester
Printed in Great Britain
by TJ International Ltd, Padstow

'Now is the day of the daughters of Eirinn passed and gone,
Forgotten are their great deeds, and their fame has faded away'

Eva Gore-Booth

For Suzie Coogan

Contents

List of illustrations

Images 1, 2, and 3 reproduced by permission of Sligo County Library. Images 4, 5 and 6 reproduced by permission of Manchester Archives and Local Studies, Central Library. Images 7, 9, 13, 14 and 15 reproduced from the Lissadell Papers by permission of Sir Josslyn Gore-Booth. Images 8 and 16 reproduced with permission from the Lissadell Collection. Image 10 reproduced with the permission of Rare Books and Manuscripts, Special Collections Library, the Pennsylvania State University Libraries. Images 11 and 12 reproduced by courtesy of the National Library of Ireland, Dublin.

Cover image, portrait of Eva Gore-Booth by her sister, Constance (later Countess Markievicz), oil on canvas, 38 x 30.5cm. Reproduced by kind permission from the Lissadell Collection.

Preface

On 1 August 2010 Leonard Cohen walked on to a stage on the grounds of a magnificent rural estate in County Sligo and recited these lines from one of Ireland's greatest poets: 'the light of evening Lissadell, great windows open to the south, two girls in silk kimonos, both beautiful, one a gazelle.'[1] The quotation was instantly recognisable and applauded by the thousands in the audience. It is of course the opening line from W.B. Yeats' much celebrated poem, 'In Memory of Eva Gore-Booth and Constance Markiewicz [sic].' The venue for the concert was Lissadell Estate, once the ancestral home of Eva and her older sister Constance. Yeats wrote it on learning of the death of Constance in 1927, one year after Eva herself had died.[2]

More than eighty years after her death, the name of Eva Gore-Booth is still known. Some people recall her purely because of Yeats' poem, others as the younger sister of Constance, the Irish nationalist icon, Countess Markievicz. Gore-Booth's name may be familiar but details of her life and achievements have, until now, remained obscure. This book is the first dedicated biography of Eva Gore-Booth, a woman of considerable brilliance and outstanding fortitude. The following pages contain a chronological account of a politically and socially radical Irish woman who possessed vision and passion for her country and fellow citizens.

The story of her revolutionary life shows a person devoted to the ideal of a free and independent Ireland and a woman with a deep sense of how class and gender equality can transform lives and legislation. Her campaigns to achieve fundamental change in these areas were often at odds with the ideals of mainstream organisations and were almost always ahead of public opinion. In some cases her behaviour was deemed to be 'unlawful' by authorities but this only served to make her more determined.

Historian Maria Luddy suggests that 'biography always fascinates in its attempt to reveal individuals navigating the often turbulent waters of life.'[3] This is certainly true of the life of Eva Gore-Booth as she attempted to change attitudes concerning such contentious issues as landlord–tenant relations, trade unions and gender equality, the Great War, the Easter Rising, military conscription, radical sexual reform and the new age religion of theosophy. Gore-Booth was unique, an Irish woman of Ascendancy class who rejected her privileged heritage to live, socialise and work amongst the industrial classes in Manchester. Throughout her many and varied political activities, Gore-Booth published volumes of poetry, philosophical prose and plays, becoming a respected and prolific author of her time.

This biography is based on a vast body of original documents belonging to Gore-Booth, much of which has been used here for the first time. Her papers are scattered throughout numerous archives, personal collections and university libraries across Ireland, England, Scotland and the United States. It has been a long and arduous task to discover the whereabouts of these manuscripts. However, it has been possible to construct a detailed life history of Eva Gore-Booth from these various sources, which include her personal and literary manuscripts, the papers of political and trade organisations, the archives of publishers and manuscript collections of her colleagues and friends. This material has been contextualised with readings of her literature and political writings, as well as newspaper reports tracing key events and activities in her life. This research has taken place over a number of years, across many miles and has been a delightful and worthwhile journey.

Sonja Tiernan
Keough-Naughton Institute for Irish Studies
University of Notre Dame
April 2011

Notes

1 W.B. Yeats, 'In Memory of Eva Gore-Booth and Con Markiewicz [sic],' in *The Winding Stair and Other Poems* (London: Macmillan & Co, 1933), p. 197. The original version is held in the National Library of Ireland, Dublin, (hereafter NLI) Yeats Papers, MS 30,149.

2 Constance Markievicz died in August 1927 and Yeats began working on the poem in November 1927 when he was in Seville. Alexander Norman Jeffares, *A New Commentary on the Poems of W.B. Yeats* (Stanford: Stanford University Press, 1984), p. 268.

3 Maria Luddy, *Hanna Sheehy Skeffington* (Dublin: Historical Association of Ireland, 1995), p. 6.

Acknowledgements

Writing a book is certainly a solitary task, but throughout the long process of researching the life of Eva Gore-Booth many people gave me invaluable support, information and advice. I owe a great deal of thanks to Maryann Valiulis for inviting me to conduct my post-doctoral research at Trinity College Dublin. To Christopher Fox, and the staff at the Keough-Naughton Institute for Irish Studies, University of Notre Dame, for providing such a warm and inspirational environment to finalise writing this book. To Mary McAuliffe, Bríona Nic Dhiarmada, Maria Luddy, Sally Munt and Ruán O'Donnell for reading various drafts of this work and providing advice and insightful comments which helped shape the final version.

I am indebted to various agencies for much needed financial support enabling me to dedicate myself to this research and to travel throughout Ireland, England and the United States for archival research. I am especially grateful to the Irish Research Council for the Humanities and Social Sciences for the award of a two-year Government of Ireland Post-Doctoral Fellowship, to the Royal Irish Academy for funding a research trip to Manchester and to the National Endowment for the Humanities for a generous one-year fellowship to complete this research.

Throughout the period of this research I was contacted by many local historians and interested parties who made me aware of unknown facts and invaluable primary source material. I owe thanks to Brendan Nelson for information on the history of the Sligo Feis Ceoil, Felix Larkin for alerting me to the exhibition of John Lavery's paintings, Richard Haworth for giving me access to his grandmother's collection of letters and Derek Clarke for his enquiries into the present whereabouts of the Eva Gore-Booth memorial window. Also I am grateful to Michael Herbert for introducing me to the Working Class Movement Library, for also generously providing access to materials in his personal collection and for organising a public talk in Manchester on Eva Gore-Booth.

I consulted many archives throughout the course of this research and I am most grateful to Sandra Stelts of Pennsylvania State University Libraries, Donal Tinney at Sligo County Library, Jane Parr and Kevin Bolton of Manchester Archives and Local Studies Central Library, Honora Faul, Keith Murphy and Sandra McDermott of the National Library of Ireland, James Peters at the University of Manchester Archives, John Hodgson at the John Rylands University Library, Darren Treadwell of the People's History Museum Archives, Pamela Cassidy of the Lissadell Estate and Kate Willson at the Parliamentary Archives in the Houses of Parliament. Many thanks also to Josslyn Gore-Booth for permission to publish from the Lissadell Papers, at the Public Records Office Northern Ireland.

Also heartfelt thanks to my many friends and family for their unwavering support and encouragement throughout this entire writing process. To my parents Chris and Marie Tiernan and my grandmother, Mollie Harmon, thank you for your constant love and support.

Abbreviations

Æ	George Russell
AFIL	All-for-Ireland League
ASL	Anti-Sweating League
CE	*Poems of Eva Gore-Booth: Complete Edition*
CMS	Church Missionary Society
CO	Conscientious Objector
EGB	Eva Gore-Booth
EGR	Esther Gertrude Roper
GPO	General Post Office, Dublin
IACC	Irish Anti-Conscription Committee
ICA	Irish Citizen Army
ILP	Independent Labour Party
IPP	Irish Parliamentary Party
IRA	Irish Republican Army
IRB	Irish Republican Brotherhood
ITGWU	Irish Transport and General Workers' Union
IV	Irish Volunteers
IWSLGA	Irish Women's Suffrage and Local Government Association
IWWU	Irish Women's Workers' Union
LCWTOWRC	Lancashire and Cheshire Women Textile & Other Workers' Representation Committee
LPF	League of Peace and Freedom
LRC	Labour Representation Committee
MG	*Manchester Guardian*
MNSWS	Manchester National Society for Women's Suffrage
NCF	No Conscription Fellowship
NESWS	North of England Society for Women's Suffrage

NIPWSS	National Industrial and Professional Women's Suffrage Society
NLI	National Library of Ireland
NUWSS	National Union of Women's Suffrage Societies
PRONI	Public Records Office of Northern Ireland
RIC	Royal Irish Constabulary
SPR	Society for Psychical Research
TS	Theosophical Society
UVF	Ulster Volunteer Force
WFL	Women's Freedom League
WILPF	Women's International League for Peace and Freedom
WSPU	Women's Social and Political Union
WTLC	Manchester and Salford Women's Trade and Labour Council
WTUC	Women's Trade Union Council
WTUL	Women's Trade Union League
YMCA	Young Men's Christian Association

Introducing the Gore-Booth family

'My soul did not grow
Out of my mother's heart'[1]

Eva Gore-Booth despised her aristocratic heritage. Even as a child she was embarrassed by her family's wealth and their privileged status as members of Ireland's Ascendancy class. When she reached adulthood, Eva dramatically rejected her family and her social position. Although estranged from her aristocratic background, her heritage was still to shape her personal, political and literary endeavours throughout her life. A brief introduction to the Gore-Booth family background, tracing the reality behind how they achieved their land and titles, explains why Eva was so troubled by her family history.

The turbulent nature of Ireland is embodied in the story of the Gore-Booths. The origin of the family in Ireland can be traced to Paul Gore, a prosperous soldier during the reign of Elizabeth I. Gore came to Ireland in 1599. Four years later, he was chosen to escort the defeated Irish chieftains Donough O'Connor and Rory O'Donnell to their place of surrender. Having successfully delivered the chieftains to Athlone, Gore was granted lands in the north-west of Ireland by James I, who had recently ascended to the throne of England. Loyal to the Crown in 1608, he followed James' orders to occupy Tory Island, then controlled by Irish forces. His plan was a sinister one. He orchestrated a quarrel amongst the two main Irish forces on the island and when the battle was over, Gore slaughtered the victors. In recognition of his loyal service to the Crown, Gore was created a baronet in 1622. He resided in Ireland and built the castle of Ardtermon on the shore of Drumcliff Bay in Sligo, just two miles from where Lissadell House now stands.

The current Gore-Booth family is directly descended from Paul Gore's fourth son, Francis. According to *The Books of Survey and Distribution*, when Francis succeeded to his father's estate, he held just over 4,000 acres of land in Ireland.[2] Through well chosen marriages and astute business decisions, the family went on to acquire considerably more land, another 28,000 acres, over the course of the next two centuries. Francis was granted lands in Sligo, Kilkenny and Mayo by Charles II after the Restoration. He became Knight of Ardtermon and an MP for Sligo in 1661. Francis was the first member of the family to reside in the Lissadell area of Sligo. After he died in 1678, his son Robert succeeded to the family estate.

Robert's son, Nathaniel Gore, married Lettice, the only child and heiress of Humphrey Booth of Dublin. It is through this marriage alliance that the family name Gore-Booth came to be adopted. Their first son, Booth, built the original house at Lissadell and was created baronet in 1760, becoming Sir Booth Gore, first baronet of Lissadell. His younger brother, John Gore, inherited Humphrey Booth's estate, which included extensive lands in Manchester and Salford.[3] In his will, Humphrey Booth bequeathed land and money to the Church of the Sacred Trinity in Salford.[4] The will also made provisions for the relief of the poor in the area.[5] The Humphrey Booth charity is active in the Salford area to this day.[6] Interestingly, Eva would dedicate herself to social reform in this same area of Manchester, at the turn of the twentieth century.

In order to show gratitude for his inheritance from Humphrey Booth's estate, John Gore adopted the additional surname of Booth. John died in 1789 and, as he was childless, the Manchester and Salford estates passed on to his nephew, Sir Booth Gore, second baronet of Lissadell. The second baronet also died childless in 1804 and the now large estate passed to his brother, Captain Robert Newcomen Gore. Robert had lived at Lissadell and managed the Sligo estate for some years previously. He was the first member of the family to officially take up the Booth name and coat of arms. Robert received special permission signed by George III to assume the additional name and arms of Booth and thus represent both families.[7]

By the time that Robert, third baronet, inherited Lissadell, he was in his sixties. Mindful of the lack of male heirs in the Gore-Booth line, he married Hannah Irwin almost immediately. She was in her twenties and was from Streamstown in County Sligo. This alliance successfully produced an heir to Lissadell and increased the size of the Gore-Booth estate more than ninety years later. The Streamstown estate came into the possession of the Gore-Booth family when Hannah's nephew, Burton Irwin, died childless in 1898.[8] Robert and Hannah, Gore-Booth had two sons, Robert and Henry, and one daughter, Anne.

Sir Robert died when his children were still young. His eldest son, also named Robert, inherited the Lissadell estate in 1814, at the age of nine. During his minority Robert, fourth baronet (grandfather of Eva), was educated at Westminster School before proceeding to Queen's College, Cambridge where he obtained an MA degree. A land agent was appointed to manage the Lissadell estate during this time. In November 1823, Robert appointed a Mr Dowdell as his agent to manage Lissadell. Dowdell's statement to the Government Commission on the condition of the poorer classes in Ireland provides an insight into the deplorable condition of the Lissadell estate before Robert took over its management:

> Nothing could exceed the miserable appearance of the tenantry, living, for the most part, in wretched small cabins, clustered together without deserving the name villages, and generally occupying the best part of the land in common. Their agriculture was of the worst kind; the men were mostly employed in making illicit whisky, and the women in scolding and quarrelling with each other, and the roads to their houses was almost impassable.[9]

The estate was suffering financial problems. The rent-roll was £33,000 per annum but the rental arrears amounted to £16,000.

When Robert Gore-Booth reached the age of twenty-one in 1826, he succeeded to the estate. Four months later he married Caroline King, daughter of the first Viscount Lorton. Robert's sister, Anne, married into the same family; she married Caroline's brother, Robert King, later second Viscount Lorton and later still sixth Earl of Kingston. Robert Gore-Booth's first marriage increased the family's wealth considerably with a marriage portion of £10,000. Caroline died in 1829 along with her newborn child shortly after giving birth. Robert married again the following year to Caroline Susan Goold, Eva's grandmother, and received a relatively smaller marriage portion of £2,000.[10] Soon after the couple married, Robert employed the services of the renowned architect Francis Goodwin, to build Lissadell House. Goodwin had recently received acclaim for his design of the Grecian revival style town hall in Manchester, constructed on King Street between 1822–25. Sir Robert visited the town hall during his travels to Manchester on business. Lissadell House mirrors the Greek revival style of the building in Manchester (see Figure 1).

Lissadell House was built in front of the old eighteenth-century Gore-Booth residence. The origin of the place name Lissadell or 'Lissadill,' is a corruption of the Gaelic 'Lios an Daill,' which Eva later translated as 'fort of the blind man.'[11] The location provided an idyllic setting for what would be Eva's childhood home. The countryside around Lissadell House had a deep impact on Eva's imagination and imbued in her a love of Celtic mythology. Josslyn Gore-Booth, ninth baronet of Lissadell, described the house as sitting 'on a gentle slope to the south giving a beautiful view over the Bay of Knocknaree and the . . . Bronze Age monument or burial ground of Maeve, the Queen of Connaught in the first century A.D. on the summit of Knocknarea.'[12] The dramatic landscape of Lissadell, reflecting the ancient history and myth linked with the local area, had a profound and lasting influence on Eva and her siblings.

The people of Sligo benefited financially from the fact that, unlike many landlords of his generation, Sir Robert lived on his Irish estate. Historian Gerard Moran observes that 'a considerable portion of his rents, not only from Sligo but also from Lancashire, were spent locally.'[13] Lissadell employed local household and estate staff as well as keeping accounts with shopkeepers and producers in the vicinity. The vast majority of landlords of larger Irish estates lived in England; the money earned from their Irish rents was generally spent in London and in other large English cities. The fact that Sir Robert lived on the Lissadell estate also ensured that he was better acquainted with the circumstances and the needs of his tenants.

Sir Robert quickly began to prove himself as a resourceful and innovative landlord. In addition to building an impressive family home, he actively engaged in a grand plan to re-structure and improve his estate. He realised that in order to improve both the living standards of his tenants and the profitability of his estate, it was crucial to dismantle the then current system of rundale. Through the old Gaelic arrangement of rundale, many people divided one plot of land. Sir Robert set about clearing land and consolidating small farms. Re-structuring, however, left many tenants destitute. In 1834, he offered his displaced tenants financial assistance to emigrate to North America. Sir Robert was accused of

1 Lissadell House, County Sligo, ancestral home of the Gore-Booth family

abusing his power in this respect. In evidence given to the Devon Commission, an inquiry into the occupation of land in Ireland, he was accused of evicting tenants because they would not vote for his nominee in the 1838 general election. It was claimed that a number of tenants were forcibly evicted from his land, given £2 and sent to North America because they voted for an opposing candidate.[14] Sir Robert vehemently denied this, claiming that the tenants in question agreed to leave as part of his land consolidation plans.

As a reforming landlord, Sir Robert was concerned at his tenants' total dependence on one subsistence crop, the potato. He viewed this dependency as a path to impending disaster. By 1845 his worst fear was realised. Potato blight swept across the country resulting in the Great Irish Famine. Local Sligo historian, John McTernan, notes that the county of Sligo was one of the last areas to be affected by the blight. McTernan pinpoints the first recording of potato blight in Sligo on 10 October 1845. Problems with crops were seen near the town and, 'potatoes which appeared sound when digging, rotted shortly afterwards.'[15] By April 1846 tenant farmers in the Sligo area were experiencing harsh conditions. A large group of local labourers descended upon the Board of Guardians' meeting begging for assistance.[16] By November 1846 the Sligo workhouse was full to capacity.[17] The British authorities had done little to relieve the situation believing that it was a local problem and should be dealt with by landowners.

The Great Irish Famine was a tragedy of mammoth proportion. It is estimated that from 1845 to 1849 over one million people died of hunger and disease and a further one and a half million people left Ireland seeking refuge in America, Canada and England. The British government's stance remains contentious. Some landlords, mainly absentee ones, acted in merciless ways, contributing to the distress of their starving tenants. In contrast others, including Sir Robert, were compassionate and actively engaged in projects to alleviate suffering in their locality. Through examination of the Lissadell estate records, Gerard Moran asserts that Sir Robert assisted the people of north Sligo in four ways, 'as a member of Sligo board of guardians, as chairman of the Sligo grand jury, as chairman of four local relief committees, and through the private relief measures he initiated around his properties.'[18]

The fact that the Lissadell estate remained solvent after the Great Famine, while many other properties went into bankruptcy and were sold off in the Encumbered Estates Court, leads some historians to believe that Sir Robert acted in his own interests. In fact Sir Robert relied heavily on rental income and the sale of lands in Manchester and Salford to finance his philanthropic deeds. It is evident that Sir Robert concentrated all of the family's capital in the Sligo area.

After the worst of the famine was over, Sir Robert was urged to enter political life. In 1850 John Ffolliott resigned his Sligo county seat at Parliament due to ill health. The *Sligo Champion* newspaper advocated for Sir Robert to stand for election. The editorial remarked:

> He is a resident landed proprietor; he spends a large portion of his income at home; the tradesman, the artisan, and the shopkeeper are benefited by him; and he is a politician of moderate views ... he has done much good during the years of famine ... He did not desert his post, but stood by the people ... his kindness to the poor, in the hour of difficulty will not be forgotten, if the hour should come to make it known.[19]

Encouraged by such public demonstrations of support Sir Robert stood for election. In his election address on 7 February he vowed to improve the local Sligo economy, observing 'that this country has been very much overlooked by the government relatively [sic] to many improvements, railway communications, and that of the harbour of Sligo.'[20]

Sir Robert was elected unopposed on 12 March 1850 and he purchased a London residence, 7 Buckingham Gate, for parliamentary sessions. When the House of Commons was in session the Gore-Booth family, accompanied by a large household staff from Lissadell, moved to London. They stayed in a house situated in the shadow of Buckingham Palace. Sir Robert entered parliament during a time of dramatic political change. Months after he was elected the Irish Franchise Act 1850 was introduced enabling tenants with land holdings valued at above £12 to vote. The act ensured that many middle-class Catholic tenants were eligible to vote, increasing the electorate in the Sligo area from 45,000 to over 132,000.

In the following election of 1852 Sir Robert was faced with stiff opposition from Liberal, Catholic and nationalist candidates. He topped the polls and held his seat comfortably.[21] Despite Sir Robert's overwhelming victory, it would be unwise to imagine that this indicated his popularity among the general population of Sligo.

Many tenants on the Lissadell estate may have felt compelled to vote for him since the secret ballot had not yet been introduced.[22] Indeed, myths demonising his emigration schemes abounded at this time. One account maintains that Sir Robert had forcibly evicted starving tenants from his land and boarded them onto a rotten ship, the *Pomona*, bound for Canada. The tale concludes that the *Pomona* sank in clear sight of Lissadell and all passengers onboard drowned. Such rumours would become too much of a burden for Eva and her siblings to carry.

Robert did continue to represent county Sligo as a Member of Parliament (MP) until his death in 1876. However, his record of contribution to parliamentary debate is relatively undistinguished as he rarely attended House of Commons sessions. Robert was more active in his local Sligo area where he acted as Lord Lieutenant, Governor of Sligo and Leitrim Hospital for the Insane, Governor of Sligo County Infirmary and he was a board member of superintendence for Sligo County Prison.

In 1861 Sir Robert's eldest son and heir, also called Robert, was involved in a tragedy on Drumcliff Bay.[23] Robert, accompanied by his younger brother, Henry, had set sail on 29 October. When they encountered harsh weather Robert was thrown overboard and drowned. Henry, Eva's father, was saved with some difficulty. Following the death of his father's land agent in 1866, Henry, now his father's heir, took over management of the vast 32,000 acre Lissadell estate. The next year, Henry married Georgina Mary, daughter of Lady Frances Charlotte Hill and John Hill, Colonel of Hussars, from Tickhill Castle, Yorkshire. Shortly after his marriage Henry travelled through Europe on a grand tour before settling at Lissadell with his new wife. Georgina and Henry had five children, Constance, Josslyn, Eva, Mabel and Mordaunt.

Notes

1 Eva Gore-Booth, 'Heredity,' in Esther Roper (ed.), *Poems of Eva Gore-Booth: Complete Edition* (London: Longmans Green & Co, 1929), p. 294. (Hereafter referred to as EGB, *CE*).

2 Public Records Office of Northern Ireland, Belfast (hereafter referred to as PRONI), Annesley Papers, MIC 532/1–13, *Books of Survey & Distribution*, 1670.

3 Title deeds, Manchester and Salford estates, 1698–1960s, Sir Josslyn Gore-Booth's Manchester solicitors, with inventory.

4 Lancashire Record Office, WCW1635, will of Humphrey Booth (the elder) proved at Chester, 17 October 1635.
5 Public Record Office, Kew, Booth 2/2/2/2, will of Humphrey Booth (the younger) proved at the Prerogative Court of Canterbury, 1676.
6 Booth Charity registered number A0798. The Booth Charities Archive is held in Chetham Library, Manchester.
7 PRONI, D4131/D/2/1, grant of arms to Robert Newcomen Gore-Booth, 1805.
8 PRONI, D4131/A/7, will of Burton Irwin, 9 June 1884.
9 *Royal Commission for Inquiring into the Condition of the Poorer Classes in Ireland: third report* (London: His Majesties Stationery Office, 1836), Appendix (C) Part II, p. 37.
10 PRONI, D4131/A/3, marriage settlement of Robert Gore-Booth and Caroline Susan Goold, 1 April 1830.
11 EGB provides a translation of the name in a footnote to her poem 'Lis-An-Doill,' in EGB, *CE*, p. 243. According to folklore the blind man was a thirteenth-century poet, Muireadhach Albanach Ó'Dálaigh, who prospered in Scotland. The place name is referenced as Lissadill on the Ordnance Survey Map for the area dated 1837.
12 PRONI, D4131/D/2, letter from Josslyn Gore-Booth, 24 June 1994.
13 Gerard Moran, *Sir Robert Gore Booth and his Landed Estate in County Sligo, 1814–1876* (Dublin: Four Courts Press, 2006), p. 13.
14 *Devon Commission*, pt ii, p. 222, q. 17–18, as cited in Moran, *Sir Robert Gore Booth*, p. 19.
15 John C. McTernan, *Olde Sligoe: Aspects of Town and Country Over 750 Years* (Sligo, 1997), p. 311.
16 *Mayo Telegraph* (6 May 1846), cited in Moran, *Sir Robert Gore Booth*, p. 21.
17 NLI, catalogue 926–30, minute books for Sligo workhouse.
18 Moran, *Sir Robert Gore Booth*, p. 23.
19 *Sligo Champion* (9 Feb 1850).
20 PRONI, D4131/Q/1, unnamed and undated newspaper cutting.
21 PRONI, D4131/Q/1, unnamed newspaper cutting, 31 July 1852.
22 The secret ballot was introduced in 1872.
23 PRONI, 'Introduction Lissadell Papers,' p. 17.

1

Life in the big house: childhood and Lissadell

'Time flows on through streams of monotonous orderly years, but it seems as if every now and then an Angel troubles the waters'[1]

At eight o'clock on the evening of Sunday 22 May 1870, Eva Selena Laura Gore-Booth was born in Lissadell House, County Sligo. The third child of Henry and Georgina Gore-Booth, she was the first of their children to be born at Lissadell. Eva's sister, Constance, and her brother, Josslyn, were born at their grandfather's London residence, Buckingham Gate. Three generations of the Gore-Booth family then occupied Lissadell House. These were Eva's paternal grandfather, Robert, fourth baronet; her maternal grandmother, Lady Frances Hill; her parents, Henry and Georgina; her paternal aunt, Augusta; her siblings, Constance then two years old and Josslyn who had just turned one. The mansion was also home to a large household staff including a butler, a housekeeper, a nurse, footmen, stable hands, grooms, house stewards, housemaids and cooks.[2]

At first glance Gore-Booth's early years appear idyllic. She was surrounded by her extended family and lived a life of opulence and privilege. However, Gore-Booth was born at a time of great political unrest in Ireland. The affluent position enjoyed by Anglo-Irish landowning families was facing real challenges. In the aftermath of the Famine the family was also slowly losing the respect of the local community as a general feeling of contempt for the powerful position occupied by landowners took grip in Sligo. As an active participant in the Anglo-Irish power structure, Eva's father, Henry, was assigned the role of High Sheriff in 1871. He also served as Justice of the Peace and Deputy Lieutenant for Sligo County. From 1873, Henry resumed his travels, often leaving his wife and young children behind at Lissadell. He became an avid Arctic explorer at a time when the North Pole was relatively uncharted. Henry's journeys were often hazardous and there was little hope of rescue should he encounter problems. He wrote about his travels and later published some of his accounts. An article by him entitled 'the basking shark' appeared in *Longman's Magazine* in 1891.[3] This may well have been the impetus which later inspired Eva to submit writings to that same magazine a few years later.[4]

Georgina did not despair at her husband's long absences. She engaged herself with industrious and worthwhile activities. Recognising that women on the Lissadell estate possessed no money of their own and had little or no training or education, she established a school of needlework during the 1870s. Georgina ran the school in one of the offices on the estate and she taught women to crochet, white embroider and darn-thread work.[5] The completed work was sold at reasonable prices, providing the women with an independent income, usually a weekly wage of eighteen shillings. This income was crucial at a time of great poverty and deprivation in the Sligo area. Moreover the skills learnt by the women helped them to secure good posts in America if they chose to emigrate.

The work of the Lissadell School was highly commended in the *Pall Mall Gazette*. The newspaper recognised Georgina's endeavour as a cottage industry which would contribute towards the 'regeneration of Ireland.'[6] This endeavour provided Eva with a positive example of economic reform through training. Her mother's work in helping to achieve financial independence for women would be echoed and indeed replicated in Eva's later trade union campaigns.

When Eva was four years of age, Mabel, her younger sister was born. By this time, her paternal grandfather, Sir Robert, had become ill and was troubled with severe gout. His illness was, no doubt, compounded by a growing concern for his own political and privileged position. Appalled by the lack of action taken by the authorities during the famine, advocacy groups were now emerging all over Ireland. Campaigns for tenant rights, home rule and the disestablishment of the church began in earnest. Although Sir Robert was charitable towards his tenants during the famine, he failed to show any compromise when his status was threatened. As a Member of Parliament for the Sligo area, Sir Robert held an obligation to represent the political interests of all of his constituents. However, he rarely attended the House of Commons and when he did he clearly favoured the interests of landowners and supported Protestant rights, against the rights of the majority Catholic population.

Sir Robert's health appeared to improve during 1876 but days before Christmas of that year, he died suddenly in Lissadell House at seven o'clock in the evening.[7] The unexpected death shocked the family but worse was still to come. While the family were coming to terms with Sir Robert's death, Eva's cousin, Isabella Gore-Booth, was found dead in her bedroom. Isabella was the daughter of Sir Robert's wayward brother, Henry, and was visiting from Scotland. In his memoirs Sir Robert's butler, Thomas Kilgallon, , sadly recounts watching Isabella saying goodnight to Sir Robert as she retired to her room. By Christmas Eve both Robert and Isabella were dead.[8]

These two sudden deaths must surely have traumatised the family. On St Stephen's Day, Eva joined her family in a grim procession of two coffins from Lissadell House to the family vault in the local churchyard of St John's. The weather was a bitter mix of hurricane, rain and sleet.[9] The funeral was reported as the largest in Sligo for many years. The cortege stretched for two miles behind the hearses. Isabella's hearse was adorned with white plumes; her sister and brother, who had also been staying at Lissadell, walked behind. The tenants from Sir Robert's estate followed the chief mourners on horseback, creating an imposing sight. The announcement of Sir Robert's death in the *Sligo Champion* best describes the contradictory way in which he was viewed by the local community. The obituary testifies that, 'in every position in life Sir Robert displayed the highest principles of integrity and humanity. Although he was conservative in his politics and strongly attached to the religion he belonged to, he never allowed his religion or his politics to interfere in his dealings with his tenantry.'[10]

Eva's father, Henry, now succeeded to the estate and the baronetcy. Just over one year later in 1878, the last of Henry and Georgina's children, Mordaunt, was born at Lissadell (see Figure 2 for a photograph of the five Gore-Booth children).

Eva spent most of her time with her maternal grandmother, who instilled in her a love of poetry and an interest in religion. She was deeply affected when Lady Hill died at Lissadell in 1879. Within months of her death, famine revisited Ireland and during the winter of 1879–80 the Sligo area again suffered badly. Sir Henry, as he was now, helped re-constitute the Carney and Drumcliffe Relief

2 Mordaunt, Eva, Josslyn, Mabel and Constance Gore-Booth, with their governess on the grounds of Lissadell estate

Committees.[11] Mindful of the devastation caused by the Great Famine, the Gore-Booths at once opened their food store and supplied maize to any tenant in need. The food was provided free and the entire family, including the nine year old Eva, became involved with the distribution. Through this act of kindness the local community once again warmed to the Gore-Booth family. Years later a former secretary of the Relief Committee in Sligo wrote to an Irish newspaper recounting the importance of Sir Henry's food donations during this time of hardship. He describes how Henry gave out food 'to the starving poor, free to all, at his own cost.'[12] This sense of responsibility had a deep impact on the Gore-Booth children who were old enough to witness and understand the famine. Eva, her sister Constance, and her brother Josslyn, all later exhibited an awareness of responsibility to others less fortunate than themselves.

During this time of famine Michael Davitt launched the Irish National Land League, with the manifesto 'the land of Ireland belongs to the people of Ireland.' The organisation defended tenant rights and aggressively campaigned against evictions. The young MP Charles Stewart Parnell was elected as president and the league launched a series of mass meetings across the west of Ireland. On 2 November 1879, leading members of the Land League including, Davitt, James Daly and James Boyce Killeen addressed a crowd of over 8,000 people on Gore-Booth land, at Gurteen in County Sligo. Davitt warned local tenants 'of impending famine and dire misfortune before us.'[13] With the enormity of the famine of 1845–50 in mind, he implored people 'to look first to the necessities of your children, of your wives, and of your homes; look to the wants and necessities of the coming winter; and when you have satisfied those wants and necessities, if you have a charitable disposition to meet the wants of the landlord, give him what you can spare, and give him no more.'[14] Davitt, Daly and Killeen were arrested under a charge of using seditious language and imprisoned in Sligo. The trial lasted a week and generated enormous public interest and the men received huge local support. The case was eventually dropped and the three men were released without charge.

The campaign for rent reform influenced Eva's father, Sir Henry. Within five years of succeeding to the estate, he had reduced his tenants' rents to the level of Griffith's valuation. Based on the Tenement Act of 1842 all properties across Ireland were subject to a valuation for local taxation purposes. The Commissioner of Valuation, Richard Griffith, devised the valuation based on the productive capacity of land and the potential rent of buildings. The results of the valuation were published between 1848 and 1864.[15] For the first time in Ireland there was a national guide to the appropriate rents which tenant farmers should pay. Davitt campaigned for rents to be charged at the rate of the valuation. Sir Henry reduced his tenants' rents accordingly, without any legal obligation to do so. If tenants' experienced difficult conditions Sir Henry reduced the rent further, well under the level of Griffith's valuation. In December 1881 he gave an extra reduction of 3 shillings in the pound.[16] This aspect alone identifies him as a caring landlord. Many reports describe Henry as well-liked and compassionate, an article in the *London Times* testifies that, 'few owners or agents have such intimate knowledge of their tenantry, their holdings or their necessities. The people have been wont to come to Sir Henry as their adviser and friend, as their arbiter in family feuds and as their depository for wills and marriage settlements.'[17]

As the famine subsided Eva, Constance and Josslyn became actively involved with the annual Harvest Home Festival, established by their grandfather. Harvest Home was a celebration for all the tenants and employees of the Lissadell estate and it became a monumental event. A report in the *Sligo Independent* illustrates the occasion with delight. 'About 300 tenant and workers would sit down to a traditional dinner of beef, mutton and plum pudding, with Sir Henry and Lady Gore-Booth and other members of the family and their friends acting as helpers and "paying every attention to their guests."'[18]

Conditions in Sligo began to improve in the spring of 1880 and life at Lissadell slowly returned to normal. During a social occasion at the home of Miss Jane L'Estrange, Lady Georgina was introduced to the young artist Sarah Purser.[19] Purser had recently returned from studying art in Paris and had just completed a portrait of Miss L'Estrange. Lady Georgina was so impressed with the painting that she commissioned Purser to paint a portrait of her two eldest daughters. Within weeks Purser arranged to paint Eva, then ten years of age, and Constance, who was twelve. In the portrait Eva is seated on the ground in a wood on the Lissadell estate admiring flowers and Constance stands behind her looking directly out of the picture.[20] Purser had only recently taken up portraiture to earn a living. She maintained that painting the portrait of Eva and Constance was a defining moment in her artistic career. Purser famously described how after completing the Gore-Booth commission, demand for her paintings soared and she 'went through the aristocracy like the measles. Then I attacked the English, and to this day you will find vestiges of the outbreak on the walls of the stately homes.'[21] Purser almost certainly had an impact on the two young Gore-Booth girls, who undoubtedly viewed this young independent woman as an exciting role model. Eva and Constance both established a friendship with Purser which was to last throughout their adult lives.

Unlike the male members of the family, Eva Gore-Booth was not sent away for schooling. She was educated at home by a governess. In 1882 a Cambridge graduate, Miss Noel, was employed at Lissadell and grounded Eva in the classics, both Latin and Greek, as well as Italian. Eva and Constance became particularly close to their governess, whom they nicknamed Squidge. Years later Noel fondly recalled Eva as:

> A very fair, fragile-looking child, most unselfish and gentle with the general look of a Burne-Jones or Botticelli angel. As she was two years younger than Constance, and always so delicate, she had been, I think,

> rather in the background and a little lonely mentally, but music was a great joy to her. The symbolic side of religion had just then a great charm for her, and always of course the mystical side of everything appealed most.[22]

In addition to their education, the Gore-Booth children enjoyed outdoor activities typical of their class, including riding and hunting. Both Eva and Constance excelled at these pursuits, earning reputations in the Sligo area as expert horsewomen. Their younger brother, Mordaunt, described his sisters taking him on 'wild expeditions in a pony-cart with ramshackle harness, tearing over rough and stony ground at a speed that would cause the hair of an ordinary quiet person to rise, but neither of them were ever perturbed, and the ponies seemed to enjoy the joke.'[23]

In her teenage years, Eva enjoyed roaming the local countryside on horseback and became taken by her surrounding nature. On their frequent horse rides, Constance and Eva stopped at cabins to speak with the local tenant farmers. During these visits Eva became enthralled with tales of Celtic legends and the history of Sligo. She thrived on folklore, in particular folk tales which recounted stories and legends of the High Queen of Connacht, Maeve, reputably buried on the cairn of Knocknaree Mountain not far from Lissadell House. Eva spent much of her time at Lissadell writing poetry and reading the classics. Her older sister showed a flair for sketching and painting, often illustrating Eva's work with watercolour paintings or line drawings, a collaboration which was to continue for years to come.

Eva was particularly aware of the plight of others less fortunate than herself. A family story of her childhood recounts how, when she was very young, she was discovered by the side of the road taking off her coat to give to another child.[24] She became particularly conscious of the oppression of the indigenous Irish at the hands of Anglo-Irish landowners. She visited inmates of the Sligo Infirmary, where her grandfather had been on the Board of Governors. An account of one such visit was reported by Dutch journalist Kees van Hoek in the *Irish Independent*. Van Hoek records that Eva 'asked an old inmate at the infirmary for the recollections of her youth. As the ugly story began to unfold itself, the nun signalled frantically for her to stop. But Eva insisted on hearing it all. "I like to realise what we have to make good," she said simply.'[25]

Gore-Booth appears to have been troubled by the fact that so

3 Eva and Constance Gore-Booth

many people in the Sligo area suffered from acute poverty during the 1880s, while she benefited from a life of great affluence. In stark contrast to the lives of local Sligo girls, Eva and Constance were presented at the Court of Queen Victoria in the monarch jubilee year of 1887 (Figure 3 shows a portrait photograph of the two sisters around this time).[26] As was the custom, the two girls spent the season in London each year. Constance relished the social gatherings and became a popular new Irish beauty. Eva did not care much for these formal occasions. She did take advantage of the opportunity to meet writers and artists. She attended concerts and the theatre as often as possible while in London. Eva became very ill in August of the next year when she contracted scarlet fever.[27]

Eva recovered her health but the Gore-Booth family was particularly blighted by premature deaths during the 1800s. They appear to have dealt with these tragedies through a strong belief in the spiritual afterlife. During the 1860s spiritualism and the occult were becoming fashionable among the elite set in London who thrilled at attending séances and table rapping events. The premature deaths of his wife and son had led Eva's grandfather to investigate spiritualism, possibly in the hope of contacting those who had died. While staying at Buckingham Gate, Sir Robert employed the services of one of the most infamous spiritualists in England, Daniel Dunglas Home. Home had an exclusive following including Elizabeth Barrett Browning, Mark Twain, Tolstoy, and the Empress Eugenie. Home organised numerous séances at Sir Robert's residence. These psychic events were later published as *Experiences in Spiritualism with D.D. Home*.[28]

When the Gore-Booth family returned home to Lissadell House they continued holding séances. Samuel Waters, a member of the Royal Irish Constabulary (RIC) at Grange, attended many of the séances for fun but soon realised that 'things occurred which were very difficult to explain.'[29] The Gore-Booth family did not organise psychic events as mere entertainment. When Sir Robert's cousin, Captain King, was murdered in Sligo during a contentious election in 1868, Sir Robert held a séance to discover who shot him.[30] Through documented accounts and popular gossip, the Gore-Booth family became publicly associated with spiritualism in the mid-nineteenth century.[31]

Sir Robert's engagement with séances and supernatural phenomena was shared by the next generation. Eva's parents were particularly open to ideas of the spirit world and the occult. Sir

Henry and Lady Georgina were friends with Frederic Myers, a founder member of the Society for Psychical Research (SPR), which had been established in 1882. Myers became one of the earliest members of the Theosophical Society, which perhaps influenced Eva to formally join the society in later life. In 1889, Lady Georgina reported to Myers that her son, Mordaunt, had a psychic encounter in the kitchen of Lissadell House. The event was recorded and published in the proceedings of the SPR and in several newspapers. Reports reached as far as New Orleans and Pittsburg.[32] Myers documented a full account of the psychic encounter in his book *Human Personality and its Survival of Bodily Death.*[33] Myers interviewed Eva's mother and her younger brother and sister, Mordaunt and Mabel, noting that the psychic encounter 'though coming from a young boy, is clear and good, and the incident itself is thoroughly characteristic.'

On 10 April 1889 as Mordaunt and Mabel were walking downstairs to the kitchen in Lissadell House, Mordaunt reportedly saw John Blaney, a hall-boy at Lissadell. He told Mabel that John appeared quite ill, 'he looked yellow; his eyes looked hollow, and he had a green apron on.'[34] In Mabel's interview she recounts, 'when I asked my maid how long John Blaney had been back in the house? She seemed much surprised, and said, "Didn't you hear, miss, that he died this morning?" On inquiry we found he had died about two hours before my brother saw him.'[35] Myers investigated the claim and confirmed from the Ballingal presbytery records that John Blaney from Dunfore was interred on the 12 April 1889, having died on 10 April.

Living in an environment receptive to occult beliefs, Eva became preoccupied by spiritualism and believed she developed a psychic ability. She records details of these abilities in a short autobiographical piece entitled 'the inner life of a child.' Among her many claims, she believes that the spirit of her dead grandmother visits her night after night. She records her experiments with telepathy, noting that she could summon her nurse through a psychic connection. 'If she fixed her mind on the old nurse upstairs in the nursery and cried out with her will and her imagination, she could almost always draw her downstairs to see her.'[36] In the text Eva claims that she often dreamt of a death before it happened, such as a prediction of the demise of her nurse the day before the woman passed away. Many historians and literary critics have credited Eva's interest in the occult to the influence of Yeats. However, it is now clear that Eva's roots in spiritualism first stemmed from her family.[37]

Eva and Constance enjoyed a close sisterly bond. When Constance suddenly left Ireland in 1893, Eva's life dramatically changed. Constance had become bored with the pursuits of the landed gentry and seasons spent in London attending formal balls. Much to the disapproval of her parents she enrolled in the Slade School of Art in London. It was while she was there that Constance first met Yeats, who was by then a respected author.[38] After pursuing her studies in London, Constance moved to Paris and furthered her studies at the Académie Julian under the guidance of Rodolphe Julian from 1898. The Académie, a private art academy, was established by Julian in 1868 as an alternative to the official École des Beaux-Arts. The Académie Julian admitted women on an equal status with men and thus Constance mixed with an elite and progressive group of artists in Paris. She was no doubt encouraged to attend because Sarah Purser had also studied there. Constance immersed herself in artistic life and 'in the spirit of the age, she wore a ring declaring herself married to art.'[39]

The year after her sister moved to London, Eva joined her father on his travels around North America and the West Indies. She diligently kept diaries in 1894, recording the extent of their travels – Jamaica, Barbados, Cuba, Florida, New Orleans, St Louis, San Francisco, Vancouver, Toronto, Niagara, Montréal and Quebec. Their arrival was often announced in the social pages of local newspapers.[40] Although Eva was intrigued to learn about faraway places, her diary displays a certain amount of boredom with these trips. She records on 19 March 'I meant to write in this diary but find nothing ever happens to write about.'[41] Many of her entries detail an aversion to sea travel noting, 'stormy – rather sea sick,' and declaring 'we rocked in a fog in close contact with iceberg.'[42] It is telling that the remainder of her diary for 1894 is filled with drawings of leaves, palm trees, flowers and descriptions of the common vegetation of different regions. It is evident from her writings, that nature was of more interest to Gore-Booth than the hotels she and her father stayed at or the many social events which they attended.

On her return to Ireland Eva encountered Yeats for the first time. The writer was visiting his maternal uncle, George Pollexfen, who lived at Thornhill in Sligo. During his six month stay in Sligo Yeats was a guest at Lissadell House on at least two occasions. He stayed at Lissadell for a number of days in November and spent his time regaling the Gore-Booth family with tales of Irish fairy lore and

Celtic mythology. Sir Henry invited him to deliver a talk to the local parishioners, which Yeats describes as a 'novel experience,' lecturing on 'Fairy lore chiefly to an audience of Orangemen.'[43] Gore-Booth was fascinated by Yeats and in turn he recognised her potential as an author, writing to his sister Lily, 'Miss Eva Gore Booth shows some promise as a writer of verse. Her work is very formless yet but it is full of telling little phrases.'[44] In private Yeats admitted to having deeper feelings for Gore-Booth; he considered proposing marriage. Recording in his memoirs that she 'whose delicate, gazelle-like beauty reflected a mind ... subtle and distinguished. Eva was for a couple of happy weeks my close friend, and I told her of my unhappiness in love; indeed so close at once that I nearly said to her, as William Blake said to Catherine Boucher, "You pity me, there[fore] I love you." "But no," I thought, "this house would never accept so penniless a suitor," and besides I was still in love with that other.'[45]

Yeats and Eva were not destined to become romantically involved but they did form a lasting friendship. Yeats, sensing her promise as a writer, decided to mentor her work. Early in 1895 he confided in Olivia Shakespeare that Eva 'has some literary talent, & much literary ambition & has met no literary people ... I am always ransacking Ireland for people to set writing at Irish things. She does not know that she is the last victim – but it is deep in some books of Irish legends I sent her – & might take fire.'[46] Under the influence of Yeats as well as her own sense of the myths and legends of the local countryside, Eva began to write poetry firmly imbued with Celtic imagery.

Around this time Eva's older brother, Josslyn, returned to Lissadell. After his education at Eton, he had spent two years living on ranches in America and Canada, learning about livestock management and agronomy. During this time abroad Josslyn became interested in co-operative farming. On his return to Ireland he befriended fellow Anglo-Irish landowner, Horace Plunkett. The co-operative movement was emerging in Ireland under the promotion of Plunkett, who began his efforts in the Irish dairy industry. Plunkett persuaded individual farmers to contribute a set amount of capital to establish a creamery. The farmers would then agree to supply all of their milk to this creamery and in return receive a share of the profits. The plan was simple but the results would create an economic revolution by giving small, vulnerable farmers, financial power. However, it was not easy to convince tenant farmers to trust an Anglo-Irish landowner or to implement the discipline required from members. Plunkett launched a propaganda campaign adopting the slogan 'Better Farming, Better Business, Better Living.'

In April 1894 Plunkett formed the Irish Agricultural Organisation Society, with Josslyn Gore-Booth becoming a leading force. In the history of the co-operative movement the secretary, R.A. Anderson, declares that Lissadell House became their headquarters.[47] With his father's help, Josslyn established the Drumcliff Creamery Co-operative Agricultural and Dairy Society in 1895. Josslyn's mother laid the foundation stone for the new building. Josslyn went on to launch two more co-operatives in the Sligo area, one at Ballinphull and another at Ballintrillick. The *Sligo Champion* reported that, 'it is gratifying to find a gentleman so young as Mr. Josslyn Gore-Booth, so vigorously exerting himself to elevate and improve the condition of the Industrial Classes.'[48]

By the end of 1895 there were a total of sixty-seven creameries and co-operative societies around the twenty-six counties in the south of Ireland. The sales of butter from the creameries amounted to a staggering £185,000 for that year. The Drumcliffe co-operative was one of the most successful in the country. The *Freeman's Journal* gloried in the success of the society, describing how farming in Drumcliffe had been transformed by the co-operative, 'not only through its medium do the farmers receive the highest market price for their milk, but they also obtained last spring seeds and manures on much better terms than from the houses in the trade.'[49] In October 1896, the people of Drumcliffe showed their appreciation and made an official presentation of a gold hunting watch to Josslyn.

Before Josslyn's involvement with Plunkett's programme for economic revival, Eva had not engaged in political activities.[50] She enjoyed the benefits of her privileged heritage and spent her days travelling, reading the classics and writing poetry, which she had not yet attempted to publish. It appears that her brother's actions sparked a new awareness in her. She and Constance posed for a photograph to promote the Drumcliffe Creamery. The co-operative movement also acknowledged the importance of Celtic cultural revival to the economic development of Ireland. Along with Father Finlay, Plunkett established the *Irish Homestead* journal in 1895 as the organ of the co-operative movement; Gore-Booth submitted her poetry.[51] The paper had offices in South Frederick Street in Dublin and was published weekly until 1923. P.J. Matthews describes the *Irish Homestead* as a 'remarkable publication, it was not uncommon to see a poem by Yeats or a short story by James Joyce published side by side with an article on bee-keeping or how to treat cattle with scour.'[52] Gore-Booth maintained her support of the *Homestead* for many years. When her friend and fellow poet George Russell (Æ) became the editor of the journal in 1905, he regularly included favourable reviews of her literature. Eva and Josslyn shared an interest in the economic advancement of Ireland and the belief that the cultural development of the country was vital to its financial success.

Eva's mother was also particularly appreciative of Irish culture and heritage and encouraged Eva's endeavours. By this time Lady Georgina was an avid supporter of the Sligo Musical Society which originally formed in 1876. When the first Feis Ceoil festival was established in Dublin in 1897, choirs from Sligo entered the competition with great success. Sligo's achievements at the Dublin festival inspired a local group to form their own Sligo Feis Ceoil in 1903.[53] Lady Georgina became a founder member and she was later nominated President for life of the organisation.[54] Records of the Sligo Feis Ceoil AGM in 1914 describe the active role Lady Georgina adopted.[55] She continued to fulfil her duties as president of the Feis and took an active role in the organisation until her death.[56]

The year after Josslyn established the Drumcliff Creamery Co-operative, Gore-Booth extended her travels to Europe. This time she travelled with her mother, Constance and a friend, Rachel Mansfield. In July 1896 the group visited Germany and the Bavarian town of Bayreuth for the Wagner Festival, attending performances of *The Ring of the Nibelung*, *Parsifal*, *Tannhäuser* and *Die Meistersingers*. She later toured the galleries of Italy viewing works of the great Italian artists. While she was in Venice she became ill. According to her governess, Eva suffered with respiratory disorders from a young age. She was advised by doctors to recuperate in a warm climate. Her family sent her to stay with the writer George MacDonald and his wife in their villa in Bordighera in Italy. MacDonald was a Scottish writer and pastor in Arundel, West Sussex from 1850 to 1853.[57] He suffered from delicate health all of his life, as did his daughter. MacDonald and his wife took their daughter to Italy in 1877 to help her recuperate from illness. His daughter never recovered and she died that same year in Bordighera. MacDonald found the Italian climate beneficial to his own health and for this reason he and his wife spent most of their time between 1881 and 1902 in Bordighera. He and his friends built a house, Casa Coraggio (House of Courage), which offered a place of respite for any person in need.

There are no records as to why Gore-Booth stayed at Casa Coraggio. It is most likely that she or her family learnt about MacDonald's villa whilst travelling in Italy. Josslyn Gore-Booth speculates that 'there was some ecclesiastical connection with George MacDonald' and the Gore-Booth rector in Manchester.[58] Certainly Bordighera was an ideal location for an Anglo-Irish woman to convalesce from illness. During the second half of the nineteenth century the number of visitors staying in Bordighera far outnumbered the local population. The gentry flocked into the area after publication of *Doctor Antonia, a Tale of Italy* by John Ruffini.[59] The novel published in 1885 caught the imagination of the British aristocracy seeking a winter sojourn in a warm climate with an exuberant setting. The seaside town in Italy is situated near the border of France and comprises a medieval area with a fishing port surrounded by lavish palm trees and orchards. The area was considered so picturesque that Claude Monet resided in the area for a time in 1884 and painted *Villa in Bordighera*.[60]

Notes

1 Pennsylvania State University Libraries, Eva Gore-Booth Collection, Box 1: Folder 16, AX/B40/RBM/00139, manuscript of 'The Inner Life of a Child,' p. 1. This autobiographical text was published posthumously by Esther Roper in EGB, *CE*, pp. 51–61. All references here are taken from the original manuscript.

2 PRONI, D4131/D/2/1, Kilgallon diaries.

3 H.W. Gore-Booth, 'The Basking Shark,' *Longman's Magazine*, 19:109 (November 1891), 59.

4 EGB, 'To May,' *Longman's Magazine*, 26: 154 (August 1895), 380–3.

5 The women produced Donegal hand-spun tweeds, hand-knitted pullovers, cuffs and collars. In 1895 the work of the Lissadell School of Needlework was officially recognised and received a grant from the Congested Districts Board. PRONI, D4131/C/11/29, papers relating to Lissadell School of Needlework, 1909.

6 'The Regeneration of Ireland,' *Pall Mall Gazette* (30 December 1896), p. 3.

7 *Irish Times and Daily Advertiser* (23 December 1876), p. 5.

8 PRONI, D4131/D/2/1, Kilgallon diaries.
9 The description of the funeral is taken from: *Irish Times and Daily Advertiser* (28 December 1876), p. 3.
10 *Sligo Champion* (29 December 1876).
11 PRONI, D4131/H/8, minute books of Lissadell, Carney and Drumcliff famine relief committees, 1847 and 1880–81.
12 EGB, *CE*, p. 5.
13 'Mr. Parnell in Sligo,' *Nation* (29 November 1879), p. 4.
14 Ibid.
15 James. R. Reilly, *Richard Griffith and his Valuations of Ireland* (Baltimore: Genealogical Pub, 2000).
16 *Irish Times* (2 December 1881), p. 5.
17 PRONI, D4131/Q1, London *Times* (March 1881).
18 As cited in Dermot James, *The Gore-Booths of Lissadell* (Dublin: The Woodfield Press, 2004), p. 76.
19 John O'Grady, *The Life and Work of Sarah Purser* (Dublin: Four Courts Press, 1996).
20 Christies sold the painting for €240,000, at a public auction of the contents of Lissadell House on 25 November 2003. In 2011 the painting is on public display at The Merrion Hotel, Upper Merrion Street, Dublin 2 in Ireland. It is an oil on canvas, Size 59.8 x 41.3 in./152 x 105 cm. *Christie's Catalogue: Country House Auction* (25 November 2003).
21 Trinity College Dublin, manuscripts department, MS 10381/81–182, letters of Thomas MacGreevey, director of the National Gallery. Partly cited in Elizabeth Coxhead, *Daughters of Erin: Five Women of the Irish Renascence* (London: Secker & Warburg, 1965), p. 129.
22 EGB, *CE*, p. 6.
23 Esther Roper (ed.), *Prison Letters of Countess Markievicz* (1934: London: Virago, 1987), p. 2.
24 Ibid, p. 7.
25 'Spectator,' *Irish Independent* (8 July 1940), p. 6.
26 According to Anne Haverty only Constance was presented at Court, while Eva remained at home in Sligo. *Constance Markievicz: An Independent Life* (London: Pandora, 1988), p. 22. It seems remarkable that Lady Gore-Booth would not have presented both daughters when the opportunity arose. Esther Roper asserts that 'both Constance and Eva were presented at Court in the usual way.' Roper, (ed.), *Prison Letters*, p. 3.
27 Pennsylvania State University Libraries, Box 1, Folder 8, AX/B40/RBM/00139, an early poetry book by EGB, includes an inscription by her 'written during my illness with scarlet fever.'
28 Windham Thomas Wyndham-Quinn, *Experiences in Spiritualism with D.D. Home* (London: Ayer Publishing, 1976).
29 Stephen Ball (ed.), *A Policeman's Ireland: Recollections of Samuel Waters*,

RIC (Cork: Cork University Press, 1999), p. 36. The original manuscript memoirs of Samuel A.W. Waters are contained in PRONI, D/4051/14.

30 For details of the 1868 Sligo election riots see: Colonel Wood-Martin, *History of Sligo: County and Town* (Dublin: Hodges Figgis & Co, 1892), p. 60.

31 Home's psychic abilities became renowned through his connection with the Gore-Booth family. At a psychic event on 13 December 1868, Home apparently levitated out of a third-floor window and floated back into the room through another window. While many sceptics were pained to accept claims of levitation, this act gained credibility because it was witnessed by a distinguished group of men. The group of witnesses included Sir Robert's son-in-law, Captain Wynne, who was then stationed at the Tower of London, and Sir Robert's nephew, Lord Adare.

32 'Facts on Phantoms,' *Times Picayune* (10 September 1892), p. 2; *The Pittsburg Dispatch* (28 August 1892), p. 15.

33 The following account of Mordaunt's psychic encounter at Lissadell is taken from Frederic Myers, *Human Personality and its Survival of Bodily Death* (London & Bombay: Longmans Green & Co, 1903), pp. 742–4.

34 Ibid.

35 Ibid.

36 Pennsylvania State University Archives, 'The Inner Life of a Child,' p. 6.

37 Although accounts of the Gore-Booth séances were published, these books are out of print and have, until now, been overlooked by researchers.

38 Letter to Constance Gore-Booth accepting an invitation to visit, 21 June 1893. John Kelly and Eric Domville (eds), *The Collected Letters of W.B. Yeats: Volume One*, (Oxford: Clarendon Press, 1986), p. 357.

39 PRONI, 'Introduction Lissadell Papers,' p. 21.

40 For example it was recorded in the 'personal notes' section of the *San Francisco Chronicle* that 'Sir Henry Gore Booth and Miss Eva Gore Booth of Lissadale [sic], Ireland, are stopping at the Palace.' (21 May 1894), p. 8. Many thanks to Glenn Rosswurm for alerting the author to this newspaper article.

41 PRONI, MIC 5/590/L/I, diary of Eva Gore-Booth, 19 March 1894.

42 Ibid.

43 Letter from Yeats to Susan Mary Yeats, 16 December 1894. Kelly and Domville (eds), *Letters of W.B. Yeats: Volume One*, p. 418.

44 Letter from Yeats to Susan Mary Yeats, 23 November 1894. Kelly and Domville (eds), *Letters of W.B. Yeats: Volume One*, p. 413.

45 Denis Donoghue (ed.), *Memoirs of W.B. Yeats* (New York: Macmillan, 1972), pp. 78–9. The 'other' with who Yeats was in love is presumably Maud Gonne.

46 Letter from Yeats to Olivia Shakespeare, 12 April 1895. Kelly and Domville (eds), *Letters of W.B. Yeats: Volume One*, p. 463.

47 Robert Andrew Anderson, *With Horace Plunkett in Ireland* (London: Macmillan, 1935).
48 As cited in James, *The Gore-Booths of Lissadell*, p. 106.
49 'Address and presentation to Mr. Joselyn [sic] Gore-Booth,' *Freeman's Journal and Daily Advertiser* (22 October 1896).
50 For a further discussion on Josslyn's political influence over his sister see; Sonja Tiernan, 'Sligo Co-operative Movements (1895–1905); the Birth of an Irish Political Activist,' in Shane Alcobia-Murphy, Lindsay Milligan and Dan Wall (eds), *Founder to Shore: Cross-currents in Irish and Scottish Studies* (Aberdeen: AHRC Centre for Irish and Scottish Studies, 2010), pp. 189–96.
51 For example EGB, 'A Celtic Christmas,' *Irish Homestead* (Dublin, 1903).
52 P.J. Matthews, 'The Irish Revival: A Re-appraisal,' in P.J. Matthews (ed.), *New Voices in Irish Criticism* (Dublin: Four Courts Press, 2000), p. 17.
53 Brendan Nelson and Regina O'Dea, *Sligo Feis Ceoil: History 1903–2008* (Sligo: Sligo Feis Ceoil, 2008), p. 49.
54 'Provincial News,' *Irish Independent* (28 July 1913), p. 6.
55 Sligo Feis Ceoil AGM speech delivered by Rev. P. O'Leary, Vice President, 1914 in *The Sligo Times*, a copy of which was kindly given to the author by Brendan Nelson on 22 January 2009.
56 *Irish Independent* (17 April 1925), p. 8.
57 C. S. Lewis, *George MacDonald: An Anthology* (London: Centenary Press, 1946).
58 PRONI, MIC 590, Reel 11, L/18: 1–76, letter from Josslyn Gore-Booth to Dr Hilary Robinson, 15 July 1986.
59 A review in 1897 describes how the novel 'was soon pronounced to be one of the loveliest, purest, and most perfect novels ever written, in its own way absolutely unique: a book which fascinated and held us captive by its rare and delicate beauty.' Ursula Tannenforst, *The Unitarian*, 12 (January 1897), 345.
60 *Villa in Bordighera, Italy* by Claude Monet, oil on canvas housed at the Musée d'Orsay in Paris.

2

A pair of oddities: meeting Esther Roper

'You whose Love's melody makes glad the gloom'[1]

It was at the villa in Bordighera that Eva met a young English woman named Esther Roper. Meeting Esther was a defining moment for Eva. Their relationship, which would last until her death, sustained Eva's creative and political work throughout her life. Yet, this relationship may be one reason why Eva's name is often overlooked in social and cultural history. It is possible that Gore-Booth's erasure from history is not a simple oversight but that it is due, in part, to an inability to clearly label her relationship with Roper. Editor of Gore-Booth's plays, Frederick Lapisardi, concurs stating that, 'a life-long companionship with Esther Roper, may well be the root cause of Gore-Booth's neglect both as an important feminist and as a literary figure.'[2] In her biographical study of Gore-Booth and Roper, Gifford Lewis notes that 'in their time Esther Roper and Eva Gore-Booth were seen as a pair of oddities who did not fit any tidy categorisation within the official women's suffrage movement and have inevitably "disappeared from history" along with many other women.'[3]

When Gore-Booth is remembered, generally those who write about her feel the need to classify her relationship with Roper as that of platonic friendship and thus fail to acknowledge the ramifications of their partnership. Lewis declares in the introduction to her book that 'Eva Gore-Booth and Esther Roper never entered each other's bedrooms except in illness.'[4] Lewis is emphatic in her assertion but she provides no evidence to support this statement. By referring to the bedroom she is implying that Gore-Booth and Roper did not have a sexual relationship. Including such a statement actually draws attention to the fact that the two women may not have been heterosexual. This inclusion is all the more curious considering that many women would have shared a bedroom and indeed a bed during this era, without being considered lesbian. Acknowledging the nature of their relationship is essential in order to understand Gore-Booth's radical views of gender, which permeate through her writings and political activities.[5] Literary historian and author Emma Donoghue is dismayed with Lewis' insistence that the pair, along with 'a long list of devoted partnerships among feminists of the time,' were platonic friends.[6] Donoghue states clearly, 'where I diverge from Lewis is in her insistence that these partnerships must have been as non-sexual as they were presumed to be at the time.'[7] Irish author, Eilís Ní Dhuibhne, accepts this premise stating that Gore-Booth 'lived with Esther Roper, probably in a lesbian relationship.'[8] The story of their lives together would appear to corroborate Ní Dhuibhne's premise.

The two women met in what Lewis, perhaps unwittingly portrays as a highly romantic situation. Roper 'standing under an olive tree in the garden,' first set eyes on Gore-Booth.[9] The two women stayed in Italy for a number of months and spent their days together walking by the seaside. They talked endlessly and Roper later wrote that, 'each was attracted to the work and thoughts of the other, and we became friends and companions for life.'[10] Gore-Booth was moved to immortalise their meeting with a poem entitled 'The Travellers,' dedicated 'to E.G.R,' Esther Gertrude Roper, and published in 1904.

Was it not strange that by the tideless sea
The jar and hurry of our lives should cease?
That under olive boughs we found our peace,
And all the world's great song in Italy?

Is it not strange though Peace herself has wings
And long ago has gone her separate ways,
On through the tumult of our fretful days
From Life to Death the great song chimes and rings?

In that sad day shall then the singing fail,
Shall Life go down in silence at the end,
And in the darkness friend be lost to friend,
And all our love and dreams of no avail?

You whose Love's melody makes glad the gloom
Of a long labour and a patient strife,
Is not that music greater than our life?
Shall not a little song outlast that doom?[11]

This poem expresses how Gore-Booth experienced their meeting, an encounter so intense that even the course of nature was disrupted, the tide ceased, as did those meaningless events of their own lives. After their first meeting, Gore-Booth and Roper spent very little time apart. Roper wrote that 'from 1896 onwards we were rarely separated.'[12] Indeed, the couple were to be inseparable until Gore-Booth's death nearly thirty years later.

Roper was a remarkable character and was clearly the greatest influence on Gore-Booth's personal, literary and political life. For this reason it is necessary to briefly diverge from Gore-Booth's life story to provide a short background of Esther Gertrude Roper. She was born in 1868 at Lindow in Chorley, Cheshire.[13] Her family circumstances are fascinating. Her unique upbringing no doubt inspired her to follow the path of political activism. Roper's father was the Reverend Edward Roper and her mother, Annie Craig, was the daughter of Irish immigrants. Although she was born in Manchester, Roper's mother identified herself as Irish and in turn Roper identified herself as half-Irish. Roper's parents were from struggling working-class backgrounds. Her father left school before he was eleven years of age to take up employment in a local factory.[14] Previous researchers have suggested that Edward was forced to leave school after his father abandoned the family; however there is no evidence to support this.[15] It was common practice for the children of a working class family to begin work at a young age. Edward's father, Thomas Roper, was a labourer and later a watchman in a local factory. Edward's three sisters became cotton weavers in Manchester and his younger brother trained as a glass blower.[16]

Edward worked hard to achieve middle-class respectability as a Church of England Minister. He received this opportunity through his commitment to a local Sunday-school, St Jude's in Manchester. When the Church Missionary Society (CMS) appealed for missionaries in the *Juvenile Instructor* magazine, Edward put himself forward. His life took an extraordinary turn. He moved from being a factory hand in Manchester to working as a missionary in Ijaye, a town in West Africa, now Nigeria. He was a dedicated social reformist and published an account of his missionary work. Edward's particular awareness of gender inequality is evident in this text as he describes how, 'domestic slavery still exists ... I knew a woman in one town who was obliged to bribe her husband not to sell her and her child, because she was his slave as well as his wife, the mother being a slave, according to native law her child was also a slave, and both could be sold at the master's will.'[17] Edward carried on his work as a lay missionary for the next three years until he became a victim of the political instability in West Africa.

In 1860 war broke out between the Abeokuta tribe and the Ibadans and fighting swept across the country. In 1862 Ibadan forces occupied the town where Edward was stationed and he was devastated as he witnessed the children in his school being bound and carried away for the slave trade.[18] He was captured by the Ibadan forces and held as a prisoner for three years. Aware of the slave trade industry, English authorities attempted to disrupt the activity and had appointed a British consular in Lagos in 1852. Britain later formally annexed Lagos as a colony. Captain John Hawley Glover took over the position as colonial secretary. Glover organised the successful escape of Edward and two other missionaries. Edward returned to Manchester in 1865 and he became renowned in the CMS community for his missionary work and successful escape from captivity. He met Annie Craig at a church function and the couple married in 1867. That same year Edward was ordained as a minister.

The next year their first child, a daughter, was born. The couple named the child after Edward's sister, Esther. Within months Edward returned to Africa with his young wife. Esther was only four months old and she was left in the care of her Irish grandparents. Her parents were stationed for a time at Lagos and her mother dedicated herself to teaching English language to the local girls.[19] Esther's parents were dedicated to the education of girls and on 1 May 1869 they founded a Female Institution for the education of Native Christian girls.[20] Within weeks Annie became ill with her next pregnancy and the couple were advised to return to their homeland. They left Lagos and on 7 June 1869 their second daughter was born on board a ship destined for England.[21] The baby girl died five months later. Edward and Annie remained in England until 1872. When Esther was four years of age her parents returned to Lagos. This time she was sent to the CMS children's home in Highbury Grove in the Islington area of North London. The home provided free education for the children of missionaries, a total of ninety-eight children were recorded as resident on the 1861 census. There is no record of what life was like for Roper during these years. Whatever the emotional effect, it did provide her with a solid basic education.

In 1874 Esther's father became ill and her parents returned to England. Edward devoted himself to the missionary interest in England and he travelled to many parishes preaching about the work of the African missions. Esther had rarely seen her parents until now and she spent much of her time accompanying her father on his travels around England. Her mother gave birth to another daughter early in 1875 and before the year was out Annie Roper was again pregnant and her recently born baby daughter had died of typhoid. Annie gave birth to a son, Reginald, in January 1876. Edward's health began to deteriorate steadily and he died in October 1877. The time spent working in the missions in Africa and the three years imprisoned under harsh conditions, had taken its toll on Edward's health; he was only 39 years old when he died. After his death, Esther lived with her mother and her younger brother, Reginald, in a house on George Street in the Broughton area of Manchester.[22] Although the house was modest, the family employed one servant and Esther's mother received a pension of £50 per year from CMS. Annie described herself as a ladies school teacher, although there are no records to show that she continued teaching after she returned to England. Roper's mother was an advocate of female education and the CMS showed their financial support of Roper's further education. With the help of the Missionary Society, Esther entered Owens College, Manchester in 1886, becoming one of the first female students at the college.

Manchester is credited with being one of the world's first industrial cities and in the nineteenth century the thriving city was in need of a high class institute for education. Through a bequest in 1846 from a Manchester textile merchant, John Owens, a college was established in his name. In his will Owens specifically requested his 'earnest desire and general object to found . . . an institution for providing or aiding the means of instructing and improving young persons of the male sex.'[23] The fact that Owens' will stipulated a provision for the education of men, alongside the prevailing notion that it was against nature to educate women, meant that women were barred from entering the university until 1883. In that year it was decided to accept female students but only as a probationary measure, to be reviewed five years from that date. Women were

4 Esther Roper

allowed to enrol in the college but there were various restrictions. Female students were kept apart from the general student population and attended classes in the college's Brunswick Street premises. Female students could only attend classes in Owens College when they were in preparation for their final exams.

Under these numerous restrictions Roper enrolled as a BA degree student in 1886. College authorities were concerned that education could be dangerous for the mental and physical health of women. The college required Esther's mother to take full responsibility for the effect that education may have on her daughter's health. Annie Roper wrote a letter confirming that Esther's 'course of study may be entered on without prospect of injury to her health.'[24] Roper became part of a student body of 714 students enrolled at Owens College, out of this number only 67 students were female and not all of these were reading for degrees (see Figure 4 for one of the few surviving photographs of Esther Roper).

Roper immersed herself in her studies and in political activities on behalf of female students. Along with Marion Ledward, she founded and edited *Iris*, the university's first ever newsletter for women, originally produced in December 1887.[25] They appointed three other students to the board. Amy Mullock was nominated as treasurer, while Alice Cooke and Edith Johnstone were appointed as journalists. The women named the magazine after the appropriate Greek mythological figure, Iris, messenger of the gods. The fact that women were separate from the predominant male student body made this a most important publication. The newsletter would become a vital means of contact between past female students and those newly enrolled. *Iris* was issued bi-annually and reported on the academic progress of female students at Owens College and at other universities.[26] The newsletters included accounts of any educational developments which related to women, such as the first graduation of female students. A reporter excitedly describes how 'our triumph had, as yet, only begun; we had still three princesses to watch to the crown of their toil. Many comments went up as they stood in line waiting their turn; but in one thing we all agreed – the costume might have been made expressly for these new aspirants to academic honours.'[27]

Iris listed individual female students enrolled each year and detailed whether or not these women registered for a degree. In the first issue of the newsletter Roper and Ledward reported that out of the sixty-one women registered at Owens that year, only eighteen were actually reading for degrees; the remainder simply attended some classes on campus. The editors also listed any awards, scholarships, prizes or degrees earned by female students. *Iris* created a network with women in colleges elsewhere, seeking to improve female education nationally. This networking is evident in an 1888 edition of the magazine which includes a letter relating to Yorkshire College, Leeds. The unnamed author points out how female students at Owens were particularly disadvantaged, noting that in Leeds, 'men and women are on an entirely equal footing, and are admitted indifferently to all classes and lectures on the Arts and Science side, and women are only excluded from the Medical School because there are not enough applicants to form a separate class, which there alone are thought necessary.'[28] *Iris* proved to be very successful and was incorporated into the *Owens College Union Magazine* in 1894. The success of Roper's newsletter was later to inspire her and Gore-Booth to found and edit various journals.

In 1888 the probationary period regarding female students at Owens expired and the College Council agreed to admit women as full students, with less restrictions. The next year Roper's mother died at home at the age of forty-three. She had developed anaemia due to several pregnancies over a short period of time. Her death certificate records death as due to Anaemia Pyrexia. This tragedy had a dramatic impact on Roper personally. She was only twenty years of age when her mother died. She now had to ensure her own financial welfare and that of her brother, who was only thirteen. Esther and Reginald Roper boarded in the Chorlton upon Medlock area of Manchester.[29] They shared the house with their landlady, Elizabeth Wright, and another lodger, Ellen Hugger, who is described on the census return as a 'lady teacher'. Even with the added stress of caring for her young brother, Roper successfully received a BA degree in 1891 which was announced in the 'University Intelligence' section of the *Manchester Guardian* (*MG*).[30] Her final exam results were outstanding; she received a first class in Latin, English Literature and Political Economy and was awarded the prize for English Literature.[31] Roper was intelligent, educated and driven by an ambition to improve the lives of women.

After graduation she joined numerous political groups which sought equality between the sexes. She kept ties with Owens College and became a leading member of their Social Debating Society. The society had a female only membership and organised many debates around issues of suffrage for women. In 1892 Roper became a graduate Associate of Owens College.[32] Associates were chosen from graduates who had distinguished themselves during their college life. Applicants for the status of Associate underwent a rigorous selection process, after approval by the College Senate candidates must then be approved by council. Once elected, Associates were granted special privileges including the right to attend lectures, access to college facilities and a vote at court. Roper's position at Owens would provide Gore-Booth with an ideal introduction to college activities.

Although Roper's father had reached a respectable professional position, the Ropers did not pass on any great wealth to their children. It was therefore essential for Roper to find employment. She decided to pursue a career campaigning for female equality. In 1893 she was appointed to the salaried position of secretary of the Manchester National Society for Women's Suffrage (MNSWS). Roper believed that Manchester was the ideal location to begin her career, describing Lancashire as the 'natural home of a women's movement.'[33] The city of Manchester had been transformed into one of the main industrial cities in Britain. The area has a strong history of female political activity and the suffrage movement developed alongside industrial growth. By the time that Roper took over the post as secretary, there had been a structured suffrage organisation in Manchester for over twenty-six years. The Manchester Committee for Women's Suffrage was formed on 11 January 1867. The committee comprised an impressive collection of members including Lydia Becker as secretary; Elizabeth Wolstenholme Elmy; Elizabeth Glyone, president of the Manchester Board of Schoolmistresses; Max Kyllman, a friend of John Stuart Mill; Dr Richard Pankhurst; and Jacob and Ursula Bright.

Within months of their establishment the committee claimed an unusual victory in the campaign for female suffrage. At a Manchester by-election on 26 November 1867 Lily Maxwell, a female shop-keeper, arrived at a polling station. She duly cast her vote for Jacob Bright, a Liberal candidate.[34] The *Englishwoman's Review* revelled in the act, describing Maxwell as 'a woman of strong political opinions . . . delighted to have a chance of expressing them.'[35] The vote generated much controversy. Maxwell's inclusion on the voting register was a clerical error. The recently formed group took advantage of the mistake as explained in a letter written by Lydia Becker, 'her name got on the register by mistake. It is spelt Lilly

– and the overseer must have thought it was a masculine name. But being on the register – her vote could not be refused. The fact that a woman was registered as a voter was discovered by Mr Bright's committee in the course of their canvass – they first wrote to me – and I called on her & took her to the poll.'[36]

The society became intensely motivated by the national focus their campaign received. They held the first ever British public suffrage meeting on 14 April 1868 at the centre of public debate in Manchester, the Free Trade Hall. At the meeting a resolution was passed to demand the vote on the same terms as it was or may be granted to men. Earning votes for women under these conditions would make no difference to the working-class factory women of Manchester who did not own property.[37] However, the Manchester society was happy to accept the vote for women under these terms, clearly favouring the rights of the middle classes. Victorian suffrage campaigners predominately belonged to the middle-class sector and often fought for their own interests, ignoring or misunderstanding the needs of the working classes. This aspect is evident in a testimony written by Becker in her capacity as secretary: 'What I desire is to see men and women of the middle classes stand on the same terms of equality as prevail in the working classes – and the highest aristocracy. A great lady or a factory woman are independent persons – personages – the women of the middle classes, are nobodies, and if they act for themselves they lose chaste!'[38] Referring to factory women as 'independent persons,' highlights Becker's ignorance as to the plight of working-class women.

Becker died in 1890 and the Manchester society lost the drive and organisation she had given the campaign. It was not until 1893 when Roper took over as secretary that the then MNSWS found direction. Under Roper's guidance the committees were rationalised and a new executive committee included Walter MacLaren, Thomas Chorlton, Reverend Samuel Steinthal, Alice Scatcherd and Emmeline Pankhurst. The MNSWS joined forces with the Central National Society in 1895 and in 1897 the society changed its name to the North of England Society for Women's Suffrage (NESWS) to show responsibility for all northern counties. The society became part of the 500 strong organisations within the National Union of Women's Suffrage Societies.[39] Roper ensured for the first time that the interests of working-class women were included in the campaign for suffrage. The North of England Society began to fight for votes for all women, regardless of whether they owned property or not. This was a fundamental change in suffrage campaigning.

In her position as secretary, Roper became solely responsible for putting the Special Appeal into practice. The Special Appeal Committee was formed in 1892 with the objective of getting women across Britain, regardless of class, to sign a petition for suffrage.[40] The goal was to submit the largest petition ever on this issue to parliament. The idea was to increase the size and effect of the original Women's Suffrage Petition which was presented to Parliament by MP John Stuart Mill. The original 1866 petition was signed by 1,499 people under a simple statement requesting 'the representation of all householders, without distinction of sex, who possess such property or rental qualifications as your honourable House may determine.'[41] After this petition was presented certain women were granted voting rights in local elections. In 1869 rate-paying spinsters became eligible to vote in borough elections, in 1882 this extended to votes for town councils and by 1888 eligibility was further extended to include county councils. Extending local election votes to unmarried women ensured that only the husband and not the wife in a rate-paying household could vote. Furthermore, all women remained excluded from voting at general elections.

Inspired by the slight improvement in women's voting rights two prominent suffragists, Isabella Ford and Millicent Garrett Fawcett, organised the Special Appeal Committee. The appeal petitioned to extend the franchise to women on the same grounds as men. The petition was headed with a more detailed notice that, 'many of the women who sign this appeal differ in opinion on other political questions, but all are of one mind that the continued denial of the franchise to women, while it is at the same time being gradually extended amongst men, is at once unjust and expedient.'[42] The main suffrage organisations across Britain combined their efforts and countless meetings were held throughout the country.

As a daughter of working-class parents, Roper held a unique insight into class structure. She was an educated woman, named after an aunt who had worked as a cotton weaver from the age of twelve. Roper respected her heritage and ensured that women working in the factories of Lancashire signed the petition. She waited outside factory gates and collected signatures from women as they left work. For the first time the petition for female suffrage included a focus on how women were disempowered in the workplace. The petition specified that because women did not have a franchise, 'power to restrict women's work [is placed] in the hands of men who are working alongside of women whom they often treat as rivals rather than fellow workers.'[43] The mammoth task was completed by the set deadline, 31 March 1894. More than 3,500 people had collected nearly a quarter of a million signatures.

The list of signatures was returned to a central office and organised into volumes for each county in Britain. The completed volumes were impressive and it was decided to display the entire collection in the library of the House of Commons. Days before the Special Appeal petition was complete, the Local Government Act (1894) was passed extending the vote in local elections to married women. The act further enabled any eligible voter to stand for election onto a town or county council. The property qualification remained and women were still excluded from the franchise at general elections. The appeal committee resolved to submit their petition to parliament alongside an appropriate bill, which came in the form of Ferdinand Faithfull Begg's Parliamentary Franchise (Extension to Women) Bill in 1896. The bill was never debated in the House of Commons and the Special Appeal petition was never officially presented to parliament. The work of the committee was not in vain, however, as they had established a nationwide network of suffrage organisations. Roper was now at the centre of this national movement.

Roper expanded her interests by becoming involved with the Manchester University Settlement in 1895. The settlement movement began in London in the 1880s with the aim of bringing people of different social classes together for the common good. The settlement encouraged past students and staff of universities to provide classes and cultural activities for people of the local area who had little or no access to education. It was hoped that the working classes would gain educationally and that university staff would learn about the experiences and difficulties encountered by the poor of the area. The first University Settlement was established at Toynbee Hall in London's East End, organised by the students and staff of Oxford and Cambridge Universities. There was a general feeling by past students of Owens College that 'steps should be taken for the organisation of some definitely social work in the poorer industrial parts of Manchester.'[44] The Principal of Owens College, Dr

Ward, was in favour of such a movement and there was considerable positive response in local newspapers.

The warden of Toynbee Hall, Canon Barnett, agreed to come to Manchester to address a meeting in support of establishing a University Settlement there. A formal association was established at the first annual general meeting on 15 July 1896 and it was named the University Settlement, Manchester.[45] At the meeting a constitution was drawn up which clearly defined the aims of the movement: 'This Settlement is founded in the hope that it may become common ground on which men and women of various classes may meet in goodwill, sympathy and friendship; that the residents may learn something of an industrial neighbourhood, and share its interests, and endeavour to live among their neighbours a simple and religious life.'[46] Amongst the vice-presidents were Arthur Balfour MP and C.P. Scott MP, editor of the *Manchester Guardian* newspaper.

It was necessary to form an executive committee to oversee management of the University Settlement. Roper was a living example of how the working classes could be empowered through education. She put herself forward for election onto the committee. At a meeting on 17 May a revolutionary move was put forward by Mr Smythe of Owens College that the committee should comprise an equal balance of male and female members. Smythe proposed that six men and six women should be elected. Roper and a Miss Wilson objected to the proposal, insisting that the female candidates should face election on equal terms with the male candidates. Roper did not want any discrimination between the sexes, she strove for unequivocal equality. This was a clever move on her behalf. There were six women standing for committee election and they were all successfully elected without the need for intervention.[47] Roper was elected to the executive committee and her brother Reginald was elected as a member of the council for three years.

The Manchester Art Museum offered rooms in Ancoats Hall and the settlement also occupied a circular building, aptly named the Round House, at 20 Every Street (see Figure 5).[48]

Under direction of the committee the University Settlement became a thriving centre of education and entertainment in Ancoats. Owens College boasted about the colourful and diverse activities held at the Settlement. In *Owens College Union Magazine* an unnamed author describes the broad range of cultural and social

5 The Round House at 20 Every Street, which housed the Manchester University Settlement

activities which brought the deprived area of Ancoats much needed entertainment:

> One room may contain an audience of twenty-five to eighty in number listening to a popular lecture with lantern slides, to a practical discourse on Local Government, to one more erudite on Psychology or Evolution. In a larger room are assembled about seventy folk of all ages and upbringings playing games, chatting, hearing or giving songs and recitations, learning to know and sympathise with one another. Upstairs some dozen men, under the leadership of a resident, are practicing the instrumental parts of an operetta to be produced by the choral society. At the end of the corridor fourteen artisans and clerks are 'treading the primrose paths' of botanical lore, under the guidance of a newly-graduated Owens man. Relegated to the attic a band of work girls are rehearsing Macbeth.[49]

Within just five years of graduating from Owens College, Roper became a highly respected campaigner for women's suffrage. She fundamentally altered the focus of the suffrage movement, including a new concentration on the needs of working-class women. She was a respected social activist who actively improved the impoverished district of Ancoats. While Roper was submerged in both paid and voluntary work she successfully raised her brother Reginald. In 1896, Reginald graduated from Owens College with a BA in Classics. It is not surprising that by the end of 1896 Roper was overworked and suffered from acute exhaustion which necessitated her respite in Italy. It is also not surprising that when she met Esther, Eva was fascinated by such a vibrant, driven and active individual. After spending months recuperating together, Roper returned to her life in Manchester and Gore-Booth returned briefly to Lissadell.

Notes

1 EGB, 'The Travellers,' *The One and the Many* (London: Longmans Green & Co, 1904), p. 82.

2 Frederick S. Lapisardi, (ed.), *The Plays of Eva Gore-Booth* (California: Mellen Research University Press, 1991), p. iv.

3 Gifford Lewis, *Eva Gore-Booth and Esther Roper: A Biography* (London: Pandora, 1988), p. 3.

4 Ibid, p. 8.

5 For an in-depth discussion regarding the relationship of Gore-Booth and Roper see: Sonja Tiernan, 'Challenging Presumptions of Heterosexuality: Eva Gore-Booth a Biographical Case Study,' *Historical Reflections/Réflexions Historiques*, 37:2 (2011), 58–71.

6 Emma Donoghue, 'How Could I Fear and Hold Thee by the Hand? The Poetry of Eva Gore-Booth,' in Eibhear Walsh (ed.), *Sex, Nation, and Dissent in Irish Writing* (Cork: Cork University Press, 1997), p. 38.

7 Ibid.

8 Eilís Ní Dhuibhne, *Voices on the Wind: Women Poets of the Celtic Twilight* (Dublin: New Island, 1995), p. 105.

9 Lewis, *Eva Gore-Booth and Esther Roper*, p. 1.

10 EGB, *CE*, p. 9.

11 EGB, *The One and the Many*, pp. 81–2.

12 EGB, *CE*, p. 65.

13 General Register Office, birth certificate: Macclesfield District (vol 8a), p. 138.

14 'Rev. E. Roper obituary,' *Church Missionary Society Gleaner* (April 1877). Edward Roper is listed as an errand boy on the 1851 census at his home, 12 Bk Woodward Street, Manchester.

15 Gifford Lewis states that 'Thomas Roper lived apart from his wife after burdening her with a large family.' Lewis, *Eva Gore-Booth and Esther Roper*, p. 29.

16 Census return for the Roper household, 16 Wesley Street, Manchester 1861, lists occupations of each family member and that Edward's father, Thomas Roper, was living in the household.

17 Edward Roper, *Facts about Foreign Missions in West Africa* (Oxford: Oxford University Press, 1871).
18 Reported in W.M. Watts, *The Church Missionary Intelligencer: A Monthly Journal of Missionary Information* (Oxford: Oxford University Press, 1862), p. 271.
19 University of Birmingham, Church Missionary Society Archive, CMS/B/OMS/C: A2 081/1–36, accounts of female institution in Lagos.
20 Annie Roper, 'Female Institution for the Education of Native Christian Girls,' *Church Missionary Society Gleaner* (October 1875).
21 National Archives, Kew, register of births at sea, 1854–87.
22 1881 Census, RG number RG1, (p. 3955, folio 100), p. 8.
23 H.B. Charlton, *Portrait of a University 1851–1951* (Manchester: Manchester University Press, 1951), p. 153.
24 Cited in Lewis, *Eva Gore-Booth and Esther Roper*, p. 53.
25 Marion Craig Ledward (later Mrs. H.S Ashburner), received a BA degree in 1888 and became an Associate of Owens College in 1892 along with Roper. *University of Manchester Register of Graduates and Holders of Diplomas and Certificates 1851–1958*, (Manchester: Manchester University Press, 1959), p. 394.
26 University of Manchester Archives, Manchester, UMP/2/5, full run of *Iris*, 1887–94.
27 *Iris*, December 1887, p. 8.
28 *Iris*, December 1888, p. 7.
29 231 Upper Brook Street. 1891 census record: RG12, (p. 3185, folio 56), p. 21.
30 *Manchester Guardian* (26 June 1891), p. 8.
31 Ibid.
32 *University of Manchester Register of Graduates*, p. 563.
33 EGB, *CE*, p. 10.
34 For a full account of Lily Maxwell see: Jane Rendall, 'Who was Lily Maxwell? Women's Suffrage and Manchester Politics, 1866–1867,' in June Purvis and Sandra Stanley Holton (eds), *Votes for Women* (London: Routledge, 2000), pp. 57–83.
35 *Englishwoman's Review*, 6 (January 1868), 359–69.
36 Manchester Central Library, Manchester, Women's Suffrage Archive, M50/1/3, (f. 138–9), letter from Lydia Becker to Mary Smith, 20 May 1868.
37 For further information see; Martin Pugh, 'Politicians and the Women's Vote 1914–1918,' *History*, 59 (1977), 358–74. Sandra Stanley Holton, *Feminism and Democracy: Women's Suffrage and Reform Politics in Britain 1900–1918* (Cambridge: Cambridge University Press, 1986).
38 Undated letter from Becker in Manchester Central Library, cited in Andrew Rosen, *Rise Up, Women!: The Militant Campaign of the Women's Social and Political Union, 1903–1914* (London: Routledge, 1974), p. 8.

39 *Englishwoman's Review* (15 January 1897), p. 18.
40 International Institute of Social History, Amsterdam, Estelle Sylvia Pankhurst Papers, 322 (1 folder), minute book of the executive committee of the Women's Franchise League, 20 January 1896 to 8 April 1987.
41 Cited in Elizabeth Crawford, *The Women's Suffrage Movement: A Reference Guide 1866–1928*, (London: Routledge, 1999), p. 756.
42 Ibid, p. 648.
43 Ibid.
44 University of Manchester Archives, MS: MUS/1/3/1, *The University Settlement Manchester: The First Annual Report* (Manchester, 1897), p. 7.
45 University of Manchester Archives, MS: MUS/1/3/1, the University Settlement Manchester: minutes of proceedings at general meetings.
46 Ibid.
47 Ibid.
48 Michael Rose and Anne Woods, *Everything Went On At the Round House: A Hundred Years of the Manchester University Settlement* (Manchester: Manchester University Press, 1995).
49 *Owens College Union Magazine*, 1900; cited in Lewis, *Eva Gore-Booth and Esther Roper*, p. 64.

3

The birth of a rebel: soc in Manchester

'I have such longing to be home again'[1]

Gore-Booth was inspired by Esther Roper's suffrage work. When she returned to Lissadell she immediately set about organising a local campaign to secure votes for women at general elections. Although voting eligibility had been extended for local government, major restrictions still applied at general elections. Women were not allowed to vote under any circumstance and only men who adhered to certain property qualifications had a political franchise, which ruled out most working-class men who did not own or lease property. The entire political system was controlled by middle-class and aristocratic men. Gore-Booth arranged a public meeting at Breaghwy Old School in Ballinfull in December. She convinced both of her sisters to attend; Constance was staying at Lissadell for the Christmas festivities. At the meeting it was agreed to form the Sligo branch of the Irish Women's Suffrage and Local Government Association (IWSLGA). Eva was elected secretary, Constance, president and Mabel, treasurer of the association.[2]

As of this date the suffrage campaign in Ireland had not gained momentum. The Dublin Women's Suffrage Society was established in 1876, founded by Anna Haslam. A branch in Belfast was founded by Isabella Tod. The Dublin society was not active from 1886 until 1895.[3] The society's annual report for 1896 notes that this inactivity was due to 'the present condition of political controversy in Ireland.'[4] By 1896 the Women's Poor Law Guardian (Ireland) Act enabled Irish women who adhered to certain property qualifications to act and vote as poor law guardians. This slight improvement in women's access to the political sphere stirred the association back into action.

Gore-Booth called the first official meeting of the Sligo IWSLGA n Friday 18 December 1896 at Milltown National Protestant School in Drumcliffe, Sligo.[5] The hall was packed with attendees, over two-thirds of whom were men, apparently against the idea of female suffrage. The walls of the hall were decorated with banners, framed in evergreen foliage, carrying wistful slogans; 'Who would be free themselves must strike the blow'; 'No taxation without representation'; and 'Liberality, justice, and equality.' The crowd came to order as Constance opened the meeting at 7.30 in the evening. She began by recounting anecdotes about extending the vote to women explaining; 'I have been told amongst other things that it [the vote] will cause women to ape the other sex, to adopt their clothes, copy their manners and peculiarities, that it will cause women, to neglect their homes and duties, and worst of all prevent the majority marrying. Of course this may be true; pigs may fly, as the old proverb says, but they are not likely birds.' The hostile crowd appeared subdued by Constance's light-hearted address and responded with laughter.

After Constance's speech Eva's younger sister, Mabel, took the stand. Mabel was not a confident public speaker and she encountered a negative reaction when she proposed the resolution to 'try to awaken in Irishwomen a sense of their responsibilities, and to encourage them by every means in our power to fulfil their public duties.' The resolution was seconded by a Mr E. Rowlette but several moves in opposition were presented by men in the crowd. A local bachelor, Percy Clarke, announced that 'no man of common sense could be in favour of seeing the franchise extended to women.' Clarke based his argument on the fact that more women than men would be eligible to vote in certain areas. Concluding that 'enfranchisement of women would be Home Rule with a vengeance – petticoat government,' he proposed that the resolution be read again in another seven years. Clarke's address stirred some of the men in the audience to voice their own opposition and the crowd turned hostile. One man protested that, 'the women's movement tended to make ladies independent, masculine and ride bicycles.'

Unshaken by this boisterous response Eva Gore-Booth took the chair and was received with warm applause. She brought the meeting to order and made a forthright resolution that she and the society 'demand . . . the extension of the parliamentary franchise to women.' Inspired by the success of Josslyn's co-operative creamery, she called on 'Irishwomen to follow the example of the farmers of

Drumcliffe, and to insist, in spite of opposition, in taking affairs into their own hands.' In what was to become typical of Gore-Booth's oratory style she addressed each point of opposition in an orderly and engaging manner. Constance's biographer, Anne Haverty, notes that while Constance adopted a theatrical style in her first public address Eva was, 'more sober, more measured and she displayed a broader comprehension of the issues.'[6]

The meeting generated much interest in the local area. The *Sligo Champion* dedicated a large section of the weekly paper to a detailed account of the events. The report entitled 'the women's suffrage movement' announced 'eloquent speeches for and against the question.'[7] However, the subtitle of 'amusing proceedings,' exhibits the journalist's prejudice on the issue. The *Irish Times* ridiculed the meeting in the column 'talk of the town,' authored by 'a lady.'[8] The events are narrated in that paper as, 'an amusing account [which] comes all the way from Sligo of a meeting held there by three young ladies.' Patronisingly it was noted that the meeting was arranged by the women, 'all on their own responsibility.' The social standing of the three Gore-Booth sisters is ridiculed with a description of their usual activities. In Sligo, 'they ride to hounds and otherwise demonstrate their personal courage and physique – and in London ... they are members of several societies and clubs, and share in all the intellectual life of the town.'[9]

It is clear from reports of this first suffrage meeting that Gore-Booth would always be judged in Ireland by her status as a member of the Anglo-Irish aristocracy. Although she identified as Irish, in Ireland Gore-Booth was viewed as part of the British ruling class. Within months of the suffrage meeting in Sligo, Gore-Booth rejected her privileged lifestyle at Lissadell and moved to the poor industrial quarters of Manchester. This move was a mammoth decision and would certainly have caused deep concerns within the Gore-Booth family, crossing culture and class boundaries at a time when society frowned on such interactions.

Meeting Roper is evidently the foremost reason why Gore-Booth chose a dramatic, driven and inspirational life course from 1897. When she arrived in Manchester, Henry Francis Gore-Booth, the son of her grandfather's wayward brother, was rector of the Church of the Sacred Trinity in Salford.[10] The charity funded by her ancestor Humphrey Booth was actively assisting the needy of the area. The Gore-Booth family still owned a considerable portion of land and property in the area. In recognition of the family's influence a street in

Salford is named Lissadel Street after the Gore-Booth seat in Sligo.[11] However, Gore-Booth was unfamiliar with Manchester and she distanced herself from her aristocratic roots. She did not have a close relationship with Henry Gore-Booth, nor was she involved with administering the family's property.[12] Gore-Booth had given up her life of luxury to be with Roper. She moved into a small three bedroom, mid-terrace property in the heart of working-class Manchester at 83 Heald Place (see Figure 6 to appreciate the contrast). The house was the home of Roper and her brother, Reginald.

Moving from a rural area with clean air and the luxuries of Lissadell, to the smoke-bound industrial quarters of Manchester may have further damaged Gore-Booth's delicate health. Aware of this she made her final will on the first day of March 1900, simply leaving all of her possessions to Roper (see Figure 7).[13]

After moving, Gore-Booth enjoyed a new lease of life. She attended her first meeting in the House of Commons in January

6 83 Heald Place, Eva Gore-Booth's first home in Manchester

(6)

TELEGRAMS.
BALLINFULL.

LISSADELL,
SLIGO.

This is the last & only will of me
Eva Selina Gore Booth of Lissadell
in the county of Sligo. I DEVISE
and BEQUEATH all the estate
and effects whatsoever & wheresoever
both real & personal to which I
may be entitled or which I may
have power to dispose of at my
decease unto my friend Esther
Gertrude Roper & I appoint her sole
executrix of this my will in
Witness whereof I have hereunto set my
hand this first day of March one thousand
nine hundred.
Signed by the above named testatrix
as her last will in the presence of
us present at the same time who in
her presence & at her request & in the
presence of each other have hereunto
subscribed our names as witnesses (E. G. B

7 Last will and testament of Eva Gore-Booth, written on 1 March 1900

1897. She was the official representative for the Sligo Society for Women's Suffrage.[14] Her literary career also took a new direction. She had written many poems while living at Lissadell and published individual verses in *The Irish Homestead*, *Temple Bar* and the *Yellow Book*. However, it was not until she moved to Manchester that Gore-Booth published her own volume of work.

Months after moving, she completed her first book, *Poems*, a compilation of seventy-two verses. Her friend Julian Sturgis presented her writings to Andrew Lang, a prolific writer and monthly contributor to *Longman's Magazine*.[15] Sturgis was delighted with the response they received and wrote to her 'that so fastidious a critic as A. Lang should call poems "good," is much. He is very powerful with Longmans, and, I suspect, with the critical brotherhood; and I think that his personal interest in the book would be valuable to you.'[16] Indeed, Lang was a highly respected literary critic and when he passed Gore-Booth's poetry on to Longmans Green & Co with a recommendation to publish, they instantly accepted her manuscript.

Publishers often required first time authors to open a financial account in order to cover the costs of printing, marketing and advertising, in case the book sales did not achieve production costs. Sturgis was so impressed by Gore-Booth's poetry that he personally opened an account for her with Longmans, sending the publisher a cheque for £30.[17] A first print run of 250 volumes of *Poems* sold for the relatively small cost of 5 shillings per book; the majority sold within the first year. Longmans ultimately became Gore-Booth's main publisher throughout her life and she became a regular contributor to *Longman's Magazine*. *Poems* was the beginning of what would become a large body of poetic work by her. She dedicated her first book to Sturgis, 'most generous of artists and kindest of friends.' Although now out of print, Sturgis was then a novelist of some distinction, from the publication of his first novel *John-a-Dreams* (1878) until his death in 1904.[18]

As well as her prose and political writings, Gore-Booth wrote occasional poetry. Poetry is perhaps the most personal of all her writings as Roper observes, 'to follow the procession of her [Gore-Booth's] poems is to see and understand the story of her inner life.'[19] For this reason it is significant that this early poetry expresses her thoughts on Irish independence. Although she is rarely thought of as a nationalist, Gore-Booth's patriotism is particularly striking in

Poems. Similar to much Celtic Revival poetry of the time, a preoccupation with national identity and political independence for Ireland is dominant. In *Poems* this is presented through a reoccurring theme of liberty. Gore-Booth's focus is republican and revolutionary, based on the ideals of the French Revolution. As an Irish Protestant, Gore-Booth was attracted to Wolfe Tone's non-sectarian principles. A short poem entitled 'Tricolor,' elucidates her position.

> In liberty of thought,
> Equality of life,
> The generations sought
> A rest from hate and strife.
> Hard work on common ground,
> Strong arms and spirits free,
> In these at last they found
> Fraternity.[20]

Gore-Booth also clearly expressed the ideals of feminist thought in her literary publications. She predominantly employed feminine imagery in her poetry and in *Poems* she casts several female goddesses, religious, historical and mythological figures. She was moved to write 'the Repentance of Eve' after viewing a picture with the same title painted by her sister Constance. There is a strong feminist theme in this poem as Gore-Booth reminds readers that Eve 'ate but half the fruit, sinned half the sin,' yet, 'eternal hunger is her punishment.'[21] She would develop this feminist reasoning both in her social reform work and in her theological prose in later life.

There was mixed public reaction to this book. The review magazine *Dome* announced that *Poems* 'is amusing, but it is not poetry.'[22] While the *Academy* warns that, 'Miss Gore-Booth has a trick of pulpiteering, which should be checked.'[23] However, *Poems* was received with praise from female quarters. Periodicals such as the *Nursing Record and Hospital World* advised their patrons to read Gore-Booth's book.[24] While in Ireland praise was more forthcoming. Gore-Booth sent Yeats a copy and he responded with an approving letter, 'your gift is for putting very serious delicate emotions into fragile rythms [sic],' but he cautioned her to 'avoid every touch of rhetoric every tendency to teach.'[25] Gore-Booth's brother, Josslyn, wrote to her that Father Finlay and George Russell are 'much pleased with your poetry.'[26] The Irish paper the *Freeman's Journal* delighted that 'the ranks of our Irish women poets have been reinforced by the accession of Miss Gore-Booth.'[27]

The publication was received with applause through an *Irish Times* review by Dublin author Jane Barlow. Barlow had become known for her novels which deplored the privileged status of Anglo-Irish landlords and for her published poetry. She welcomed Gore-Booth's collection of *Poems* declaring, 'although George Eliot discouragingly calls prophecy "the most gratuitous form of folly," we venture to predict that this small volume, in its pleasant green covers, will some day be sought and prized by the collector of First Editions.'[28] Although Barlow highlights some problems with the poetic style, she offers high praise by deciding that 'the verse and diction have in some passages a stateliness which recalls that of Emily Bronte at her best.'[29]

After the publication of *Poems*, Gore-Booth concentrated on social and economic reform in Manchester. Over the next few years she submitted only small items of prose and individual poems for publication to the *New Ireland Review* and to *Longman's Magazine*.[30] Now Gore-Booth was living in the heart of working-class Manchester and she witnessed first-hand the growing socioeconomic problems that stemmed from the industrial revolution. While Roper was campaigning on behalf of women workers in the textile industry, Gore-Booth became aware of another marginalised group living in Manchester, Irish immigrants. When Gore-Booth moved to Manchester there were more Irish people living in that city than in her entire home county of Sligo.

Liverpool was one of the main ports of call for Irish people travelling to England. The port of Liverpool was especially favoured by people from Sligo because a steam ship departed from Sligo Bay bound for Liverpool, weekly. It was a difficult route, steaming along the north and north-west coast of Ireland where the boat was at the mercy of the Atlantic gales. However, this route was so popular with passengers that the Sligo Steam Navigation Company built their largest ship, the *Liverpool*, in 1892 to accommodate the increased demand in passenger crossings. Once they reached the port of Liverpool, tens of thousands of Irish refugees travelled thirty miles to Manchester, where employment was to be had in abundance.[31] By the early 1860s more than 806,000 Irish people were living in England and of this number almost half were to be found in Lancashire and Cheshire. From 1851 to 1901 the number of people living in central Manchester doubled and the population continued to grow well into the 1920s.[32] The population explosion brought with it many social and living concerns for the working classes, especially for the downtrodden Irish.

Wealthy manufacturers built themselves grand houses around the Mosley Street area of Manchester city and designed cheap buildings for labourers' cottages near to the factories. Friedrich Engels managed his father's textile factory, Ermen and Engles, in Manchester. Although he was the son of an industrialist, Engels was a forward thinking socialist. He published an account of the living conditions of the working population in Manchester. *The Condition of the Working Class in England* provides us with a unique insight into Manchester in 1844:

> 350,000 working people of Manchester and its environs live, almost all of them, in wretched, damp, filthy cottages, that the streets which surround them are usually in the most miserable and filthy condition, laid out without the slightest reference to ventilation, with reference solely to the profit secured by the contractor. In a word, we must confess that in the working men's dwellings of Manchester, no cleanliness, no convenience, and consequently no comfortable family life is possible; that in such dwellings only a physically degenerate race, robbed of all humanity, degraded, reduced morally and physically to bestiality, could feel comfortable at home.[33]

In his detailed account Engels notes the vast number of Irish workers in Manchester. He highlights the ghettos of the New Town, which was aptly branded as Irish Town, a cramped area which was home to over 20,000 Irish people.[34] He also describes the smaller area of Little Ireland which housed about 4,000 Irish people.[35]

Although these Irish immigrants had escaped the consequences and aftermath of famine at home, their living standards did not improve greatly after they arrived in Manchester. The Irish worked in large, cramped and unsanitary conditions in factories under the control of British employers. Living in tenement houses owned by their employers, their lives were akin, if not worse, to their lives back in Ireland. The callous landlord prevalent in their native land had simply been replaced by the profiteering industrialist in England. At least in Ireland they had the support of their local community and extended family. In England the Irish were often viewed with hostility and fear. These negative views were not surprising because Irish people would work for less money and concern grew that they would take employment away from English workers. Due to the alarming physical condition of Irish people when they arrived in England it was feared that they would spread disease. Gore-Booth had lived through the famine of 1879–80 in Sligo and she was deeply aware of the conditions from which these people had fled. She was appalled at the environment they now encountered in Manchester.

She became involved with social reform in the densely populated and dismally poor working-class district of Ancoats, the population of which was over 40 per cent Irish. She was drawn to the work of the University Settlement and in 1898 she began organising social evenings for young women and girls at the Manor Street premises of Owens College. Along with Alice Cooke and Elizabeth MacGowan, Gore-Booth organised a dramatic evening every Monday.[36] Within a year she took over the evenings and formed a class for young women, which she called the Ancoats Elizabethan Society. The society was applauded by the committee of the University Settlement who described, 'its object being the revival of a dramatic spirit, Elizabethan in the boldness of its aim and its independence of nineteenth-century machinery.'[37] The dramatic society comprised of about sixteen women who worked in the textile factories.[38] The group staged their first performance on 28 June 1899. The performance of scenes from the *Merchant of Venice* received much acclaim. The women were praised for 'the courage and spirit with which the parts were sustained.'[39]

Gore-Booth cast an imposing image; she was tall, slender and strikingly beautiful. Surprisingly her aristocratic background and genteel manner did not create a barrier for her interacting with the labouring classes. Her quick wit and engaging personality made her popular with her students. Louisa Smith, a member of the Elizabethan Society, recalls:

> We were very raw material but keen on acting; she [Gore-Booth] showed such patience and love that we would do anything to please her and she got the best out of us . . . I don't think I exaggerate when I say we worshipped her, but she never knew it, she was so utterly selfless . . . She was always sympathetic with the downtrodden, and worked and lectured might and main, interviewing Members of Parliament, etc., on their behalf till conditions were mended. She was very frail and delicate herself, but full of pluck and determination, and would stand up for people she knew to be unjustly treated, even though the world was against them.[40]

Gore-Booth became aware of the deplorable working conditions that these women endured in the factories of the textile industry in Manchester. She soon became more politically active, joining the executive committee of the National Union of Women's Suffrage Societies (NUWSS) in 1899. Gore-Booth stressed the importance of gaining votes for women in order to improve their position in the workplace. She became actively involved with the work of the NUWSS, attending a conference of their parliamentary friends in the House of Commons on 7 February 1899.[41] The meeting was called by Faithfull Begg, who had not been deterred by his failure to introduce the Parliamentary Franchise Bill in 1896. At the conference Begg sought support from other MPs to ballot in favour of another women's franchise bill. Twenty-five MPs supported his request. However, once again Begg was not successful in having his bill read to the House.[42]

Within two years of moving to Manchester Gore-Booth had established herself as a voice of the working classes. She joined any organisation which would further her goal of social reform and became a regular speaker at the Manchester Women Student's Debating Society. Elizabeth Parker, a first year undergraduate at Owens College, was secretary of the society in 1899. Parker describes Gore-Booth as an effervescent speaker, with an endearing personality who always put people at ease. After one of her first debating sessions Parker was to recollect how, 'I had not even made her acquaintance by correspondence. She read her paper, sat down by me and proceeded, during the rather active debate that followed, to send me into suppressed ripples of laughter by the vivacious stream of comments which she whispered into my ear. At the close of the debate, a new planet had swum into my little world. I had made a new friend.'[43] Gore-Booth was at the cutting edge of social and political activities which were integral to economic reform in Manchester. The importance of the Women's Student's Debating Society is evident from the list of people who addressed the group. Speakers included Millicent Garrett Fawcett, who led a debate on women's suffrage at a meeting on 13 February 1899.[44]

Through her contact with suffrage campaigners and with female factory workers, Gore-Booth was open to the idea that those who suffered the most in the industrial world were working women. One woman who worked in the Manchester factories at this time was Selina Cooper. She began employment at the age of eleven and later described how conditions in the factories were far worse for women than for men. Not only did women receive less pay than their male counterparts, they were subjected to frequent sexual harassment and unsanitary crudities. Cooper portrayed the cotton mills as cramped, filthy quarters, describing how the winding room floor was invariably drenched with menstrual blood because women rarely had access to sanitary protection.[45] The Manchester and Salford Trades' Council was not entirely sympathetic to the plight of women in the workplace. The councils' president, R.W. Walters, believed that 'the proper place of woman was not in the workshop but at home.'[46]

In January 1895 a group of local influential radicals took matters into their own hands. The group distributed a circular around Lancashire highlighting the need for a women's trade union organisation:

> As you are perhaps aware, women's trades in this large district are almost entirely unorganised, if we except the Textile Workers and the Shirtmakers' Union, founded in Manchester several years ago. At the same time, the rate of wages for women's labour is exceedingly low. It is therefore important, not only in the interest of the women themselves, but also for the sake of all other workers, that they should no longer continue without the protection that well-organised unions can give. It has been constantly found by those who have tried to organise women's trade that it is impossible for the women to struggle through the first years of a union unless assisted by outside help.[47]

The signatories included the Bishop of Manchester; Mrs H. Arnold and her husband Matthew Arnold of the Manchester and Salford Trades Council; G.D. Kelly, secretary of the Trades Council; Reverend Steinthal, an active suffrage campaigner and treasurer of the MNSWS; and C.P. Scott MP, an avid supporter of Irish home rule and editor of the somewhat avant-garde *Manchester Guardian* newspaper.[48]

The group called a meeting to be held in Manchester Town Hall in February. At that meeting the Manchester and Salford Women's Trade Union council (WTUC) was officially formed. The objects of the council were clearly defined by the Committee:

> To promote new and encourage existing organisations among women workers.
>
> To collect and publish information as to the condition under which women work, with a view to influencing public opinion and

> promoting legislation for the improvement of their conditions of labour.
> To endeavour by all legitimate means to improve such conditions by obtaining for women workers fair and uniform wages, shorter hours and sanitary workrooms.[49]

The council appointed Amy Bulley as chair and began to successfully organise women into trade unions. In 1900, Miss Ashwell resigned as secretary of the WTUC after her marriage. The council appointed Gore-Booth as co-secretary, along with Sarah Dickenson, in June 1900.[50] In the annual report the council announces Gore-Booth's appointment with pride, noting that she 'brings to her task considerable acquaints with the condition of working women's lives.'[51] Gore-Booth was now responsible for the main function of the council, 'to bring trade-unionism within the reach of scattered individuals working in unorganised trades, and to draft them off into their own unions once they are formed.'[52] She immediately took over responsibility for organising the tailoresses, fancy box makers and printers into unions and attended their meetings frequently. She was a dedicated organiser, holding a conference of trade union officials at her and Roper's home on 12 July that year.[53]

The joint post for the WTUC carried a salary of £70 per annum and the offices were based at 9 Albert Square in Manchester. Dickenson understood the issues facing women workers as she herself was employed in Howarth's cotton mill in Salford, where she had worked since the age of eleven. Under the leadership of Gore-Booth and Dickenson, the WTUC helped to form trade unions for women; primarily for cotton operatives and weavers. The two women launched their own investigations into how women were treated in various work places, often uncovering unacceptable practices. In one of their first investigations they examined the brushmaking industry which employed about fifty women. Gore-Booth and Dickenson discovered that women in this industry were paid considerably less than their male counterparts and were banned from joining the appropriate union. The two women's report to the WTUC highlighted the importance of establishing a union to represent this growing sector of female workers.[54] Dickenson was extremely impressed with her colleague's drive and resourcefulness; recounting the impact of Gore-Booth's work she testified, 'the friendly way that she treated all the women trade unionists endeared her to them. If she was approached for advice or help she never failed. She is remembered by thousands of working women in Manchester for her untiring efforts to improve their industrial conditions, for awakening and educating their sense of political freedom, and for social intercourse.'[55]

Gore-Booth was particularly aware of the value of social intercourse and arranged for the women of the Elizabethan Society to meet with recently recruited female trade unionists. In the summer of 1900 the society performed *Macbeth* for various trade union groups.[56] On 28 July of that year Elizabeth MacGowan invited the women of the trade union council to a garden party at the Knoll, Bowdon where the Elizabethan Society performed for them.[57] Gore-Booth sought more suitable material for the society to perform for the trade unionists. She penned a five act play entitled *Fiametta*, the plot of which reflects on issues of gender equality and the subordinate position of women in marriage. The drama is set in the early twentieth century and therefore the women could relate more readily to Gore-Booth's play than to works by Shakespeare. Along with MacGowan, Gore-Booth rehearsed and discussed *Fiametta* with the drama society.[58] *Fiametta* remained unpublished until 2010 and there is no record of any performance of the play to date.[59] The committee of the University Settlement recognised the Elizabethan Society as one of their most successful groups and they elected Gore-Booth onto their committee.

In order to promote greater social reform Gore-Booth actively encouraged factory workers to become involved in the campaign for their own equality. Under the auspices of the NESWS, she and Roper launched a new petition for suffrage. This time only women working in the cotton mills would be included. In May 1900, the two women launched their petition and recruited mill workers, including Selina Cooper, to help them collect signatures at factory gates, in mill yards and in women's homes. The group distributed thousands of leaflets. Gore-Booth held open air meetings outside of factories. Through her engaging oratory style she convinced many women to sign the petition asserting that, 'the continued denial of the franchise to women is unjust and inexpedient. In the home, their position is lowered by such an exclusion from the responsibilities of national life. In the factory, their unrepresented condition places the regulation of their work in the hands of men who are often their rivals as well as fellow workers.'[60]

Gore-Booth and Roper argued that women trade unionists paid

the same parliamentary levy as men yet women were not represented at parliament.[61] This fact was all the more disturbing considering that the vast majority of members of the textile trade unions were women. In 1900, there were 96,820 female and only 69,699 male members of textile trade unions.[62] Within months of the campaign, 29,359 signatures had been secured from women workers in the cotton factories.[63] Gore-Booth and Roper accompanied by a group of petition workers, including Selina Cooper, Sarah Dickenson and Sarah Reddish, travelled to London in March 1901 to present their petition to the House of Commons. Like many of the party, Reddish had also worked in the cotton mill factories from the age of eleven. She was chosen to officially present the petition to the Lancashire MPs. This was the first petition of working women to be presented to parliament. As Bertha Mason, an executive committee member of the NESWS, was to later observe, 'there can be no doubt that this active and enthusiastic demand ... made a deep impression on parliament, and caused many who had hitherto treated the agitation as an "impracticable fad" and "the fantastic crochet" of a few rich and well-to-do women, to inquire seriously into the why and wherefore of the movement.'[64]

The campaign not only influenced MPs, who were now made aware of working women's issues, but this move also impacted on the highest echelons of the suffrage movement. When Gore-Booth and Roper arrived in London, along with fourteen members of their petition group, they were met by executive committee members of the NUWSS. The group were dined by Lady Frances Balfour, Isabella Ford and Millicent Garrett Fawcett at the stylish *Florence Restaurant*.[65] This social gathering generated much needed contact between factory women and the elite organisers of the suffrage movement. Through the work of the WTUC Gore-Booth began the process of taking suffrage out of the preserves of middle-class concerns, making it also a working woman's issue and thus forming gender critique into a Marxist analysis. Suffrage historians Jill Liddington and Jill Norris stress that the group of women campaigning with Gore-Booth shared 'considerable industrial experience and a political radicalism that set them apart from other non-militants.'[66] This new movement of female activists are now known as the radical suffragists.[67]

The WTUC successfully organised many unions for women cotton operatives throughout Lancashire. The development of organised unions had far-reaching consequences. Gore-Booth observed that 'the total lack of organisation in such an important centre had long been felt as more than a mere local disadvantage, and had its effect in tending to depress the rate of wages all over Lancashire.'[68] The turn of the century had seen a bigger growth of trade unions in Britain than at any other time. However, the unions cannot be credited with organising women workers; this mission was accomplished by women such as Gore-Booth, Dickenson and Cooper. By the year 1914 over 50 per cent of all women in trade unions in Britain were workers in the textile industry.

As well as attracting textile workers into her campaign for social reform, Gore-Booth attracted an individual who would dramatically change the direction of the suffrage movement in Britain and Ireland. During a Women's Students' Debating Society meeting on 11 October 1900, a twenty year old newcomer, Christabel Pankhurst, spoke at length during the question-time. The topic of 'the politics of poets' was addressed by Sir Alfred Hopkins, the Vice-Chancellor of the University of Manchester. Pankhurst's articulation and energy impressed the chair of the society, Roper. Pankhurst describes how Roper 'descended from the platform at the close of the meeting and overtook me.'[69] Roper brought Pankhurst home to meet Gore-Booth that evening. Pankhurst was so impressed by Gore-Booth that she began attending her poetry circle in the University Settlement and her Sunday morning reading class at the Ancoats Brotherhood House. Pankhurst realised that Gore-Booth and Roper 'were conducting something of a woman suffrage revival.'[70] .

Christabel was the daughter of Dr Richard Pankhurst, one of the founding members of the Manchester Women's Suffrage Committee, and Emmeline Pankhurst, an active member of the suffrage movement. After Roper had taken over as secretary of the NESWS, Mrs Pankhurst became an executive committee member. She helped to organise the Great Demonstration in the Free Trade Hall, supporting the Special Appeal led by Roper. Both Richard and Emmeline were dedicated supporters of the Independent Labour Party (ILP), a socialist political group led by Keir Hardie. In July 1895 Richard Pankhurst stood in the general election as an ILP candidate for Gorton; he was overwhelmingly defeated. He died suddenly in 1898 and his wife was forced to retire from political activity. Without a family income Mrs Pankhurst was obliged to re-open the family business, Emerson's, an inexpensive art and furnishing shop. Christabel was the oldest of the Pankhurst children. After finishing her schooling in 1897, she was sent to Geneva to improve her French. She was staying there when she learnt of her father's untimely death. Within months Christabel returned to Manchester and began working in the family shop at 30 King Street.

Shop work bored Pankhurst and she began attending courses in logic and classics at Owens College, though she did not register for a degree. It was through this involvement that she had first attended the Women's Debating Society. Gore-Booth inspired her to become active in the labour and suffrage movements. Pankhurst joined both the WTUC and the NESWS. Gore-Booth continued to mentor Pankhurst from 1900 until 1904. Under Roper's direction Pankhurst registered for a law degree at Owens College, finally graduating with an LL.B honours degree in 1906.[71] This was a cunning move for the suffrage campaign. Pankhurst's educational success proved that women could graduate with a law degree and enter the realms of a male dominated profession. It also provided her with legal knowledge, invaluable for the campaign to gain votes for women.

Pankhurst and Gore-Booth developed a particularly close relationship. Pankhurst's sister, Sylvia, recalls the unusual but charismatic style of Gore-Booth as, 'tall and excessively slender, intensely short-sighted, with a mass of golden hair, worn like a great ball at the nape of her long neck, bespectacled, bending forward, short of breath with high-pitched voice and gasping speech, she was nevertheless a personality of great charm.'[72] Sylvia describes her sister as being smitten by Gore-Booth; 'she adored her, and when Eva suffered from neuralgia, as often happened, she would sit for hours, massaging her head.'[73] This relationship amazed the Pankhurst family as Sylvia observes, 'Christabel had never been willing to act the nurse to any other human being. She detested sickness.'[74] This close bond was not to continue. Driven by her eventual power within the suffrage campaign and her mother's attempt to discourage their friendship, Pankhurst would eventually split from Gore-Booth in a dramatic fallout. The split between the women would send ripples through the labour and suffrage movements in Manchester. However, Pankhurst always maintained that her time with Gore-Booth 'was a stage in my political apprenticeship of great and lasting value.'[75]

Indeed, Gore-Booth treated Pankhurst as an apprentice, encouraging her to become involved with the work of the Elizabethan

Society. Together the women oversaw a production of *Macbeth* at the Owens College Women's Debating Society and at Collyhurst Recreation Rooms. Pankhurst, Margaret Kemp and Gore-Booth later prepared the women of the society for a production of *Romeo and Juliet*.[76] In 1902, the Elizabethan Society expanded and elected Louie Smith as president, Lil Alexander as treasurer and Alice Dixon as secretary. The society continued to perform Elizabethan works for women's trade union groups, generating much needed social and political interaction between various groups of women. It was reported at the University Settlement annual general meeting that the society, 'has somewhat widened its scope, and many interesting discussions on vital political and social questions have been held.'[77] Pankhurst continued organising the Elizabethan Society with Gore-Booth until 1903.[78]

As well as improving the physical and material lives of the working classes, Gore-Booth was concerned with improving their spiritual lives. She became involved with progressive religious movements. Along with Roper, she attended services at the Upper Brook Street Unitarian Church in Manchester. The two women befriended the minister, John Trevor. Gore-Booth's socialist ideals were shared by Trevor. The minister believed that organised religions were not accessible to the working classes and he vowed to form a church for the workers. After an initial meeting in Chorley Town Hall he founded the Labour Church on 4 October 1891. Two months later he resigned from his position as a Unitarian minister.[79] Trevor produced *The Labour Prophet* as the newsletter of the church, adopting the motto 'let labour be the basis of civil society.'[80] The Labour Church was founded as the spiritual expression of the Labour movement. The object of the church was to provide a 'good democratic or socialistic sermon.'[81] Gore-Booth threw herself into this ideal. From its formation she and Roper delivered talks at Sunday sermons.

Gore-Booth joined other movements which were viewed as radical or New Age at the turn of the twentieth century. She became a vegetarian in 1900 and remained so for the rest of her life.[82] The vegetarian movement in England has its roots in Manchester and the first official organisation, the Vegetarian Society, was based there from 1847. Although vegetarianism is now often linked with the women's movement, the Vegetarian Society had a predominately male membership during the nineteenth century. The first women's vegetarian union was not formed in England until 1895.[83] Female membership of the society did not become significant until after the formation of militant suffragette organisations in 1905. Research by historian Leah Leneman suggests that suffragettes often chose to become vegetarian for various reasons, 'ranging from the psychological identification of women with animals as victims of male brutality, to the empowering idea that women confined to a homemaker's role could still help create a new and more compassionate world by adopting a vegetarian diet.'[84] Gore-Booth chose to become vegetarian because of her love of nature and her socialist commitment to create a better world.

Notes

1 EGB, 'From a Far County,' *Poems* (London: Longmans, 1898), p. 17.
2 *Sligo Champion* (19 Dec 1896), p. 9.
3 For a detailed discussion of the conflict between Irish national politics and the suffrage movement, particularly the role of Irish Party in deferring franchise for women see: Elizabeth Crawford, *The Women's Suffrage Movement in Britain and Ireland: A Regional Study* (London: Routledge, 2006).
4 *Irish Women's Suffrage and Local Government Association Annual Report*, 1896.
5 The following account of the suffrage meeting is taken from a report in *Sligo Champion* (26 December 1896), p.8.
6 Haverty, *Constance Markievicz*, p. 41.
7 *Sligo Champion* (19 Dec 1896), p. 9.
8 *Weekly Irish Times* (30 Jan 1897), p. 4.
9 Ibid.
10 Henry Francis Gore-Booth was rector of the Church of the Sacred Trinity from 1885 until 1902. PRONI, D4131/H/5, diary of Henry Francis Gore-Booth, 1875–1903.
11 Lissadel [sic] Street in Salford is positioned just beside Pendleton Town Hall, Manchester.
12 EGB, *CE*, pp. 9–10.
13 PRONI, Mic 590, Reel/10, will of Eva Gore-Booth, 1 March 1900.
14 'Political Notes,' *The Times* (21 January 1897), p. 5.
15 A monthly column by Andrew Lang, 'At the Sign of the Ship,' was published in *Longman's Magazine* from 1886 until 1905.
16 PRONI, Mic 590, Reel 10, L/11:1, letter from Julian Sturgis to EGB, 7 May 1898.
17 University of Reading, Berkshire, Records of the Longman Group,

ON/11981, account book entry, 26 May 1898.

18 Julian Sturgis' novels were mainly set in Eton and Oxford. The novels were light comedies which provided an insight into the minds of young men of the time.

19 EGB, *CE*, p. 31.

20 Ibid, p. 118.

21 EGB, 'The Repentance of Eve: A Picture by Con Gore-Booth,' in *Poems*, p. 19.

22 'Reviews,' *Dome* (March 1899), p. 87.

23 'Poems and Verses,' *Academy* (3 June 1899), p. 602.

24 *The Nursing Record & Hospital World* (10 December 1898), p. 481.

25 Letter from Yeats to EGB, 26 December 1898. Warwick Gould, John Kelly and Deirdre Toomey (eds), *The Collected Letters of W.B. Yeats: Volume Two* (Oxford: Clarendon Press, 1997), p. 332.

26 PRONI, Mic 590, Reel 10, L/11:101, letter from Josslyn Gore-Booth to EGB, 17 March 1899.

27 *Freeman's Journal* (9 December 1898).

28 *Irish Times* (28 November 1898), p. 6.

29 Ibid.

30 See appendix of works by EGB.

31 Sligo Steam Navigation Company Ltd offices were based in Wine Street, Sligo. John Kennedy, *History of the Steam Navigation* (Liverpool: Charles Birchall Ltd, 1903), pp. 290–2.

32 The first decennial census in 1801 showed the population of Manchester to be 75,275; in 1851 it soared to 303,382 and the census for 1901 records a population of 606,824.

33 Friedrich Engels, *The Condition of the Working-Class in England in 1844* (London: Penguin Classics, 1987), p.100.

34 Located north-east of Manchester city between the River Irk and St George's Row (now called Rochdale Road).

35 Little Ireland was south of the city centre, located beside an inlet off the River Medlock. There is a plaque on Great Marlborough Street in memory of those who lived in the ghetto.

36 University of Manchester Archives, MUS/1/3/1, 'University Settlement Manchester: The Second Annual Report for year ending 30 June 1898,' p. 15.

37 University of Manchester Archives, MUS/1/3/1, 'University Settlement Manchester: The Third Annual Report for year ending 30 June 1899,' p. 20.

38 EGB, *CE*, p. 14.

39 'University Settlement Manchester: For year ending 30 June 1899,' p. 20.

40 EGB, *CE*, p. 14.

41 *The Nursing Record & Hospital World* (4 March 1899), pp. 180–1.
42 Begg eventually succeeded in having the bill read in February 1900. *Parliamentary Franchise (Extension to Women): A Bill* (House of Commons, 2 February 1900).
43 Pennsylvania State University Libraries, Eva Gore-Booth Collection, box 1, folder 1: AX/B40/RBM/00139, letter from Elizabeth Parker to Esther Roper with recollections of EGB.
44 Millicent Garrett Fawcett, *Women's Suffrage: A Speech Delivered to the Women's Debating Society, the Owens College, Manchester* (Manchester: North of England Society for Women's Suffrage, 1899).
45 Jill Liddington, *The Life and Times of a Respectable Rebel: Selina Cooper 1864–1946* (London: Virago Press, 1984), p. 58.
46 'City Clerks and Trade Unionism: A Meeting,' *MG* (3 December 1895), p. 12.
47 *MG* (29 January 1895), p. 7.
48 Charles Prestwich (CP) Scott became a Liberal MP for the Leigh division of Lancashire in 1895 and he represented the area in parliament until 1905.
49 'Manchester, Salford, and District Women's Trade Union Council,' *MG* (16 February 1895), p. 10.
50 EGB, *CE*, p. 11.
51 Working Class Movement Library, Manchester, 331.88/F4 Box 17, *Women's Trade Union Council: Sixth Annual Report 1900*, 26 January 1901, p. 6.
52 Ibid, p. 7.
53 Ibid, p.12.
54 Ibid, p. 11.
55 EGB, *CE*, p. 11.
56 University of Manchester Archives, MUS/2/1/4, 'University Settlement Manchester: The Fourth Annual Report for year ending 30 June 1900,' p. 22.
57 *The Women's Trade Union Council: Sixth Annual Report 1900*, 26 January 1901, p. 6.
58 There are at least two exact typed copies of this play; the first copy of the play was discovered among Gore-Booth's personal and literary papers. PRONI, Mic 590, Reel 8, 1–56. A second copy was originally in the possession of Elizabeth MacGowan (Mrs Alfred Haworth), a graduate and associate of Owens College. The second copy was given to Michael Herbert of the North West Labour History Group by Giles Haworth grandson of MacGowan on 17 February 2002. Herbert kindly leant the author this copy in April 2010. The copy is signed at the front by Gore-Booth with the address 83 Heald Place in her handwriting, which means that the play was most probably written sometime between 1898 and 1907.
59 Sonja Tiernan (ed.), *Fiametta: A Previously Unpublished Play by Eva Gore-*

Booth (New York: Edwin Mellen Press, 2010).

60 As cited in Lewis, *Eva Gore-Booth and Esther Roper*, p. 87.

61 Esther Roper, 'The Suffrage for Women,' *MG* (4 February 1903), p. 10.

62 North of England Society for Women's Suffrage, *Report of the Executive Committee*, Manchester, 1901, p. 4.

63 Ibid.

64 EGB, *CE*, p. 13.

65 Lancashire Record Office, Preston, Papers of Selina Jane Cooper, DDX 1137/2/35, menu from the *Florence Restaurant*, 18 March 1901.

66 Jill Liddington and Jill Norris, *One Hand Tied behind Us: The Rise of the Women's Suffrage Movement* (London: Virago, 1978), p. 15.

67 A term coined by Liddington and Norris in 1978 to describe the group including Gore-Booth, Roper, Sarah Dickenson, Selina Cooper and Sarah Reddish.

68 'The Women's Trade Union Council,' *MG* (28 January 1903), p. 7.

69 Christabel Pankhurst, *Unshackled: The Story of How we Won the Vote* (London: Hutchinson, 1959), p.40.

70 Ibid.

71 Roper advised Emmeline Pankhurst that Christabel should study law. Mrs Pankhurst was so delighted by the idea that she contacted Lord Haldane to sponsor her daughter's application. See *University of Manchester Register*, p. 498.

72 Sylvia Pankhurst, *The Suffragette Movement* (1931; London: Virago Press, 1977), p. 164.

73 Ibid.

74 Ibid.

75 Pankhurst, *Unshackled*, p. 41.

76 University of Manchester Archives, MUS/2/1/5, 'University Settlement Manchester: The Fifth Annual Report for year ending 30 June 1901,' p. 23.

77 University of Manchester Archives, MUS/2/1/6, 'Manchester Art Museum & University Settlement: Annual Report for year ending 30 April 1902,' p. 33.

78 University of Manchester Archives, MUS/2/1/7, 'Manchester Art Museum & University Settlement: Annual Report for year ending 30 April 1903,' p. 26.

79 John Trevor, *My Quest for God* (London: Labour Prophet Office, 1897), p. 245.

80 *The Labour Church Hymn Book* (London: Labour Prophet Office, 1892), p. 1.

81 Ibid.

82 *Vegetarian Messenger and Health Review*, 29 (1938), 258.

83 Formed by Madame Alex. Veigele in November 1895, the Women's

Vegetarian Union was based at 96 Crawford Street, Bryanston Square, West London. 'The Women's Vegetarian Union,' *Woman's Signal* (21 November 1895), p. 324.

84 Leah Leneman, 'The Awakening Instinct: Vegetarianism and the Women's Suffrage Movement in Britain,' *Women's History Review*, 6:2 (1997), 271.

4

Sadder and wiser women: Lancashire trade unions

'And the Little Waves of Breffny go stumbling through my soul'[1]

Gore-Booth travelled back home to Sligo on short visits when the opportunity arose. It is evident from her poetry that she missed the beauty and peace of rural Ireland. She published two poems in *New Ireland Review* in 1899. The first poem, 'The Place of Peace,' expresses a dark uncomfortable feeling about the crowded streets of Manchester:

> The Fear that lurks in the crowded street
> And hides in the market-place,
> And follows the stranger with unseen feet
> And a half-averted face,
> Shall fly from the silence that sanctifies
> The lonely wood and the wind's held breath,
> From the sorrows of fools, and the dreams of the wise,
> And the shadows that darken the gates of death.[2]

Life at Lissadell had changed dramatically since Eva originally left Ireland. Her father had become seriously ill shortly after her departure. In 1899 her parents moved to a health resort in St Moritz, Switzerland due to her father's declining health. On 13 January 1900 Sir Henry died.[3] The Ballinfull Co-operative Dairy Society, of which Sir Henry was president, issued a statement of their condolence. Describing Sir Henry 'as landlord between whom and his tenants there have always existed the most friendly relations; as a kindly local gentleman who always evinced the keenest interest for the well-being of his tenantry and the people among whom he lived.'[4]

Eva and Constance remained particularly close and Constance visited her sister often in England. Figure 8 shows the two sisters relaxing in Wasey Sterry's garden in London, with their dog, Satan.[5]

Months after the death of her father, Constance's engagement to Casimir Joseph-Dunin de Markievicz, was announced. Casimir was the second son of a Polish noble, Peter Dunin de Markievicz. Constance met him in Paris the previous year. Casimir was a young widower with a son, Stanislas (Staskow). Casimir was also studying art in Paris after dropping out of law school from the University of Kiev. There were questions concerning Casimir's nobility and the Gore-Booth family did not approve of the impending marriage. Aware of the possible reaction, Constance wrote to Josslyn notifying him of her impending marriage. She asserted that if necessary she would live at the Markievicz family estate near Kiev after the marriage. Eva wrote to her sister in delight that, 'I can't help being frightfully amused when I think of the bomb bursting.'[6]

In September 1900 Constance and Casimir married at the Church of St Marylebone in London, followed by a service at the Russian Legation and at a registrar's office.[7] Although Casimir was Polish by race, he was a Russian subject and such formalities were necessary.

8 Eva and Constance Gore-Booth with their dog, Satan. Photograph taken by Wasey Sterry possibly at his house, High Ashes, circa 1898

Eva and Mabel acted as bridesmaids and Josslyn gave the bride away.[8] After the marriage Constance assumed her husband's name and title, becoming Countess Markievicz. The marriage was closely followed by the wedding of the youngest Gore-Booth daughter, Mabel, in December. She married Percy Foster, of the Royal Scots Greys, son of John Foster, JP of Coombe Lodge, Reading. Eva acted as bridesmaid along with her cousins, the Wynnes and Miss Appleton.[9] Again Josslyn gave the bride away. Markievicz and her new husband attended the wedding as guests, along with Eva's friend and literary mentor, Julian Sturgis.

As was usual, Josslyn, as the eldest Gore-Booth son, became owner of the Lissadell estate on the death of his father. Eva, Constance and Mordaunt each received £2,500 inheritance from their father and an equal value which would be held in trust for them and paid annually at a rate of £33. Mabel received a somewhat larger inheritance which amounted to nearly £300 per year, possibly as a reward for choosing a more conventional life than her older sisters. The yearly income wasn't considerable, but it would provide Eva with a welcome supplement to her salary. The fact that Josslyn had become a landowner caused him much concern. Yeats had observed that Josslyn 'is "theoretically" a homeruler & practically some kind of humanitarian, much troubled by the responsibily [sic] of his wealth & almost painfully conscientious.'[10] Josslyn attempted to make good the ugly acts perpetrated by landlords. He became one of the first landowners to adopt a scheme set up by the Wyndham Land Act in 1903, encouraging tenants to buy out their land holdings.[11] He assisted more than 1,200 tenants to buy 28,000 acres of land from the Lissadell estate, despite criticism from his less liberal-minded friends.[12] The tenants' payments for the purchase were spread over sixty-eight years. Even the earliest tenants to avail of the scheme did not make their final payments until 1971. Gore-Booth supported her brother's actions and published a poem the next year, entitled 'The Land to the Landlord.' Her rejection of landownership and of her own heritage is evident from the opening stanza:

> You hug to your soul a handful of dust,
> And you think the round world your sacred trust–
> But the sun shines, and the wind blows,
> And nobody cares and nobody knows.[13]

By the start of the twentieth century Gore-Booth had completely rejected her advantaged heritage and was submerged into her new life in Manchester. Her dramatic change of lifestyle is particularly evident in the census return forms for 1901. Gore-Booth and Roper used the census to make a particular feminist statement about their relationship. The women drew a bracket around both of their names and under the heading 'relation to head of house,' they entered, 'joint, both heads of the house.'[14] They were living at 83 Heald Place. Gore-Booth's occupation is recorded as secretary of women's trade society. Roper is recorded as secretary of a women's suffrage society. Both of these occupations did not return huge earnings. In order to supplement their income the two women boarded out a room of the house. A hydraulic worker and his wife are listed as their boarders. Reginald Roper had moved out of the house and was working as a school master in Mostyn House School at Parkgate in Chester; he lived on the premises.[15]

The Moss Side census return shows Gore-Booth as an employed worker. She was sharing a three bedroom terraced house with her female partner and a working-class couple, in the midst of a poor industrial area. In contrast, the Sligo census for her family records the lifestyle from which she left. The returns show that her aunt Augusta, a single woman living in rural Sligo, had six servants one of whom was only twelve years of age. In total contrast, under the section for employment Augusta's income is recorded simply as derived from land.[16] Josslyn's census return shows him and his mother living at Lissadell House with thirteen servants, including a butler, stable hands, a housekeeper, a lady's maid and four house maids. Josslyn's occupation is listed as baronet.[17]

The year 1901 marked a change in Gore-Booth's political campaigning tactics. She decided it was time to 'adopt newer and more forcible methods.'[18] Dismayed with the lack of response to their parliamentary petition, she describes how 'deputations of enthusiastic workers,' arrived at the House of Commons and 'could not believe in the indifference of the well-to-do world to the claims of unenfranchised wage-earners.' The deputations 'came back to Lancashire sadder and wiser women.'[19] Gore-Booth resolved to secure a representative for women in the House of Commons. She looked to the recently formed Labour Representation Committee (LRC) as the best chance of gaining the franchise for women. The Independent Labour Party had joined forces with trade unionists to establish the LRC in

1900, a precursor group to the modern British Labour Party. The new organisation demanded representation for working men in parliament.[20]

The first annual conference of the LRC was held in Manchester.[21] Gore-Booth recognised this event as a turning point for working-class men. Consecutive Reform Acts of 1832, 1867 and 1884 extended parliamentary franchise to men who met certain property criteria. By the time of the LRC's formation, approximately 60 per cent of all men were entitled to vote at general elections. The men who remained unenfranchised now had representatives in the House of Commons to look after their interests. Gore-Booth sought the same representation for female workers and petitioned the LRC. The party could not appreciate why working women would need representation in government. The LRC assumed that men were the bread winners of the family and therefore working-class men supported women financially. Gore-Booth was forthright in her condemnation of this view. In her pamphlet *Women Workers and Parliamentary Representation*, she observed 'the theory that working men keep their families, and that the earning of women are merely an extra help to family finances, may in the past have been quoted as justification for the low wages of women, but it has grown to be wholly untrue to the facts of life.'[22] In fact, it was primarily women's wages which funded the newly formed LRC.

The LRC was affiliated with the textile trade unions; the unions agreed to pay an affiliation fee of 10 shillings per thousand members. Furthermore, a levy of 4 pence per annum was to be paid by individual members of the union; 1 penny of this levy would fund salaries and expenses of Labour MPs in parliament.[23] In return the LRC would select trade union members as their election candidates. A huge fund was secured from union members and by January 1903 they had amassed over £715 for their parliamentary account.[24] The fact that the majority of textile trade unionists were female created an unfair anomaly. Factory women were expected to fund election campaigns and to pay the wages of politicians, many of whom did not support female suffrage. Additionally women were not even entitled to vote at general elections or to stand as parliamentary candidates. Roper at once highlighted this inconsistency to the Executive Committee of the NESWS. In her annual report to the Committee she bluntly questioned if 'the women pay, why should their interests not be attended to?'[25]

This situation intensified in the summer of 1902 when a by-election was called in the working-class constituency of Clitheroe. At a conference of trade unionists David Shackleton was proposed as the Labour candidate. Shackleton was a working-class man who began working in the cotton factories at the age of nine. He was an elect member of the Central Committee of the Weavers' Amalgamation, an important post within the trade union movement. The Trade Union Council proposed to introduce a supplementary fund to finance Shackleton's salary and expenses. There were 18,000 trade unionists in Clitheroe and the vast majority were female. Each member would be obliged to pay an additional sixpence towards the fund for Shackleton.[26] Gore-Booth, Roper, Cooper, Reddish, Pankhurst and Emmeline Pankhurst approached Shackleton. They informed him that if women were to finance his election campaign, he must represent women's interests. Shackleton was dependent on the support of female unionists, a detail which Gore-Booth reinforced with the unions. She pointed out the 'incontestable fact that before the Cotton Unions could subscribe £900 a year to the Labour Representation Committee, and before a candidate could be run and his salary paid as a Labour candidate for Clitheroe, a ballot had to be taken of the women who far outnumbered the men in Unions.'[27]

Gore-Booth and the radical suffragists offered to campaign for Shackleton amongst female trade unionists, if in return Shackleton guaranteed his support of women's suffrage. Shackleton acknowledged 'how large a burden fell on the shoulders of these unrepresented workers.'[28] He agreed that, if elected to the House of Commons, he would seek enfranchisement for women on the same grounds as men. Gore-Booth, Roper, Cooper, Reddish and the Pankhursts organised several meetings with female trade unionists. The meetings generated positive local media attention. In the *Nelson Chronicle* it was reported that the resolution to support Shackleton was carried by a mass majority; only one woman voted against it.[29] In the popular socialist paper the *Clarion*, Mrs Myddleton-Worrall under the pseudonym Julia Dawson, wrote a favourable account of suffrage developments in Clitheroe.[30]

Union members voted overwhelmingly in favour of financially supporting Shackleton. He was officially put forward as the LRC candidate for the by-election on 3 July. In his election address Shackleton outlined his policies. If he successfully entered the House of Commons he vowed to work for the interests of trade unionists. He undertook to fight for factory workers' rights including restricting the working day to eight hours and improving housing and old-age pensions. He made a long speech detailing many worthwhile political policies, only mentioning franchise for women at the last minute.[31] This was a fore-warning of what was to come.

Shackleton's appointment as the Labour candidate generated immense support from trade unions. The huge show of co-operation between the unions and the LRC convinced Philip Snowden, a proposed candidate for the Independent Labour Party, to stand down from the by-election. Sensing the strong community backing for Shackleton, Philip Stanhope decided not to stand as a Liberal candidate. In response the Conservative Party resolved that it was pointless to contest the by-election. Shackleton was elected unopposed and entered government on 1 August 1902, becoming the third Labour candidate to enter parliament. The party declared that Shackleton's election was one 'of the greatest triumphs which Labour has ever had in its political history.'[32] This may well have been the case. However, Shackleton proved to be a bitter disappointment for female trade unionists and for the suffrage movement in general. He failed to raise the issue of female enfranchisement in the House of Commons despite several petitions from female trade unionists. He not only proved to be unsupportive of women workers, Shackleton later advocated for further restrictions to be placed on working women, including a ban on married women working.[33] If introduced, this restriction would force a huge percentage of female cotton operatives out of work. In 1902, there were 74,000 married female cotton workers in Lancashire.[34] This proposal was an extraordinary move for Shackleton who was personally aware of the importance of married women's wages. In his early career Shackleton had become dependent on his wife's income. After he was elected onto the committee of the Accrington Weavers' Association he was dismissed by his employer, who objected to trade unions. Shackleton survived on his wife's earnings for seventeen weeks while he was unemployed.[35]

In her autobiography, the socialist feminist Dora Montefiore highlights the events of the Clitheroe by-election as a particular blow to the women's trade union movement. Montefiore describes how the Lancashire women were 'suffering under the double injustice of having, through the Textile Union, to help to pay the larger share of the levy which formed the parliamentary salary of their so-called representative, Mr (now Sir David) Shackleton. There being more women than men in the Textile Union, the heavy burden of the levy fell on the women members.'[36] Gore-Booth and her group of followers were appalled at Shackleton's betrayal. Along with Roper and Pankhurst, Gore-Booth took a well deserved break in Venice after the by-election. During this time the three women re-assessed their campaign. On their return, a letter from the secretary of the LRC awaited Gore-Booth at the Women's Trades Council office. The LRC had the audacity to request that the Women's Trades Council officially affiliate with them. Gore-Booth responded that the Council would agree to this affiliation if the LRC assured them that 'the representation of female labour is part of your programme.'[37]

The women mounted retaliation for Shackleton's betrayal. Roper wrote to the *Manchester Guardian* noting that 'when Mr. Shackleton was elected to parliament for the Clitheroe division . . . it was pointed out that out of the textile trade unionists in Lancashire and Cheshire 96,000 are women and 69,000 are men. The women pay the same Parliamentary levy as the men.'[38] She concluded with the apt question, 'can anyone with the most elementary knowledge of labour questions and of modern trade competition doubt the necessity of the franchise to protect the industrial interests of these women trade unionists?'[39] In response more than 5,500 women unionists petitioned Shackleton to press the issue of women's enfranchisement in the House of Commons. The women supposed it their right to share in the benefit of Parliamentary Representation.[40] Gore-Booth was sickened by the actions of the LRC and accused the party of being 'built in sin and founded on unrighteousness.'[41]

Dismayed, Gore-Booth continued to act as co-secretary of the Women's Trade Union Council. She dedicated herself to organising the women cotton operatives in Manchester and Salford by increasing membership of the council. It was imperative to increase the number of working women in the WTUC as Sylvia Pankhurst had pointed out, 'the Council itself was mainly composed of well-to-do people desirous of encouraging working women to join.'[42] Gore-Booth and Dickenson both realised that there were practical reasons which stopped working women from attending the WTUC meetings. The work at the cotton mills was gruelling and the women worked long hours. Not surprisingly, at the end of the working day the women wanted to go directly home. It was expensive and inconvenient for them to return to the council offices for meetings in the evening. In order to solve this problem Gore-Booth and Dickenson began to offer the women tea and cake at the meetings. This had an immediate effect and the council's annual report announced that, 'the tea has had good results in introducing a social element that promoted good fellowship and a friendly feeling among the members, and the attendance has largely increased.'[43] Through various efforts membership of the council doubled during the year 1902.

Gore-Booth's work at the WTUC was highly successful. She orchestrated the establishment of dozens of thriving unions for women workers. Manchester historian Michael Herbert maintains that the most successful union established during this time was the Salford and District Association of Power Loom Weavers. The Weavers union was founded in April 1902 and Nellie Keenan became the first Treasurer. The wages of female weavers were notoriously low and all previous attempts to organise them had failed. The women relished the opportunity of joining the new union and soon more than 1,000 women signed up for membership. Weeks after its establishment members protested at the Free Trade Hall in Manchester against the introduction of a corn tax. Herbert highlights that 'the women's resolution not only protested against the tax and the fact that it would fall heavily on women "the worst paid workers in the country" but also objected to the fact that their exclusion from the franchise prevented them "from making an effective protest at the Ballot Box."'[44]

The actions of the Weavers union soon drew the attention of a powerful trade unionist, William Wilkinson from Burnley. Wilkinson was secretary of two large unions, the Northern Counties Amalgamated Association of Weavers, which had a membership of over 80,000 and the even larger United Textile Factory Workers' Association. Wilkinson was so impressed with the Association of Power Loom Weavers that he attended their general meeting in October 1902. He appealed to the 500 women in attendance to become affiliated with the Northern Association of Weavers. The women decided to remain independent. If they chose to join Wilkinson's organisation they would have lost their sickness benefit and the weekly union dues would increase from 2d to 3d per member. Wilkinson was so encouraged by the organisation and objectives of the women's association that he became particularly friendly with Gore-Booth and Dickenson. Through this friendship Wilkinson became a supporter of the suffrage movement; he would later champion the cause at an annual LRC conference.[45]

At the WTUC annual meeting in January 1903 it was announced that membership of the council had increased to over 2,000 members. The chair, Amy Bulley, gloried in the fact that there were more women joining the organisation.[46] This was of little consolation to Gore-Booth, whose report depicts depressing and unsanitary working environments for women. Her report concludes by pointing out the inadequacies of the WTUC, 'the fact that the council had been able to double its membership during that time went far, however ... the council was hampered by the want of adequate financial support.'[47] Gore-Booth continued to orchestrate positive change for women through the organisation. In the spring of 1903 she became the council's representative on the Technical Instruction Committee of Manchester City Council. In this capacity she ensured that girls were not excluded from scholarships to attend the Municipal School of Technology.

Positive change for women was a slow process and Gore-Booth began to realise that the work of the WTUC could only achieve basic advances for women in the workplace. She again focused on securing a Member of Parliament to advocate for women's suffrage. In preparation for the next general election Gore-Booth, Roper, Reddish, Cooper and Dickenson formed a group to sponsor and support an election candidate pledged to women's enfranchisement. They chose a rather cumbersome title for their organisation; the Lancashire and Cheshire Women Textile and Other Workers' Representation Committee (LCWTOWRC). The title reflected that this was a local female equivalent to the Labour Representation Committee. The group officially formed in the summer of 1903 and acted independently, not receiving any financial support from the NESWS. In July 1904 the Committee released the following manifesto addressed to 'Fellow Workers':

> During the last few years the need of political power for the defence of the workers has been felt by every section of the labour world. Among the men the growing sense of the importance of this question has resulted in the formation of the Labour Representation Committee with the object of gaining direct Parliamentary Representation for the already enfranchised working men. Meanwhile, the position of the unenfranchised working women, who are by their voteless condition

> shut out from all political influence, is becoming daily more precarious. They cannot hope to hold their own in industrial matters, where their interests may clash with those of their enfranchised fellow-workers or employers.[48]

The manifesto notes that the committee was formed in order to secure representation for female textile workers in the House of Commons and concludes with a positive assertion that 'what Lancashire and Cheshire Women think today England will do tomorrow.'[49]

The committee sought donations from working women. They required £500 to cover the election expenses of a suitable candidate. This call for finances could not have come at a worse time. The cotton trade was undergoing a major depression. Roper estimated that women, who normally earned 24 or 25 shillings a week in the factories, were now only receiving six or seven shillings a week.[50] The group was not dissuaded. In a further attempt to secure funds a circular was sent to every individual who had signed the graduate's petition in 1902. The appeal explained that 'for a long time we have been uselessly supported by a majority of MPs – a little soul in a great body, – and we think more could be gained by one man absolutely devoted to our interests who would be a connecting link between us and the Government.'[51] Although financial support was not forthcoming, Katharine Thomasson donated money to support the work of Gore-Booth and Roper. Thomasson did not necessarily support the ethos of the committee but she was a dedicated disciple of the two women.[52] Elizabeth Wolstenholme Elmy offered to seek funds for the organisation stating that 'what is being done amongst the women workers of the North is of more value to our cause than all the work of the N.U. [National Union of Women's Suffrage Societies] put together.'[53]

Gore-Booth wrote the first official pamphlet of the committee, aptly entitled *Women Workers and Parliamentary Representation*. She announces in the opening paragraph that 'amongst those who have for their present ideal, in industrial matters, a fair day's wages for a fair day's work, the low payment of women remains one of the great problems of our modern civilisation.'[54] Gore-Booth then launched directly into an analysis of the social problems created by low incomes, describing 'the wretched houses, insanitary and overcrowded, that disfigure our great towns, the children going hungry to school, the old people left penniless and uncared for, the numbers that sleep out every night of the year, these and many other evils are the direct result of poverty.'[55] Discussing the various unions with which she had worked, she asserted that 'Trade Unionists must agree that there is something radically wrong with the present position of women in the labour market.'[56] Yet, in reality male trade unionists openly discriminated against female workers. Male workers often viewed low paid female workers as a threat to their own job security and labour rates. The situation in industrial cities was becoming deplorable and the gap in pay between men and women positioned family members against each other.

A number of female members of the ILP did not support Gore-Booth's new committee. Emmeline Pankhurst was inspired to form her own organisation devoted to achieving votes for women. She called a meeting on 10 October 1903 at her home, 62 Nelson Street, in Manchester. During this first meeting it was agreed that the new organisation would be named the Women's Labour Representation Committee. This name was overturned by her daughter, Christabel, who had not attended the meeting but later pointed out that the title was too similar to that of Gore-Booth's committee. Mrs Pankhurst decided instead to call her new organisation the Women's Social and Political Union (WSPU). In her autobiography, she claims that the WSPU was the first and only name chosen for the organisation; she neglects to mention that the original title was overturned because of Gore-Booth. This is not surprising, as by then Mrs Pankhurst had become envious of her daughter's close relationship with Gore-Booth. Sylvia Pankhurst later wrote that her mother was 'intensely jealous of her daughter's new friendship.'[57] Indeed Mrs Pankhurst's biographer, David Mitchell, maintains that it was this jealousy which actually drove her to form the WSPU. In later years she attempted to write Gore-Booth out of suffrage history altogether. In her autobiography, Mrs Pankhurst names the American suffragist, Susan B. Anthony, as the inspiration behind Christabel's suffrage work; there is no mention of Gore-Booth.[58]

1903 thus witnessed the formation of two new groups based in Manchester, both dedicated to securing votes for women. Although the groups sought the same ultimate goal, the way in which they campaigned would differ immensely and cause a division through the centre of the suffrage movement. The committee, especially Gore-Booth's involvement with it, also generated a division within women's trade unionism. During her campaign on behalf of the Representation Committee, Gore-Booth continued in her position as co-secretary of the WTUC. The council were adamant that improvements for women's working conditions would be achieved solely through trade unionism. They viewed the campaign for women's suffrage as a separate and unrelated issue.

On 11 July 1904 Gore-Booth's involvement with both the council and the committee was publically challenged by Amy Bulley. Bulley was not only chair of the council she was also a respected journalist for the *Manchester Guardian*. Bulley printed a disclaimer in the pages of the newspaper. The article begins, 'it has been erroneously stated that the Council is connected with the movement for the enfranchisement of women, and leaflets written on behalf of a woman's suffrage society in the textile districts have been attributed to our initiative.'[59] Bulley was at pains to point out that the WTUC was not connected 'in any way with women's suffrage or any political movement.' She highlights that 'Miss Eva Gore-Booth, one of our organising secretaries, has taken some share in propaganda connected with women's suffrage but her action in this regard is entirely unconnected with the work of the Council.'[60]

This public attack on Gore-Booth's work angered one committee member of the WTUC. In retaliation Christabel demanded that the council include women's suffrage as one of its objectives. The council denied the request reiterating that however desirable the advocacy of women's suffrage, their goal was the organisation of women's labour. Christabel resigned from the council in protest. Gore-Booth and Dickenson were left with no alternative but to resign from their positions as joint secretaries. This meant that Gore-Booth also had to resign from associated positions including her presidency of the Manchester and Salford Association of Patent Cop Winders and as co-secretary of the Women's Textile and Representation Committee.[61]

Together Gore-Booth and Dickenson formed the Manchester and Salford Women's Trade and Labour Council (WTLC), in 1904. The Labour Council was based at the same address as the LCWTOWRC, at 5 John Dalton Street. The office was just across the road from the offices of the WTUC at 9 Albert Square. Significantly, eight unions which Gore-Booth represented including the bookbinders, tailoresses and the power loom weavers left the WTUC and joined the new Labour Council.[62] Nellie Keenan, treasurer of the Salford and

District Association of Power Loom Weavers, was appointed treasurer of the new council. Gore-Booth and Dickenson had forsaken their wages as joint secretaries of the WTUC but financial support for the new agency was forthcoming. Local socialist and labour organisations including the Manchester branch of the National Union of Clerks, the Women's Co-operative Guild and the Nelson Labour Representation Committee financially supported the new council. Gore-Booth appealed to her brother, Josslyn, for help. In response Josslyn paid an annual subscription fee of £5.[63] Amy Bulley wished the new organisation well. She wrote in the annual report of the Women's Trade Council: 'We shall watch their progress with friendly interest, hoping that eventually the change may help to consolidate the women's trade union movement.'[64]

The new council had a very clear objective, to improve the working conditions of women by securing their parliamentary franchise. In the meantime the council intended to protect working women in any way possible. They established a Women's Insurance Society to provide financial security for individuals who lost their jobs. Perhaps even more importantly, council members publicly responded to negative propaganda about working women. At the turn of the twentieth century, working women, especially married working women, were viewed with suspicion. During times of increased economic or social struggle, politicians often blamed working women for a range of problems, from high unemployment rates to various social concerns. The fact that women were unenfranchised meant that they became an easy target for politicians. An influx of proposed measures to restrict women's access to employment began in the first decade of the twentieth century.[65]

By the end of 1903 Gore-Booth was totally engaged with political activities and union campaigns. However, she still found time to write. While on a short trip home to Lissadell she wrote a poem, 'The Little Waves of Breffny.'[66] George Russell was so impressed by the verse that he asked permission to publish it in *Celtic Christmas*, a special literary edition of *The Irish Homestead*. On reading the poem fellow Irish author Katharine Tynan noted that it 'will go singing in the human heart so long as the heart answers to poetry. It is a small masterpiece.'[67] Indeed numerous composers set the poem to music, including the British composer, Edgar Leslie Bainton.[68]

The success and interest of this volume of *The Irish Homestead* inspired Russell to compile a volume of poetry, 'not only on account of the beauty of much of the poetry, but because it revealed a new mood in Irish verse.'[69] He requested that Gore-Booth and seven other poets submit a selection of their poetry. Russell published the volume entitled *New Songs, a Lyric Selection made by A.E.* Gore-Booth's poems were published alongside the poetry of esteemed Irish authors including, Padraic Colum, Thomas Keohler, Alice Milligan, Susan Mitchell, Seumas O'Sullivan, George Roberts and Ella Young, accompanied by a sketch from Jack B. Yeats. In the introduction Russell predicted that, 'among these new writers are names which may well be famous hereafter.'[70] Yeats wrote to *Æ* praising the volume, especially Gore-Booth's poem 'the little waves of Breffny,' which he declared is 'charming and delights my conscience.'[71] However, Russell himself later wrote to Tynan that Gore-Booth now 'writes too much, but she has flashes and splendid lines occasionally.'[72] *New Songs* was published in Dublin by the small press O'Donoghue & Co., and sold for one and sixpence.

Russell was delighted that Gore-Booth had begun to adopt a Celtic manner of writing, insisting that this 'ought to be natural for you to do so – a West of Ireland woman and Co. Sligo at that.'[73] This may have inspired her to write more Celtic-style literature. She began to produce plays which imbue the Celtic literary revival style, while still advocating radical feminist principles. Her first play, *Unseen Kings*, was published by Longmans Green & Co in 1904 with a print run of 250. The play was published alongside a selection of her poetry which previously appeared in *The Irish Homestead* and in *Longman's Magazine*. This one act play is subtitled 'the enchantment of Cuculain,' however it differs immensely from the versions of the Cuculain story penned by male Irish authors.[74] Gore-Booth's feminist perspective overturns the conventional gender hierarchy of Celtic Revival drama, typified in Yeats' later play *The Death of Cuchulain*.[75] In Yeats' version Cuculain's main adversary, Queen Maeve, never actually appears on stage.

Gore-Booth often manipulated the traditional version of Celtic mythology in order to present female characters as central to the drama. In T.W. Rolleston's traditional account of Cuculain's death, Queen Maeve sends the children of the druid Cailitin to avenge their father's murder by Cuculain.[76] Cailitin's daughter, Badb, discovers Cuculain resting in a glen with Niamh. Using her newly acquired magic skills, Badb adopts the appearance of Niamh's handmaiden and beckons Niamh away. Badb then assumes the form of Niamh and returns to Cuculain. She convinces Cuculain to enter into battle with Maeve, which ultimately leads to his death. Gore-Booth centres her play not on the death of Cuculain but on the seduction of Niamh by Badb.[77] Badb does not appear as a distorted witch as in traditional legends, rather she appears as a seductive temptress.[78] In Rolleston's version Niamh is portrayed as a secondary character; she is the wife of Cuculain's friend Conaill. Gore-Booth presents Niamh as a powerful and intelligent Prophetess.[79]

The play was applauded by distinguished authors of the Celtic Literary Revival. Russell wrote at once to Gore-Booth, 'I congratulate you on your *Cuculain*. I think it is very beautiful and full of mystery. I always thought that your imagination would incarnate finally in its best form in Irish subjects ... curiously, though, I had been planning out a drama in three acts on the death of Cuculain when your MS. came. I had no ideas half as imaginative as yours, I am sorry to confess.'[80] He wrote again that he hoped Gore-Booth's play would be performed in the Abbey Theatre during a week of performances including his own *Deirdre*, Edward Martyn's *Enchanted Sea*, *Cathleen ni Hoolihan* by Yeats and *The Tinker and Faery* by Douglas Hyde.[81] This never materialised and James and Margaret Cousins accounted for this in their autobiographical account, *We Two Together*. The Cousins maintained that the Abbey Theatre could not produce the play due to technical complications. It appears that the Abbey production team could not work out how to make 'a fog ... condense into a living figure,' or indeed, how to make a huge crow 'fly across the stage.'[82] The Independent Theatre Company, founded by Constance and her husband Casimir Markievicz, later performed *Unseen Kings* in the Abbey Theatre on 25, 26 and 27 January 1912.[83] The play was performed along with Edward Martyn's *Grangecolman*. The programme announces, 'two new productions, first time on any stage.'[84] Constance played the role of the temptress, one of the daughters of Cailitin. Casimir acted as stage manager for the production. (See Figure 9, which shows the complete cast during rehearsals.)

In the same year that *Unseen Kings* was published, Gore-Booth produced a collection of forty-five poems in a volume entitled *The One and the Many*.[85] At the time of publication the *Journal of Education* praised the collection, noting that 'this book brims over with the mystery and poetry of the East and of the ancient religions . . . The over-long crooning lines of some of the chants – Whitman-like and

9 Scene from Gore-Booth's play *Unseen Kings*, performed at the Abbey Theatre in Dublin, January 1912

fascinating ... Miss Gore-Booth is a poet for poets.'[86] Gore-Booth produced yet another drama a year later in 1905. *The Triumph of Maeve: a Romance* was published by Longmans in a single volume with a collection of spiritual poetry, *The Three Resurrections*.[87] Included on the first page of the book was the print of a painting by Gore-Booth's brother-in-law, Casimir Dunin de Markievicz, under the heading 'and amid Unseen Armies reaped and sowed.'[88] The central story of the play focuses on the relationship between women; this time it is Queen Maeve's relationship with her daughter, Fionavar. In the play, Maeve unsuccessfully attempts to shield Fionavar from the atrocities of her brutal and bloody battle with Cuculain. When Fionavar witnesses the aftermath of the battle led by her mother, she dies from heartache. Gore-Booth successfully appropriates the image of a warrior Queen to advocate for pacifism and highlight the brutality and inhumanity of war.

Maeve was a significant influence on Gore-Booth's Celtic writing. She was born near Knocknarea mountain where the warrior queen is reputably buried. A review in The *Irish Homestead* observes the special affinity which she held for the mythical queen, remarking 'that Maeve retains her old dominion over those born under the shadow of her burial place on Knocknarea is clear from the beautiful verses which are already familiar to readers of Gore-Booth's work.'[89] Indeed, her sister also had a special affinity with the warrior queen and she named her only daughter Maeve Markievicz.[90]

Similar to her other Celtic literary works, Gore-Booth manipulates the original Celtic myth of Maeve. In traditional mythology Maeve fought with the men of Ulster in order to win their great brown bull. Maeve wanted to possess the bull so that her property would equal that of her husband's. In Gore-Booth's play, Maeve goes to war not for selfish reasons but to avenge the death of Deirdre of the Sorrows, who was betrayed by the King of Ulster. There is no mention of Maeve's husband in *The Triumph of Maeve*. Maeve's daughter takes centre stage and the mother–daughter relationship becomes central to the story. This is a dramatic change from the traditional version in which Maeve offers her daughter, Fionavar, to the warrior Ferdia as his wife if he will fight Cuculain. This female re-imagining is most obvious in Gore-Booth's cast list. All of the main characters in the play are female; Maeve, her daughter, the female warriors, Fleeas the female captain and a number of druidesses. The female characters exhibit the perceived masculine characteristics of strength and assertiveness along with perceived feminine characteristics of faithfulness and sympathy. In contrast, the minor male characters rarely appear on stage and are portrayed either as weak and passive such as Nera, who longs for his harp rather than a sword, or they are depicted as damaged in some way, such as the characters of the blind man and the lame man.

This manipulation of the traditional story of Maeve caused controversy among members of the Irish Literary Society some years later. Gore-Booth was asked to address the society in Dublin and she chose to read from *The Triumph of Maeve*.[91] In her introduction to the text she discussed how she had taken liberties with the original legend, insisting that 'whilst treating historical subjects in poetic form, facts should be rigorously adhered to, yet myth or legends lent themselves to, and had always been treated with a wide poetic license.'[92] In this way she explained how she 'placed her own constructions on the actions of the characters as they appeared to her, from her studies of all the available sources of inform action.'[93] The chair of the meeting, Emily Hickey, acknowledged 'the poetic beauty' of Gore-Booth's writing but took exception to her manipulation of legends claiming that this 'placed her heroes, Fergus and Cuchullin, on an altogether lower plane than any of the legends warranted.'[94]

Gore-Booth's literature was experiencing popularity in the United States. From as early as 1901 her poems appeared in prestigious newspapers including the *New York Times*, the *New York Tribune* and the *Boston Daily Globe*.[95] Her poetry was often published in impressive American journals including *Living Age*, *Dial* and *Literary Digest*.[96] Her work remained intrinsically female centred, reflecting her drive to protect women whom she described as 'politically the helpless toy of the amateur philanthropist, of the exploiter of cheap labour, and of that narrow spirit of exclusion and oppression that is bred among the very workers themselves by the severity of our present industrial competitive system.'[97] Gore-Booth was clear that while all women suffered the consequences of being politically unenfranchised, the negative consequences were more serious for the poor. Stressing that, 'though the opportunities of educated women may be stunted, and their careers spoilt and their ambitions thwarted, they can at least possess their own souls' light.'[98]

Notes

1 EGB, 'The Little Waves of Breffny,' *CE*, p. 244.
2 Eva Gore-Booth, 'The Place of Peace,' *New Ireland Review*, 11 (May 1899), 176.
3 *Freeman's Journal and Daily Commercial Advertiser* (20 January 1900).
4 *Irish Times* (19 January 1900).
5 Wasey Sterry was a friend of Josslyn Gore-Booth's from Eton. Sterry took numerous photographs of Eva and Constance, many of which are now contained in the Sterry album in the Lissadell Collection. Many thanks to Pamela Cassidy for sending the author a copy of this picture.
6 PRONI, D4131/K/1, correspondence of Constance Markievicz.
7 Roper, (ed.), *Prison Letters*, p. 8.
8 'Fashionable Marriage,' *Irish Times* (1 Oct 1900), p. 7.
9 'Fashionable Marriage,' *Irish Times* (3 December 1900), p. 6.
10 Letter from Yeats to Susan Mary Yeats, 16 December 1894. Kelly and Domville (eds), *Letters of W.B. Yeats: Volume One*, p. 418.
11 The Wyndham Land Act, 'fundamentally transformed the nature of land holdings in Ireland: the Treasury invested over £70 million in Irish land purchase, 200,000 tenant farmers became owner-occupiers under the Act, and the system of dual ownership created by the 1881 Land Act was replaced by a peasant proprietorship.' Fergus Campbell, 'Irish Popular Politics and the Making of the Wyndham Land Act, 1901–1903,' *The Historical Journal*, 45:4 (2002), 755.
12 James, *The Gore-Booths of Lissadell*, pp. 102–3.
13 EGB, *CE*, p. 238.
14 1901 census return for Lancaster, Moss Side.
15 1901 census return for Cheshire.
16 National Archives of Ireland, Leitrim – Roscommon Census return 1901.
17 Ibid.
18 EGB, 'The Women's Suffrage Movement among Trade Unionists,' in Brougham Villiers (ed.), *The Case for Women's Suffrage* (London: T. Fisher Unwin, 1907), p. 51.
19 Ibid, p. 52.
20 The resolution was passed at the Labour Representation conference on 27 February 1900. *The Labour Party Foundation Conference and Annual Reports 1900–5* (London: Hammersmith Ltd, 1967), p. 14.
21 First Annual Conference of the LRC held in the Co-operative Hall, Downing Street, Manchester on 1 February 1901.
22 EGB, *Women Workers and Parliamentary Representation*, Textile Tracts No 1, (Manchester: Lancashire & Cheshire Women Textile and Other Workers' Representation Committee, c.1905), p. 3.
23 Rosen, *Rise Up Women*, p. 26.

24 An amount of £715 19s 9d was recorded in the annual report. *The Labour Party Foundation Conference*, p. 94.
25 Esther Roper, 'The Cotton Trade Unions and the Enfranchisement of Women,' *Report of the Executive Committee* (Manchester: North of England Society for Women's Suffrage, 1902), pp. 13–14.
26 *Women's Suffrage Record* (October 1903), p. 1.
27 EGB, 'Women's Suffrage Movement,' p. 54.
28 Ibid.
29 *Nelson Chronicle* (18 July 1902).
30 Julia Dawson, 'Our Women's Letter,' *Clarion* (15 August 1902).
31 *Cotton Factory Times* (25 July 1902).
32 *The Labour Party Foundation Conference and Annual Conference Reports, 1900–1905* (London: Hammersmith Reprints, 1967), p. 91.
33 Ross Murdoch Martin, *The Lancashire Giant: David Shackleton, Labour Leader and Civil Servant* (Liverpool: Liverpool University Press, 2000), pp. 176–7.
34 EGB, *Women Workers*, p. 3.
35 Joyce Bellamy and John Saville, *Dictionary of Labour Biography: Volume II* (London: MacMillan, 1974), p. 335.
36 Dora Montefiore, *From a Victorian to a Modern* (London: E. Archer, 1927).
37 People's History Museum, Manchester, LP/LRC/5/402, letter from EGB to secretary of the LRC, 9 Oct 1902.
38 Esther Roper, 'The Suffrage for Women,' *MG* (4 February 1903), p. 10.
39 Ibid.
40 EGB, 'Women's Suffrage Movement,' p. 54.
41 Ibid, p. 55.
42 Sylvia Pankhurst, *The Suffragette Movement*, p. 164.
43 Working Class Movement Library, Manchester, 331.88/F4 Box 17, *Women's Trade Union Council: Eighth Annual Report 1902* (20 January 1903), p. 17.
44 Michael Herbert, *The Wearing of the Green: A Political History of the Irish in Manchester* (London: Irish in Britain Representation Group, 2001), p. 77.
45 Liddington and Norris, *One Hand Tied behind Us*, pp. 159–60.
46 EGB, 'The Women's Trade Union Council: The Annual Report, *MG* (28 January 1903), p. 7.
47 Ibid.
48 'Lancashire and Cheshire Women Textile and Other Workers Representation Committee Manifesto' (July 1904).
49 Ibid.
50 Esther Roper, 'Lancashire and Cheshire Women Textile and Other Workers' Representation Committee Circular' (June 1904).
51 Ibid.

52 As cited in Crawford, *Suffrage Movement*, p. 332.
53 Ibid.
54 EGB, *Women Workers*, p. 1.
55 Ibid, p. 2.
56 Ibid, p. 4.
57 Sylvia Pankhurst, *The Suffragette Movement*, p. 134.
58 Emmeline Pankhurst, *My Own Story: The Autobiography of Emmeline Pankhurst* (1914: London: Virago Ltd, 1979), p. 37.
59 Amy Bulley, 'Women's Trade Union Council: A Disclaimer,' *MG* (11 July 1904), p. 12.
60 Ibid.
61 *The Reformers' Year Book* (London: Taylor, Garnett, Evans & Co., 1907), p. 155.
62 Working Class Movement Library, Manchester, 331.88/F4 Box 17, *Women's Trade Union Council: Tenth Annual Report 1904* (15 Jan 1905), p. 14.
63 PRONI, Mic 590, Reel 10, L/13/67, letter from EGB to Josslyn Gore-Booth, 16 April 1904.
64 *Women's Trade Union Council: Tenth Annual Report 1904*, p. 14.
65 Through various amendments of the Factory and Workshop Act, 1901.
66 EGB, *CE*, p. 17.
67 Ibid, p. 18.
68 EGB, *The Little Waves of Breffny*, music by Edgar L. Bainton (London: Elkin & Co, 1927).
69 George Russell (ed.), *New Songs: A Lyric Selection made by AE from Poems by Eva Gore-Booth and others* (Dublin: Donoghue & Co, 1904).
70 Ibid.
71 John Kelly and Ronald Schuchard (eds), *The Collected Letters of W.B. Yeats: Volume Three* (Oxford: Clarendon Press, 1994), p. 576.
72 Katharine Tynan, *The Middle Years* (Boston: Houghton Mifflin Company, 1917), p. 355.
73 EGB, *CE*, p. 18.
74 The spelling of Cuculain often varies, for the purpose of clarity I use Gore-Booth's version throughout.
75 David Clark and Rosalind Clark (eds), *The Collected Works of W.B. Yeats: Volume II, The Plays* (New York: Scribner, 2001), pp. 545–55.
76 T.W. Rolleston, *Myths and Legends of the Celtic Race* (1911: London: Constable, 1992), pp. 228–30.
77 Emma Donoghue, 'How could I fear and hold thee by the hand? The poetry of Eva Gore-Booth,' in Eibhear Walsh (ed.), *Sex, Nation, and Dissent in Irish Writing* (Cork: Cork University Press, 1997), p. 27.
78 Miranda Green, *Celtic Goddesses: Warriors, Virgins and Mothers* (London: British Museum Co, 1997), p. 151.
79 EGB, *CE*, p. 205.

80 Ibid, p. 16.
81 Ibid, p. 17.
82 James and Margaret Cousins, *We Two Together* (Madras: Ganesh, 1951), p. 74. In act one, a huge crow flies violently against the window at which Cuculain sits. This bird is an integral part of the play as it represents Morrigan the goddess of death, destruction and war.
83 PRONI, Mic 590, Reel 10, L/9:102–3, Abbey Theatre Programme, 25, 26 and 27 January 1912.
84 Ibid.
85 EGB, *The One and the Many* (London: Longmans Green & Co, 1904).
86 'Review,' *Journal of Education* cited in EGB, *The Perilous Light* (London: Erskine MacDonald, 1915), p. 7.
87 EGB, *The Three Resurrections and the Triumph of Maeve* (London: Longmans, 1905).
88 Ibid.
89 EGB, *CE*, p. 19.
90 For further information on Maeve Markievicz (1901–62) see: Clive Scoular, *Maeve de Markievicz: Daughter of Constance* (Down: Clive Scoular, 2003).
91 Gore-Booth read to the Irish Literary Society on 20 January 1915.
92 *The Irish Book Lover*, 6:7 (February 1915), 111.
93 Ibid.
94 Ibid.
95 For example, 'A Monk's Lament for Maeve,' *New York Times* (27 October 1901), p. 19; 'A Song of Ireland,' *New York Tribune* (21 August 1904), p. 2 and 'The Little Waves of Breffny,' *Boston Daily Globe* (8 December 1923), p. 6.
96 For example, 'Roads of Cloonagh,' *Living Age*, 9 July 1904; 'Reincarnation,' *Living Age*, 13 August 1904; 'Beyond,' *Dial*, 16 May 1906; 'Poverty,' *Dial*, 16 May 1906 and 'Romance of Maeve,' *Literary Digest*,' 15 March 1913.
97 EGB, 'Women's Suffrage Movement,' p. 52.
98 Ibid, p. 64.

5

Women who kick, shriek, bite and spit: suffragists and suffragettes

'Long has submission played a traitor's part'[1]

After a long and arduous battle to gain equality, Gore-Booth's perseverance was rewarded in 1904. At the Labour Representation Committee conference, her friend and supporter, the powerful trade unionist William Wilkinson put forward the proposal to support the franchise being extended to women. Wilkinson insisted that it was now time for the LRC members of parliament to introduce a bill for women's suffrage in the House of Commons.[2] The motion was seconded by Isabella Ford, a suffragist and an elected member of the National Administrative Council of the ILP. The motion was carried by an overwhelming majority. The Labour movement now officially supported the votes for women cause. The party had been slow to officially support women's suffrage, viewing the movement as a middle-class cause. The Labour Party had feared that if women were granted votes on the same terms as men there would be an increase in middle-class voters. This was a major turning point in the suffrage campaign, however this development would not appease the WSPU.

Mrs Pankhurst had become disillusioned with incessantly lobbying MPs for the introduction of a women's suffrage bill. Members of the WSPU did not want to wait any longer to achieve votes for women. In desperation she warned then British Conservative Prime Minister Arthur Balfour 'that if facilities for the passing into law of the Women's Enfranchisement Bill were not granted, the WSPU would work actively against the Government at the next General Election.'[3] Balfour was not moved into action by this threat and the WSPU inaugurated a series of militant tactics from October 1905. The move to adopt militant actions would have far-reaching consequences for the suffrage movement and would cause an irreversible rift between Gore-Booth and Pankhurst.

Within days of Mrs Pankhurst's threat, Christabel and WSPU member Annie Kenney arrived at a Liberal Party meeting in the Free Trade Hall in Manchester. The Liberals held high hopes for securing a victory at the next general election. A leading Liberal politician, Sir Edward Grey, was due to speak to a packed hall. The women took their seats in the gallery. When Grey pleaded his case for a return of the Liberal Party to government, Pankhurst and Kenney produced a banner with the words 'Votes for women' emblazoned across it. Ignoring the banner, Grey continued speaking. Kenney shouted, 'will the Liberal Government give women the vote?' Her question was ignored and she repeated herself loudly until she was dragged from her seat by a steward and a number of men from the audience. At this point Pankhurst took over and began shouting the same question; again Grey did not respond. Eventually the two women were forcibly removed from their seats and brought outside of the hall where they began addressing an inquisitive crowd who had gathered.

Pankhurst and Kenney were arrested and released without bail. They were ordered to appear for sentencing the next day. On Saturday 14 October, the two women presented themselves at Manchester City Police Court. Pankhurst was charged with 'spitting at a police superintendent and a police officer and hitting the latter in the mouth.'[4] She was fined 10 shillings and 6 pence plus costs or seven days imprisonment. Additionally both women were fined 5 shillings for obstruction or seven days imprisonment. The women refused to pay the fines and were transferred immediately to Strangeways Jail in Manchester. The entire event gained the desired effect by attracting a huge media interest. It was the first time that suffrage campaigners adopted militant tactics and it was, therefore, the first time that a member of a suffrage organisation was imprisoned for the cause. The media attention impacted dramatically on the WSPU. Membership of the organisation increased but due to the militant tactics adopted, public support for the suffrage plight declined.

When the two women were released from Strangeways, Gore-Booth and Roper were waiting outside the prison gates along with a crowd of over 200 supporters.[5] Gore-Booth presented Pankhurst with flowers. Pankhurst and Kenney immediately set about organising a protest meeting for the following day. Gore-Booth and Roper agreed to act as sponsors for the event. The evening after their release Pankhurst and Kenney were back at the Free Trade Hall, this time they were on the stage addressing a large crowd. At the meeting Keir Hardie, now a prominent LRC member, put forward a motion 'that this meeting of men and women of Manchester condemns the action of the Liberals responsible for the meeting in the Free-trade Hall on Friday last in ignoring the legitimate question asked by two women.'[6] Hardie further declared 'that the treatment which Miss Pankhurst and Miss Kenney received was brutal and unjustifiable; and further, this meeting emphatically approves of their brave and determined protest.'[7] Gore-Booth seconded the resolution and was supported by a Mr A. Ogden.

Pankhurst was still an executive committee member of the North of England Society for Women's Suffrage. At their annual general meeting in 1905 the NESWS condemned her behaviour. She instantly resigned from the society and was supported in this action by Gore-Booth, Dickenson, Reddish, Haworth, Nellie Keenan, Katherine Rowton and Reverend Steinthal. This was the last time that Gore-Booth would support Pankhurst in any way. The group, led by Gore-Booth, all refused to condemn her actions and formally resigned from their positions on the committee. Roper submitted the annual report on 24 November and later resigned as secretary, forfeiting her £100 a year income. Wolstenholme Elmy summed up the situation in a letter to Harriett McIlquham, 'the North of England Society for WS [Women's Suffrage] has been captured by a Liberal gang . . . Esther and Eva, and dear old Mr Steinthal, at whose house in [18]65 the original Committee was formed, and who has ever since been connected with, have all resigned, and will henceforth work through the Women's Trade and Labour Council – which happily is full of the most vivid life.'[8]

In fact Gore-Booth and the group of dissenters decided to establish a replacement society for anyone who did not wish to remain aligned with the NESWS. Before the end of 1905 they formed the National Industrial and Professional Women's Suffrage Society (NIPWSS). The society was the ideal organisation for middle-class radical suffragists, who were not directly related with trade unionists or factory workers. The inclusive nature of the organisation is evident in the *Suffrage Annual and Women's Who's Who*, which describes it as 'a society composed of women workers of all grades, and of others interested in the industrial aspect of the Suffrage question.'[9] The NESWS Committee appeared bitter about this move and included a postscript to their annual report. The postscript, included after Roper submitted the original report, notes that 'since the annual meeting certain members of the executive committee have resigned, and have issued a circular to the subscribers asking them to leave this society and transfer their support to a new society which they have formed.'[10]

The new society acted as an umbrella organisation to the radical suffragists' Representation Committee and their Trade and Labour Council. All three organisations were based in the same offices at 5 John Dalton Street, near Albert Square, a prosperous shopping and commercial district of Manchester. These offices were now a thriving base of political activity and an Irish couple, William and Alice Sullivan, were employed as live-in caretakers.[11] Katherine Thomasson again helped finance the organisation; she contributed £210 to successfully establish the NIPWSS. Roper was appointed as secretary and Howarth became treasurer.

Pankhurst and Kenney continued to organise public speeches defending their militant actions. Pankhurst had abandoned the Elizabethan Society and stopped attending Gore-Booth's literary events. Gore-Booth still continued to attend some of the proceedings organised by Pankhurst, but she soon lost her appetite for such meetings. It quickly became apparent to her that, depending on where she was speaking, Pankhurst's story of the spitting incident changed. Spitting was considered foul in many social circles and it was a particularly venomous action considering the health concerns caused by the outbreak of tuberculosis at the time. Although Pankhurst was arrested for spitting at two police officers she later changed her version of the event, claiming that she merely pursed her lips at the men. In her book *Unshackled*, she gives an account of what happened on the afternoon of Friday 13 October 1905 after being removed from the Free Trade Hall:

> I must use the infallible means of getting arrested, I must 'assault the police.' But how was I to do it? The police seemed to be skilled to frustrate my purpose. I could not strike them, my arms were being held. I could not even stamp on their toes – they seemed able to prevent that. There could be no compromise at that moment of crisis. Lectures on the law flashed to my mind. I could, even with all limbs helpless, commit a technical assault and so I found myself arrested and charged

> with 'spitting at a policeman.' It was not a real spit but only, shall we call it, a 'pout,' a perfectly dry purse of the mouth. I could not have *really* done it, even to get the vote, I think.[12]

At one of the WSPU events in Lancashire Gore-Booth could not take the deceit any more, she 'dramatically seized' Theresa Billington and pleaded with her to 'tell Christabel not to vary her defence from one meeting to another.'[13] Gore-Booth insisted that Pankhurst 'cannot fit her explanation to her audience. She either deliberately invited imprisonment or she was a victim; she either spat at the policeman or she did not. She can't tell one tale in Manchester & another in Oldham.'[14]

Gore-Booth immediately distanced herself from this new, militant wing of the feminist movement and from Pankhurst. She was concerned that her reputation would be damaged by association with the Pankhurst family. Gore-Booth was justified in her concern as apparent in a letter from Margaret Ashton of the Women's Liberal Federation to Millicent Fawcett. Ashton clearly associates Gore-Booth with the new wave of militant actions; she writes that she is appalled at 'the actions of these few violent women . . . a small clique calling themselves the Votes for Women Election Committee and including I believe Eva Gore-Booth, two Miss Pankhursts and other seceders from the North of England Suffrage Society which disowns them.'[15] The situation intensified when on 4 November Balfour resigned due to his party's growing unpopularity. Balfour did not dissolve the government and so Edward VII commissioned the Liberal Party, under the leadership of Henry Campbell-Bannerman, as interim government. A general election was called for January 1906. Two days before the election the *Daily Mail* reported that, 'It was not surprising that Mr. Balfour should receive a deputation of the Suffragettes.'[16] Through this article a new and rather unflattering term 'suffragette' was coined. The term is loaded with negative connotations and was used to describe women who adopted militant or even violent tactics in pursuit of female franchise. In contemporary popular discourse the term suffragist and suffragette are often confused and the non-militant band of first wave feminism is often under-represented.[17]

The LCWTOWRC, in line with suffrage ideals, did not adopt militant tactics, believing that political franchise would be achieved through constitutional means. They had been working towards putting a suffrage candidate forward at the next general election. Once the election was called, the Workers' Representation Committee sprung into action. They had already chosen to contest the Wigan jurisdiction, mainly because that area had high employment in the cotton mills and the LRC were not contesting the constituency. Now that the LRC officially supported women's suffrage, the Workers' Representation Committee did not want to stand against them at elections. The radical suffragists had selected Hubert Sweeney as their independent suffrage candidate two years previously. Sweeney was a teacher, a trainee barrister, a member of the London Ethical Society and he was dedicated to the cause of women's suffrage. However, Sweeney had no links with trade unions or to the cotton industry – indeed, he had no connection with the Wigan area at all. The committee attempted to address this and sent a circular assuring voters that although 'the candidate is pledged, if returned to parliament, to work in season and out of season to secure the enfranchisement of the women workers of the country ... on all general questions he will vote in the interests of Labour.'[18]

Sweeney assured voters that his election would improve the rights of all workers, announcing that 'there was no security so long as women were without a voice in the selection of their legislators. Woman suffrage would mean protection to the trade unionists of Lancashire.'[19] Sweeney was not as dedicated to the cause as he first appeared. He withdrew from the election at short notice, placing the committee in a difficult situation. Just as their cause seemed hopeless, Thorley Smith approached the committee and offered to stand as a suffrage candidate. Smith seemed to be the ideal replacement; he was a councillor and chairman of the Wigan branch of the LRC. Smith was respected in local trade union circles and he gained support from temperance parties and from non-conformists.[20] In his opening address on 3 January 1906, Smith expressed his commitment to women's suffrage declaring that 'the women who are paying the piper are entitled to call the tune.'[21] Gore-Booth and Roper both took to the podium after Smith's speech and addressed the electors of Wigan on his behalf.

Gore-Booth organised a team of twenty women and three men to canvas for a period of two weeks before the election. One of the most vibrant campaigners was Selina Cooper, who summed up the ethos behind the radical suffragist movement in her speech supporting Smith. Cooper stressed that 'women do not want their political power to boast they are on equal terms with the men. They want to use it for the same purpose as men – to get better conditions. Every woman in England is longing for her political freedom in order to make the lot of the worker pleasanter and to bring about reforms which are wanted. We do not want it as a mere plaything.'[22] As an independent candidate Smith was not assisted financially by any of the main parties or organisations. However, he was encouraged by the support of the LRC. Hardie published a letter in the *Wigan Observer* strongly endorsing Smith's election.[23] Yet, Wigan Trades' Council refused to support him. The coal miners were a large and powerful part of the Trades' Council and they remained loyal to the Liberal Party. The entire electorate was male and Smith was standing as the women's candidate, unsurprisingly he did not win the election. The seat in Wigan was won by the Conservative candidate, Sir Francis Powell. Smith did, however, come a respectable second defeating the Liberal candidate by over 300 votes.[24] Wigan returned an unusual result during this election. Throughout the country the Liberal candidates topped the polls. Under the leadership of Henry Campbell-Bannerman, the Liberals achieved a landslide victory securing 400 seats they regained power from the Tories.

Only three members of the Conservative Cabinet managed to hold on to their seats. Balfour lost his Manchester seat. Winston Churchill's position was safe as he had left the Conservative Party in 1904 to join the Liberals. Churchill won a seat in the North-West division of Manchester. The LRC also did exceedingly well securing twenty-nine seats, after which they reformed as the Labour Party, under the leadership of Hardie. The 1906 election is now considered one of the most significant elections in twentieth-century British history, marking a turning point in politics. Consecutive Reform Acts had reduced the threshold for eligibility to vote, dramatically increasing the number of working-class and Irish men entitled to vote. The Conservative Party did not represent the interest of either group. The Tories were opposed to Irish Home Rule and they had alienated trade unionists through the Taff Vale judgement of 1902. The Taff Vale case undermined the stability of unions by making them responsible for any financial losses due to industrial action. Not surprisingly the change of voter demographics generated a dramatic change in voting patterns. The landslide victory was a stroke of luck for the Liberal Party. Voters were less concerned about securing a Liberal government than with voting the Tories out of power.

The Liberal Party did, however, offer the chance of social and economic reform to a Britain which was experiencing increasing unemployment and a steady decline in living standards. This new government would come to implement the most forward thinking social reform measures, which can now be seen as the foundation of the welfare state. Both the WSPU and the NUWSS were hopeful that such a dramatic change in government would help advance the cause of suffrage for women. In preparation for a new and improved relationship with government, the WSPU moved their headquarters to London and suffrage societies set about organising a delegation to the new Prime Minister. Roper was appointed as a member of the organising committee for the deputation. She considered it important to include as many representatives from suffrage organisations as possible, however she was concerned about associating with suffragette agencies. She wrote to Dora Montefiore, 'with regard to the Political and Social Union, there is no quarrel between us, but it seems undoubtedly better that the attack on the Government should come from as many quarters as possible, independently of one another . . . We therefore think it better that the first demonstration that we have, we should do without joining forces with the Union.'[25]

On 19 May 1906, women from suffrage organisations all over Britain arrived in London to meet with Campbell-Bannerman. The deputation was a great spectacle. Women carried banners announcing that '306,000 women in the cotton trade want votes' and declaring 'women produce the wealth in Lancashire.'[26] The Manchester and Salford Women's Trade and Labour Council's banner led a procession from the Embankment to the Foreign Office. Gore-Booth was one of fifty delegates from Lancashire. After the processions, the women held mass meetings in Trafalgar Square, Hyde Park and Exeter Hall. Ten delegates were presented to Campbell-Bannerman and each was allocated five minutes for an address. Hardie was present in support of female franchise. Labour had not yet managed to distinguish themselves as a separate political identity and acted almost as a division of the Liberal Party.

The speakers were introduced by Sir Charles McLaren MP. In his opening address McLaren declared to Campbell-Bannerman that 'I have every hope that you will see your way to do something to give practical effect to the aspirations of those who have a heart in this matter.'[27] The first speaker was Emily Davies, founder of Girton

College, who spoke on behalf of the Women's Suffrage Societies. Eva McLaren followed, representing the Women's Liberal Federation. Margaret Ashton appeared for the Joint Conference of Women's Liberal Associations. She was followed by Gore-Booth, who addressed the Prime Minister on behalf of the working women's societies of Lancashire. Gore-Booth explained that 'industrial questions were more and more becoming political questions, and it is a grave disability upon the six million women who were earning their own living that they had absolutely no voice in the settlement of these questions.'[28] She pleaded with the Prime Minister to grant women political franchise now and continued:

> I am a trade union secretary in Manchester, and know from personal experience what women's wages are and the sort of money they get for their work. Six or seven shillings a week is not a sufficient sum of money to live on. This is not the rate of wages that could possibly be enforced upon the enfranchised citizens of a free country. We feel, and I think women in other classes, who are working, also feel that our industrial status is being brought down. It results from the fact that we have no political power. That is the lesson which the working women of Lancashire have learned, and that is the thought they want to bring before you and want you to consider.[29]

Her address was followed by Mrs Gasson for the Women's Co-Operative Guild. Mrs Pankhurst spoke for the WSPU, followed by Mary Bateson on behalf of female university graduates. The final speakers included Mrs Rolland Haney of the Scottish Women Liberals, Sarah Dickenson representing women wage earners and Mrs Watson for the Scottish Christian Union of the National British Women's Temperance Association.

A detailed account of the deputation was reported on in the labour annual, *The Reformers' Yearbook*, noting that of all the speeches the one by Gore-Booth and the speech given by Mrs Pankhurst were of special importance.[30] However, a report in an American newspaper clearly favoured Gore-Booth's delivery style. A correspondence, by Clara Esmonds for the *Times Dispatch* in Richmond, describes how when Gore-Booth spoke she:

> scored an instant success. Stooping slightly, she threw all her soul into her words, declaring with intense feeling that the franchise was the only cure for women's low wages. Turning to the Premier, she said eagerly: 'We can't wait. The working women of Lancashire want you

> to consider that this is a question that touches their lives the very bread they eat; and they can't go on like this. It is impossible to go on like this in England. That's why we ask you to do something now. Do it soon! Do it soon! Do it now!' As she sank back in her chair, exhausted by her remarkable effort, a great burst of applause broke out.[31]

In complete contrast Esmonds describes Mrs Pankhurst as 'a quiet, sad-faced woman, dressed in a Quaker-gray cloak.'[32]

After hearing the final speaker Campbell-Bannerman took the stand to a riotous applause. He complemented the speakers on their oratory abilities and agreed with many assertions made by them. The Prime Minister made special reference to the trade unions of Lancashire and noted that it was now time to recognise 'the practical injustice of imposing a disability upon women, while allowing and even inviting women to share the same responsibilities and circumstances as men. From the universities at one end of the line and the mill and the workshop at the other that surely applies.'[33] The female delegates were delighted with his response. However, their happiness was short lived. Campbell-Bannerman told the gathered crowd that although he was in favour of granting political franchise to women, his party was not. He appealed to the women to embrace the 'virtue of patience.' At this point Hardie took the stand and expressed his disappointment that the Liberal Party would not see fit to grant women political franchise now. He pointed out that in 1884 there was also a feeling in favour of female franchise from the political party in government. Suffragists were told then to have patience and yet, 'displaying patience their opportunity passed away. I merely mention that, as indicating that patience, like many other virtues, can be carried to excess.'[34]

The deputation to the Prime Minister was reported in many national and local newspapers, gaining much needed publicity for the suffrage campaign. The women involved were publicly praised for their organisational skills and it was generally agreed that the groups should be 'satisfied both with their own remarkable achievement and with the able personal championship of the head of the Cabinet.'[35] Attention was drawn to the fact that a class change was occurring within the suffrage movement. The liberal review journal, *The Speaker*, noted that 'armies of women recruited from much wider classes are giving the demand for the vote an indefinitely wider currency. It is in Lancashire, where women's part in modern industry is most important and best organised, that the voice of the working women is naturally more articulate.'[36] Special mention was given to Gore-Booth's role in this development.

Gore-Booth herself was not only disappointed with the Prime Minister's response but she was also disappointed with her own performance on the day. Her sense of personal failure is best reflected in her aptly titled poem 'A Lost Opportunity.'

> Others there were who spake with fire and art;
> I stammered, breaking down beneath the weight
> Of that great stone that lies upon my heart
> When with one passion all my nerves vibrate.[37]

The lack of government action propelled Gore-Booth to write many poems that year about her involvement with the suffrage campaign. 'Women's Trades on the Embankment,' is subtitled, '"Have patience!" – The Prime Minister to the Women's Franchise Deputation, 19th May 1906.' The last verse proves that Gore-Booth is not content to simply be patient:

> Long has submission played a traitor's part–
> Oh human soul, no patience any more
> Shall break your wings and harden Pharaoh's heart,
> And keep you lingering on the Red Sea shore.[38]

Gore-Booth published these poems in a volume the next year. The book of verse entitled *The Egyptian Pillar* is dedicated to her sister Constance.[39]

Her poetry was by now gaining recognition from an international audience. In 1905, the composer Max Myers began translating her poetry into German and setting the verse to music.[40] *The Egyptian Pillar* marked a change in Gore-Booth's publishing. Until then all of her books were published through Longmans Green & Co. This volume is one of only two books which Gore-Booth published through Maunsel & Co, a Dublin press based at 96 Middle Abbey Street. The press was founded in 1905 and dedicated to publishing Irish works. According to literary historian David Gardiner this was 'the only publisher of Irish writing at the time, Maunsel *was* Irish literature.'[41] Indeed Maunsel was an intrinsic part of the Celtic Literary Revival, apparent in a list of their published authors including: Lady Gregory, Padraic Colum, J.M Synge, Douglas Hyde, Padraic Pearse, Austin Clarke and Stephen Gwynn. Significantly both the editor and sub editor of *The Irish Homestead*, George Russell and Susan Mitchell also published with Maunsel. The press embraced the ideals of socialism, Irish nationalism and women's suffrage. The ethos behind Maunsel attracted Irish female authors to publish with them, including Katharine Tynan, Dora Sigerson Shorter, Alice Milligan, Susan Mitchell and Ella Young. *The Egyptian Pillar* was the third book in Maunsel's Tower Press Booklet Series.[42] Maunsel were committed to ensuring that books by Irish writers could be easily accessed by Irish readers, keeping the cost of each book to a minimum. Gore-Booth's volume sold for one shilling. The press instigated a subscription service. In return for five shillings subscribers would receive all six books in the Tower Press series, with free postage.

The Egyptian Pillar reflects Gore-Booth's dismay with the suffrage campaign. After the deputation to the Prime Minister, she was faced with the reality that women would not receive full political franchise in the short term. She did not accept Campbell-Bannerman's invitation to have patience, realising that working conditions for women needed to be improved immediately. In her capacity as co-secretary of the Manchester and Salford Women's Trade and Labour Council, Gore-Booth began examining legislation which affected women at work. She was anxious that without political franchise, women's work would be controlled and restricted by male trade unionists and politicians, in the interests of male workers. She outlined her concerns in *Women's Wages and the Franchise and Certain Legislative Proposals*. In this pamphlet Gore-Booth aptly summarises the negative effect that women's 'political disability,' has on female income.[43] Applying the basic economic principle of the law of supply and demand, Gore-Booth asserts that the main reason why women are paid less than men is because women are only allowed access to certain occupations.

In her pamphlet Gore-Booth identifies three categories where women's labour is being restricted and displaced – 'married women's work; work in which women undercut men; and work supposed to be injurious to health or morals.'[44] She set out her concerns for each of these categories and her observations were particularly apt. Not long after their succession to power, the Liberal government began considering legislation to ban married women from working. Attempts to restrict married women working began a year previous in 1905, when infant mortality rates had reached a crisis point in

England and Ireland. That year, a quarter of all deaths in England were children under the age of one, a total of 137,392 children, excluding still births, had died.[45] It was an appalling situation and the campaign to reduce the high rate of infant mortality was impacted on by the appointment of John Burns to the Local Government Board in December 1905. Burns was a socialist and a union activist. He originally represented Battersea in the House of Commons and helped to establish the LRC. However, Burns remained aligned to the Liberal Party and thus he greatly disappointed the Labour movement.

In his position as president of the LGB Burns addressed two National Conferences on Infantile Mortality in 1906 and 1908. The first conference was held in Westminster between 13–14 June 1906. In his opening speech Burns was unequivocal as to where the blame lay for the high death rate of babies. He announced that this tragedy was the responsibility of married women leaving the home in order to work. Burns claimed that not only did working mothers cause infantile deaths to double but that 'if mothers were working for nine, ten, or twelve hours in a factory, it not only contributed to produce a high mortality among their infants, but the effect on the children who survived was seen in gangs of anaemic, saucy, vulgar, ignorant, cigarette-smoking hooligans.'[46] In his speech Burns degraded not only the idea of married women working but blamed them on creating the majority of social problems in Britain. He further asserted that 'married women's labour manufactured loafers, who might be seen buttressing a beer shop or French polishing the outside of a public-house; married women's labour was an individual injury, a social mistake, and a commercial blunder.'[47]

Burns offered a solution to this deplorable situation. He proposed that women should be banned from working for three months before giving birth and for a further five months after confinement, which initially appears to be a progressive proposal. There was already in place a section of the Factory and Workshop Act prohibiting employers from knowingly letting a woman work within four weeks of childbirth.[48] There was an instant call in the House of Commons to implement Burns' proposal. Colonel Josiah Wedgwood, quoting Burns' speech, noted that the president of the LGB 'attributes infantile mortality and other evils largely to the employment of married women.'[49] Wedgwood begged the Secretary of State, Herbert Gladstone, to consider Burns' proposal at an early date.

Gore-Booth was appalled at the suggestion of enforcing such a restriction on women workers. She wrote to the newly formed *Women's Tribune* noting that 'it is this question of "allowing" that alarms the ordinary citizen.'[50] She was incensed at what she termed Burns' 'somewhat smug ideals,' which led him to believe that infant mortality and drunkenness of working-class men was the fault of married women in employment. She publicly attacked Burns' notion that the 'ideal woman of the working class is clean, sober, dependent, and has a talent for cookery.'[51] Gore-Booth's main concern with Burns' proposal was the fact that there was no provision for maternity benefit, therefore whatever benefit a child may obtain from having a mother at home would be counteracted by a severe shortage of money and therefore malnourishment. In *Women's Wages and the Franchise* Gore-Booth highlights the long-term implications of this proposed legislation, stressing that no employer would consider it worthwhile to employ anyone who could be absent from work for eight months out of twelve. The introduction of such restrictive legislation could possibly affect 74,000 married women working in the Lancashire cotton trade. As an alternative, Gore-Booth suggested a rather pioneering method of practical reform including 'crèches with trained attendants.'[52]

Burns' proposal was viewed by many as a measure of protection for women and children. Ethel Snowden, a socialist and a suffragist, agreed with the proposal maintaining that women with children would not want to work in a factory, 'they will not wish to do so, for they will be free and their children will claim them.'[53] This idea of protecting women in the workplace was to become steadily more popular with politicians and philanthropists alike over the next number of years. Gore-Booth looked upon legislative proposals not as protection but as restriction for women workers. One of the most contentious cases involved Gore-Booth's campaign against a proposed amendment to the Dangerous Performances Acts in 1906. These acts comprised the Children's Dangerous Performances Act of 1879, which regulated the 'employment of children in places of public amusement' and the Dangerous Performances Act of 1897 which extended the age limit to include boys under the age of sixteen and girls under the age of eighteen. The acts made it illegal to employ children to partake in a public performance which would endanger their life or limbs.

Herbert Samuel, under secretary at the Home Office, presented a proposed bill to the House of Commons on 25 June 1906, which if introduced, would alter the basis of these acts.[54] Samuel was intent on reforming social conditions for children.[55] Now Samuel proposed 'to consolidate and amend the Law relating to the employment of girls, boys, or women in Dangerous Performances.'[56] Samuel's inclusion of women was meant as a measure of protection for female performers employed in theatres, circuses or other places of entertainment. No doubt Samuel was instilled by the spate of high profile accidents involving female acrobats and tightrope walkers during the nineteenth century.

In 1862 a woman using the stage name Madame Genevieve, fell while attempting to cross a tightrope with fireworks. The woman was crippled for life after the accident in north London. Five years later another young woman, Selena Powell, performed a tightrope act at Aston Park near Birmingham. Powell fell from a rope tied between two trees, thirty feet above the spectators. Powell died as a result of the fall. Restrictions were almost instantly placed on women performing such activities, as attested to by Lady Augusta Gregory. Gregory notes that her patent to open the Abbey Theatre in Dublin in 1904 specifically stated that she could not allow 'dangerous performances or to allow women or children to be hung from the flies or fixed in positions from which they cannot release themselves.'[57]

Gore-Booth viewed this new bill as yet another restriction which would reduce the livelihoods of 10,000 female performers in Britain. She highlighted that 'this bill provides that any person causing any woman of any age to take part in a public performance dangerous to life and limb should be fined £10. (This when there is no accident.) It is left entirely to the discretion of the local magistrates to decide what performances are dangerous, and to enforce the fine.'[58] In order to expose the proposed legislation as a ridiculous measure which would not protect women, Gore-Booth conducted her own research. She interviewed Dr Albrecht, a medical doctor whose practice was based almost entirely among music-hall artists in Manchester theatres. Reporting back to the *Manchester Guardian* newspaper, Gore-Booth describes how Dr Albrecht 'expressed his surprise at such a measure being brought forward. From his personal experience during the last ten years, he said, there had been only one serious accident in any theatre or music-hall in this neighbourhood. This accident happened to a man, and was therefore no proof that the profession was especially dangerous to women.'[59] In her report, Gore-Booth includes testimony from Mr Broadhead, whom she describes as the '"manager" of nine variety theatres in the neighbourhood of Manchester, Preston, Ashton, and Bury.' Mr Broadhead 'remembers in the course of twenty years' experience only one serious accident, where the sufferer was again a man.'[60]

Gore-Booth was not opposed to protecting women, she was opposed to any legislation which discriminated against women and negatively affected their livelihoods. This new bill did not enforce any restrictions protecting male performers, or attempt to curtail men's incomes. Yet, as Gore-Booth points out, 'the laws of gravity apply to men and women alike.'[61] Gore-Booth concludes her pamphlet by stressing that the members of the House of Commons will only ever legislate in favour of their voters. 'Therefore, it follows that women's wages are depressed, and their low rate accounted for by their entire want of the most elementary political rights.'[62] She followed this with an article entitled 'Fair Pay for Women,' which she published in the *Women's Tribune* and which includes examples of women's low pay in certain occupations.[63]

In contrast with Gore-Booth's strategic approach, the WSPU stepped up their disruptive activities. Their militancy hit an all time high when a group of women forcibly disrupted a parliamentary session in Westminster in October 1906. The women were all arrested and the event was reported in the *Daily Mirror* with the headline 'Riotous Suffragettes Evicted after an Onslaught on House of Commons.'[64] By the end of 1906, twenty members of the WSPU were serving prison sentences for similar parliamentary raids. The media attention given to this event caused a dramatic increase in membership of the WSPU. Millicent Fawcett offered her public support to the imprisoned women. Fawcett wrote a letter to *The Times* testifying that the women 'have done more during the last 12 months to bring it [women's suffrage] within the realm of practical politics than we have been able to accomplish in the same number of years.'[65] Disgusted by this public support Gore-Booth wrote a strongly worded letter to Fawcett:

> There is no class in the community who has such good reasons for objecting and does so strongly object to shrieking and throwing yourself on the floor and struggling and kicking as the average working woman, whose dignity is very real to them. We feel we must tell you this as we are in great difficulties because our members in all parts of the country are so outraged at the idea of taking part in such

> proceedings that everywhere for the first time they are shrinking from public demonstrations. It is not the fact of demonstration or even the violence offered to them, it is being mixed up with and held accountable as a class for educated and upper class women who kick, shriek, bite and spit.[66]

Days later Gore-Booth organised a suffrage demonstration on 3 November at Trafalgar Square on behalf of the LCWTOWRC and the WTLC. To ensure that working women would support the event, Gore-Booth and Roper wrote a letter to the editor of the *Manchester Guardian* announcing that the demonstration is in 'no way connected with the Women's Social and Political Union.'[67]

The WSPU did not give in so easily. Louisa Smith, a member of the LCWTOWRC, organised a trade union meeting later that month in support of the women workers at the Royal Army Clothing Factory in Pimlico. The tailoresses were facing a reduction in their wages and the committee came out in full support. Pankhurst and Billington insisted on attending the event and agreed that they would only address issues relating to the tailoresses. However, the WPSU members proceeded to dominate the event and spoke of nothing but their fellow suffragettes who were imprisoned. The next day the newspapers misreported the trade union meeting as a 'suffragette meeting on Pimlico Pier.' Gore-Booth articulated her disgust at such behaviour to fellow suffragist Edith Palliser.[68] The split between Gore-Booth and Pankhurst was now irreconcilable.

Notes

1 EGB, 'Women's Trades on the Embankment,' *CE*, p. 405.
2 *Labour Representation Committee Conference Report* (1904), p. 73.
3 Sylvia Pankhurst, *The Suffragette Movement*, p. 15.
4 'Disturbance at a Political Meeting,' *The Times* (16 October 1905), p. 4.
5 *The Manchester Evening Chronicle* (20 October 1905).
6 'Votes for Women: Speech by Mr. Keir Hardie,' *Guardian* (21 October 1905), p. 5.
7 Ibid.
8 Letter from Elizabeth Wolstenholme Elmy to Harriett McIlquham, cited in Crawford, *Suffrage Movement*, p. 250.
9 AJR (ed.), *The Suffrage Annual and Women's Who's Who* (London: Stanley Paul, 1913).
10 NESWS Annual Report, cited in Liddington and Norris, *One Hand Tied behind Us*, p. 195.

11 British Census 1901, RG13, Piece 3748, Folio 131, p. 8.
12 Christabel Pankhurst, *Unshackled*, pp. 51–2.
13 The Women's Library, London Metropolitan University, box 7: TBG, Teresa Billington-Greig papers, undated holograph notes.
14 Ibid.
15 Manchester Central Library, M50/2/1/225, Fawcett Manuscripts, letter from Margaret Ashton to Millicent Fawcett, 16 January 1906.
16 *Daily Mail* (10 January 1906).
17 For further discussion see: Sonja Tiernan, 'Tabloid Sensationalism or Revolutionary Feminism? The First-wave Feminist Movement in an Irish Women's Periodical,' *Irish Communications Review*, 11 (2010), 74–87.
18 *North of England Society for Women's Suffrage Annual Report*, 1903.
19 'A Woman's Candidate for Wigan,' *MG* (7 January 1904), p. 8.
20 Liddington and Norris, *One Hand Tied Behind Us*, p. 197.
21 *Wigan Observer* (3 January 1906).
22 Bob Whitfield, *The Extension of the Franchise, 1832–1931* (Oxford: Heinemann Educational Publishers, 2001), p. 150.
23 *Wigan Observer* (6 January 1906).
24 Wigan Parliamentary Election Results 1906: F.S. Powell (Conservative) 3,573, Thorley Smith (Women's Suffrage) 2,205 and Will Woods (Liberal) 1,900.
25 Montefiore, *From a Victorian to a Modern*, p. 46.
26 'Votes for Women,' *Guardian* (21 May 1906), p. 1.
27 Ibid.
28 Ibid, p. 3.
29 *The Reformers' Year Book* (London, 1907), p. 146.
30 Ibid.
31 Clara T. Esmonds, 'English Premier for Woman Suffrage but cannot Promise Government Aid,' *Times Dispatch* (10 June 1906).
32 Ibid.
33 'Votes for Women,' *Guardian* (21 May 1906), p. 1.
34 Cited in Lewis, *Eva Gore-Booth and Esther Roper*, p. 125.
35 'Votes for Women,' *Speaker* (26 May 1906), p. 176.
36 Ibid.
37 EGB, 'A Lost Opportunity,' *CE*, p. 407.
38 EGB, 'Women's Trades on the Embankment,' *CE*, pp. 404–5.
39 EGB, *The Egyptian Pillar* (Dublin: Maunsel, 1907).
40 EGB, 'The Little Waves of Breffny – die kleinen wellen von Breffny'; 'Nera's Song – Nera's lied; 'Song of Cuculain's Enchantment – die lockung zum kamf.' All three songs were published in London and Melbourne by Chappell & Co in 1905.
41 David Gardiner, 'The Other Irish Renaissance: The Maunsel Poets,' *New Hibernia Review* 8:1 (Spring 2004), 56.

42 This was the second series of the Tower Press Booklets. Series two includes *About Women* by Charles Weekes, *Studies* by Padraic Colum and *Verses: Sacred and Profane* by Seumas O'Sullivan. Series one includes *Some Irish Essays* by Æ, *Songs of a Devotee* by Thomas Keohler, *Reminiscences of the Impressionist Painters* by George Moore, *Poems* by Ella Young, *Bards and Saints* by John Eglinton and *Criticism and Courage and Other Essays* by Frederick Ryan.
43 EGB, *Women's Wages and the Franchise and Certain Legislative Proposals* (Manchester: Manchester, Salford, and District Women's Trade and Labour Council, 1906), p. 1.
44 Ibid, p. 3.
45 Edward Bunnell, *A Statistical Study of Infant Mortality* (Boston, 1908), p. 2.
46 'Proceedings of Conference on Infantile Mortality,' *British Medical Journal* (16 June 1906), p. 1422.
47 Ibid, p. 1423.
48 Section 61 of the Factory and Workshop Act (1901).
49 Hansard, House of Commons Debate, 158: c1368, (18 June 1906).
50 EGB, 'The Symposium: Mr Burns and Infant Mortality,' *Women's Tribune* (23 June 1906), p. 138.
51 Ibid.
52 Ibid.
53 Ethel Snowden, *The Woman Socialist* (London: George Allen, 1907), p. 81.
54 'Dangerous Performances Bill,' *20th Century House of Commons Sessional Papers* 1.611, (25 June 1906), p. 269.
55 Herbert Samuel's most influential change came about in 1908 when he was instrumental in passing the Children's Act, which essentially ended child imprisonment, restricted corporal punishment and enforced State responsibility for all children.
56 Hansard, House Commons Debate, 159: c668, (25 June 1906).
57 Lady Augusta Gregory, *Our Irish Theatre: A Chapter of Autobiography* (New York & London: G.P. Putnam's Sons, The Knickerbocker Press, 1913), p. 75.
58 EGB, 'The Dangerous Performances Bill,' *Manchester Guardian* (4 July 1906), p. 5.
59 Ibid.
60 Ibid.
61 EGB, *Women's Wages*, p. 5.
62 Ibid, p. 7.
63 EGB, 'Fair Pay for Women,' in *The Women's Tribune*, 1906.
64 *Daily Mirror* (24 October 1906) as cited in Jill Liddington, *Rebel Girls: Their Fight for the Vote* (London: Virago Press, 2006), p. 70.
65 *The Times* (27 October 1906) as cited in Liddington, *Rebel Girls*, p. 72.

66 Manchester Central Library, M50/2/1/230, Fawcett Manuscripts, letter from EGB to Millicent Fawcett, 24 October 1906.
67 EBG and Esther Roper, 'The Suffragist Demonstration in Trafalgar Square,' *MG* (6 November 1906), p. 4.
68 Liddington and Norris, *One Hand Tied Behind Us*, p. 206.

6

Defending barmaids: legislative proposals and Winston Churchill

'The Rich, the Great, the Wise are here, the Living and the Dead, Where the Great Towers of Westminster hold the high heavens at bay'[1]

The Yorkshire cotton town of Huddersfield was the scene of the first direct political battle between the radical suffragists and the militant suffragettes. In November 1906, Sir James Woodhouse, Liberal MP for Huddersfield, was appointed as a Railway Commissioner. He duly resigned his seat from the House of Commons. The resulting by-election positioned Gore-Booth and the Pankhurst family in unequivocal opposition for the first time. The NUWSS decided not to become involved with any electioneering at Huddersfield. Fawcett maintained that all three candidates standing in the by-election, Conservative, Labour and Liberal, supported female suffrage.

The WSPU, under the leadership of Mrs Pankhurst and Hannah Mitchell, were the first to descend upon the town of Huddersfield. Mrs Pankhurst addressed a crowd on 20 November at the market centre. She aggressively asserted that the WSPU would oppose all Liberal candidates standing for election, in the hope that the Liberal government would fall. She forcefully criticised the government, regaling the gathered crowd with stories about mistreatment of WSPU members in prisons around the country. The WSPU placed a prominent advertisement in the *Huddersfield Examiner* imploring, 'Working Men of Huddersfield, will you allow the Liberal Government to treat the women of this country so unjustly?'[2] The government reacted swiftly, that evening they arranged for the early release of suffragette prisoners from Holloway. Government officials must have been horrified to discover that the released prisoners travelled directly to Huddersfield and joined their colleagues electioneering against their party's candidate.

The ethos behind the Women's Representation Committee was entirely different to that of the WSPU. Gore-Booth's strategy was to either run a suffrage candidate at election or support an existing candidate, regardless of party, who advocated for women's suffrage. Since the Labour Party now officially supported the cause of women's suffrage, Gore-Booth was sensitive to the party's interests. The week of the Huddersfield by-election she wrote to Labour member W. Henderson reassuring him that 'our policy is briefly this; the candidate is pledged to put women's franchise before all other questions. As regards his position on general questions he will represent Labour ... our policy is practically identical with the attitude of the Labour Party except that our candidate is pledged to put our question first.'[3]

The radical suffragists actively supported the Labour candidate at the by-election. Gore-Booth and Cooper conducted open-air meetings in the town. The Liberal candidate, Arthur Sherwell, was supported by his party. A young Liberal MP from Manchester North-West arrived in Huddersfield and conducted meetings in the town hall on Sherwell's behalf. This was Gore-Booth's first encounter with Winston Churchill. The energetic electioneering generated much public interest. Frank Gillett, an artist for the illustrated *Daily Graphic*, drew impressive pictures of Churchill, Kenney, Gore-Booth and Cooper at their various campaign posts. The illustrations appeared on the front page of the newspaper announcing 'closing scenes of a short campaign.'[4] The picture included a mention of the LCWTOWRC (see Figure 10).

On the day before the election, Gore-Booth and members of the LCWTOWRC marched through Huddersfield with placards seeking votes for the Labour candidate. Members of the WSPU drove through the streets in a horse drawn carriage with placards stating 'Oppose the Government that imprisons women, and vote against the Liberal candidate.'[5] During the election on 28 November, WSPU members positioned themselves outside of the polling stations and the Liberal candidate's room. The radical suffragists and the WSPU were both disappointed when the Liberal candidate, Arthur Sherwell, won the election and was appointed MP for Huddersfield.

Gore-Booth was never deterred by defeat. She began the year 1907 on a positive and lively note. She and Roper had moved from

10 *Daily Graphic* front page depicting the closing scenes of the Huddersfield Election in 1906. Winston Churchill, Annie Kenney, Eva Gore-Booth and Selina Cooper are all featured

the industrial quarters of Heald Place to the leafy middle-class suburb of Victoria Park.[6] The two women jointly purchased a large house called Cringle Brook from the mother of Marion Ledward.[7] Mrs Pankhurst's bitterness may well have been compounded by this action. She had lived on this very road until the death of her husband, Richard, in 1898. Due to reduced finances Mrs Pankhurst was forced to move to a smaller house in the less affluent area of Nelson Road.

In January 1907, Gore-Booth launched a quarterly paper, the *Women's Labour News*, as the organ of the Women's Trades and Labour Council. This was a strategic move. Lydia Becker had proved that there was a need for a regular news-sheet to inform suffrage groups of current events. Becker edited the *Women's Suffrage Journal* from 1875. The journal ceased publication one month after Becker's death in 1890 and it had not been successfully replaced. Secretary of the NUWSS, Edith Palliser, established the *Women's Suffrage Record* in 1903. She edited and self-financed the journal. Palliser, an Irishwoman from County Waterford, had worked closely with Roper on the parliamentary campaign in 1895. She was a supporter of the radical suffragists and attended the LCWTOWRC annual conference in 1906. That same year the *Women's Suffrage Record* ceased publication, possibly because Palliser took over the more demanding role as chair of the committee of the London Society for Women's Suffrage in 1907 or simply because the publication became too much of a financial drain. Gore-Booth instantly launched the *Women's Labour News* hoping that the news-sheet would provide 'a full account of all that was going on and the varied activities, industrial and political, of the Women's Trade Unions.'[8]

Gore-Booth edited the paper with vigour, announcing with pride 'our new little venture.'[9] She was not a lone voice advocating for the rights of women in the workplace and she noted in the editorial of the first edition, 'those who are working for the betterment of political and industrial conditions of women have great need of fellowship, of coherency and free discussion, and the ventilation of pressing grievances.'[10] Gore-Booth anticipated that the *Women's Labour News* would provide a forum to air grievances and establish consistency throughout campaigns for gender equality in the workplace.[11] She set out the guiding principle of the paper in a rather literary form, 'to light a few street lamps here and there in the darkest ways, to let us at all events see one another's faces and recognise our comrades, and work together with strong, organised and enlightened effort for the uplifting of those who suffer most under the present political and industrial system.'[12] The fact that mainstream newspapers rarely printed details of suffrage activities compounded the importance of the paper. The *Women's Labour News* remained the sole organ of the radical suffragist movement until the *Common Cause* was launched by Helena Swanwick in 1909. The existence of the *Labour News* may well have inspired the WSPU to establish a journal. The official organ of their organisation, *Votes for Women*, was launched in October 1907, edited by Mrs Pankhurst and Frederick Pethick-Lawrence.

Shortly after the launch of the *Labour News*, Gore-Booth organised another suffrage demonstration including the LCWTOWRC, the WTLC and the Lancashire and Cheshire Women's Suffrage Society. The event took place on 26 January 1907 at the Free Trade Hall in Manchester. Gore-Booth invited her sister to address the meeting. Markievicz spoke alongside Gore-Booth, Roper, Cooper and Reverend Steinthal. This was almost certainly Markievicz's first serious political venture. Her stepson, Stanislas, later recalled the campaign of 1907–08 noting that 'any struggle against authority and for those suffering injustice, appealed to Madame [Markievicz], though unlike her pacifist sister, she was not primarily a feminist, nor specially interested in the women's cause as such, but she rallied to the militant call always, and joined her sister in this campaign. Without doubt Madame's debut into politics dates from this visit to Manchester.'[13]

Although the demonstration drew a huge crowd it did not achieve noteworthy media attention. By now the militant activities of the WSPU were making daily appearances in national and local newspapers. However, all was not well within the organisation. There was a growing concern that the WSPU was being run by a small, closed group of middle-class women. In a letter to Adelaide Knight, Dora Montefiore warned that 'it was perhaps foolish to believe that the W.S & Pol. Union was really democratic, but it is governed by a clique, and that clique will allow no inside criticism, so that any one who criticises, even in the best spirit, must go.'[14] The controversy over democracy within the union intensified throughout the year, until a group of members led by Teresa Billington Greig called for the adoption of a democratic constitution. When the Pankhursts and Emmeline Pethick-Lawrence denied the request, a group of WSPU members broke away to form their own organisation, the Women's Freedom League (WFL), led by Billington Greig and Charlotte Despard. The group announced in *The Times* that 'we have found it necessary to withdraw from the WSPU in consequence of the unconstitutional method of a section of the committee.'[15]

It was becoming imperative for non-militant suffrage organisations to increase their public profile. The NUWSS adopted a new constitution in January 1907, strengthening and re-arranging the organisation. Fawcett, as leader of the organisation, arranged a series of open-air protests calling for political franchise. The first march was organised on 7 February 1907 from Hyde Park to Exeter Hall in London. This was the first national demonstration organised by the NUWSS and it became the largest outdoor protest on the issue to date. On a rainy Saturday afternoon more than 3,000 women marched through the streets of London to advocate for women's suffrage. The deplorable weather meant that the shoes and clothes of thousands of women became covered in mud and the demonstration infamously became known as the Mud March. The procession stretched for over a mile long. It was led by Lady Strachey, an ardent feminist campaigner, along with Millicent Fawcett, Keir Hardie and Lady Frances Balfour, suffragist leader and sister-in-law to the previous Conservative Prime Minister.[16] Gore-Booth addressed the crowd and made a special appeal to members of the Labour Party 'not to forget their pledge to the working women.'[17] The event included constitutional suffragists only. Members of the WSPU were deliberately excluded from the demonstration.[18] The absence of suffragette organisations was noted as a positive development by various newspapers reporting the event. The *Observer* recorded that the suffragettes 'were not officially invited to take part in the proceedings for fear of alienating a number of supporters who do not approve of their extreme methods.'[19]

Within days Gore-Booth stepped up her own attack on WSPU activities. This time she publicly ridiculed their election strategy through the pages of the *Manchester Guardian*. Pankhurst initially wrote to the paper on 15 February outlining the WSPU electioneering policy, which was to oppose any politician standing for by-election as a government candidate. In this way she maintained that the WSPU's 'growing influence with the working-class electors will enable us in the near future to prevent the return of all Liberal candidates.'[20] In fact the WSPU policy was to oppose any government candidate, regardless of which party they represented. Suffrage historian Elizabeth Crawford maintains that Pankhurst adopted this approach after witnessing the Irish Home Rule campaign led by Charles Stewart Parnell. Parnell opposed all government candidates at elections until Gladstone introduced a Home Rule Bill for debate in the House of Commons. Pankhurst imposed the same standard hoping that the government would eventually succumb to the WSPU demands.

Gore-Booth read Pankhurst's letter in the *Manchester Guardian* and prepared a response that same day. In her letter, Gore-Booth outlines why the northern industrial organisations are in complete disagreement with the WSPU's 'entirely negative' electioneering policy.[21] Gore-Booth's public attack on Pankhurst and the WSPU enraged a huge response. The letter pages of the *Manchester Guardian* became a battleground between supporters of the WSPU on one side and followers of Gore-Booth on the other. Members of the WSPU, including Evelyn Sharp, took exception and directly addressed Gore-Booth in their responses.[22] Sharp, herself a columnist for the *Manchester Guardian*, was later to describe the difference between suffragettes and suffragists in rather unflattering terms for non-militant campaigners. She maintained that because suffragists had waited for decades to receive political franchise for women, they were content to wait a bit longer. While suffragettes 'suddenly aware of an imperative need, could not wait another minute.'[23]

Within days the campaign for women's suffrage took a new and urgent direction. W.H. Dickinson, Liberal MP for St Pancras, introduced a proposed Women's Enfranchisement Bill. The bill was due for a second reading in the House of Commons on 8 March.[24] Dickenson proposed to alter the wording of the current legislation regarding political franchise qualifications. The new wording would simply include women as well as men, without disqualifying married women.[25] If passed, this bill would guarantee that a large proportion of working women would be granted a vote at general elections. It was crucial to act fast. Gore-Booth, Roper and Sarah Dickenson led a women's suffrage demonstration to Trafalgar Square in London. The women called for public support of the enfranchisement bill. The gathered crowd were not receptive. Gore-Booth faced a particularly boisterous response when she took the platform.[26] She warned that the government would soon attempt to legislate against women working in certain occupations, highlighting the employment of barmaids as a particular area of concern.

Gore-Booth, Roper, and Dickenson decided to tackle the issue head on and wrote to each member of the House of Commons. The letter was signed on behalf of the Women's Representation Committee, the Women's Labour Council and the Lancashire and Cheshire Women's Suffrage Society, stating:

> May we earnestly request you to consider the urgent and growing need of working women for the franchise, in order that they may protect their industrial interests? Their trade unions are disabled, their wages are depressed, and their industrial status lowered by their political rights. Close on five million women are suffering in this way.
>
> The growing tendency to submit all trade questions to Parliament for decision, the influence of the Government as the largest employer of female labour in the country, and the rapid increase in the number of women who are obliged to earn their livings, make it imperative that this large and important body of workers should no longer be denied that measure of political power which alone can improve their industrial position and make it secure. We therefore earnestly beg you to be in your place on March 8 in order to support the second reading of Mr. Dickinson's Women's Enfranchisement Bill.[27]

The next day a letter opposing the proposed bill was sent by the novelist Mrs Humphry Ward to the secretary of the Women's Anti-Suffrage Movement. Numerous groups actively campaigned against extending the vote to women. Ward's letter was printed in *The Times* and it clearly summarises the female anti-suffragist approach, explaining that 'women are entitled to vote in the one sphere, because they are fully competent to take a practical part in its administration.'[28] However, Ward stressed that this is not the case with the Imperial Government, 'simply because women are women, and their work in the world is different from that of men.'[29] Dickinson's bill was debated in the House to riotous arguments. Dickinson himself was shouted down on numerous occasions, with the result that the bill was dropped without ever being voted on. The anti-suffrage campaign got what they desired.

With no possibility of female franchise in the short term, Gore-Booth focused her attention on the plight of the barmaids. The proposal to ban women working as barmaids in Britain and Ireland was now becoming a real possibility. During the 1890s the House of Commons legislated to restrict women's access to bar work and four separate bills were introduced attempting to solve what was seen as the barmaid problem. In 1902, Glasgow implemented a ban on employing barmaids. The only females then permitted to work in Glaswegian licensed premises were relatives of the publican. Groups including the National British Women's Temperance Association, the Joint Committee on the Employment of Barmaids and the Male Waiters Association called for legislation to ban women from working in any capacity on licensed premises in Britain and Ireland. Ramsay MacDonald, Chairman of the Labour Party, and his wife, Margaret, actively campaigned to abolish the employment of barmaids. Temperance groups were inspired both by Glasgow's new legislation and by the upcoming change in the licensing laws in Britain.

The role of alcohol and of public houses had altered dramatically since the end of the nineteenth century. New laws to control opening hours, grant licences and restrict services were required. The Liberal government proposed to overhaul the entire licensing arrangements. Gore-Booth was concerned that politicians would use the new Licensing Bill in order to place further restrictions on female workers. A number of articles and pamphlets advocating the evils of bar work for women were produced around this time.[30] Many religious and temperance organisations believed that women were being exploited by the alcohol industry. The Bishop of Southwark protested that 'the nation ought not to allow the natural attractions of a young girl to be used for trading purposes.'[31] Many senior members of the Labour Party agreed with this assessment, including Ramsay MacDonald and Gore-Booth's old adversary, David Shackleton. The Labour MPs were part of a group who published their opposition to women working on licensed premises, insisting that the lives of barmaids often ended in 'drunkenness, immorality, misery and frequently suicide.'[32] Comments like these attempted to situate the occupation of barmaid as a starting stage towards prostitution and moral ruin.

Gore-Booth organised a great gathering of barmaids in Holburn on 14 March 1907. A series of meetings followed at which resolutions were passed denouncing any proposal to abolish or restrict the employment of barmaids. The meetings attracted huge media attention and reports of Gore-Booth's activities appeared in newspapers across England, Ireland and America.[33] The *Washington Post* highlighted the difficulty of organising women of 'the barmaid type,' who 'have not learned the fine art of expressing approval or disapproval at a public meeting, and it was somewhat disconcerting to hear laughter and cries of "Hear, hear," when Miss Esther Roper, B.A., was explaining that only four barmaids in ten years had committed suicide.'[34] Indeed, barmaids were not unionised and previously had no cause to organise themselves. Gore-Booth immediately established the Barmaids' Political Defence League under the auspices of the Women's Trades and Labour Council. The object of the league was set down 'to defend all women working on licensed premises from legislative attempts to restrict or abolish their employment.'[35] It was agreed that the league would defend the rights of barmaids by 'direct practical organised resistance to any specific measure of interference, by securing for these workers the political position that is necessary to make such attempts impossible in future.'[36] It was further agreed to fund the organisation through a small membership subscription of 1 shilling per year.[37]

Gore-Booth's determined organisation of barmaids caused concern in political quarters and she received a rather condescending and particularly nasty letter from Ramsay MacDonald, who wrote:

> You are reported in some score of papers to have stated that Mr. Gladstone and we desire to deprive barmaids of their living. You must know that that is untrue as we only desire to prevent new barmaids being taken on. Your letter, however, does appear to show that you did not intentionally misrepresent us, but rather that you had not the capacity to understand us. When you innocently go on to say that the barmaids would have their employment gradually abolished it does seem as though you had still to pick up the real meaning of our proposals.
>
> I am simply amazed that one who poses as you do as a friend of working women should talk such unmitigated rubbish about the effect of closing the barmaid trade to women, but so long as you are content to be a tool in the hands of the worst kind of publicans I dare say you will carry on your little campaign. Some elementary lessons in economics would, however, save you from much that you now say and do.[38]

Days later, at a meeting of barmaids in Memorial Hall, Manchester, Gore-Booth referred to MacDonald's letter describing how these 'are not the letters of people who are impartially and scientifically looking into a question of great importance ... they are angry, foolish, violent letters, and they do not appeal to any reasoning, but are merely and simply personal abuse.'[39]

Gore-Booth sought volunteers to attend a deputation to the Home Secretary, Herbert Gladstone. Nine women were selected from a large number of volunteers. Later that year Gore-Booth, Roper, and Dickenson led the deputation to meet with the Home Secretary. On 28 November, Gore-Booth addressed Gladstone pointing out the economic implications of abolishing barmaids, effectively throwing thousands of women 'upon a labour market already overcrowded.'[40] She argued against the idea that bar work was an immoral occupation for women which threatened 'health, morality, and the economic disadvantage of the trade.'[41] Explaining to Gladstone with clarity that 'the worst temptation to immorality,' is not working behind a bar, it is 'a state of unemployment, absence of wages, and starvation.'[42]

Gladstone appeared to be sympathetic with the plight of the deputation. He assured the group that the Licensing Bill would not be put before government until the next year and that any changes to the licensing legislation would be under the charge of the Chancellor of the Exchequer, Henry Asquith. Gladstone assured the group that he was well acquainted with Asquith who would not introduce 'any drastic provisions to check or diminish or put an end to the employment of women on licensed premises.'[43] Gladstone appeared confident that the government did not intend to put any women out of work. He stressed that the intention of a new Licensing Bill would be to reduce the number of 'undesirable' public houses that are 'sources of evil and danger.'[44] The meeting ended on a positive note and in friendly terms. After the meeting Gore-Booth and her group proceeded to Caxton Hall, where they met with a larger group of barmaids. Gore-Booth chaired the meeting to inform the women as to the Home Secretary's response. It is obvious from her address that she did not trust Gladstone's assurances. In fact, Gladstone's carefully chosen response to the barmaid deputation heightened Gore-Booth's concern. She energetically addressed the group alerting them to be 'keen to fight, for when a Cabinet Minister talked about sympathy it was dangerous, and they must not rest in their efforts until they had seen the Licensing Bill.'[45]

News of the deputation reached other female trade unionists and interested parties, who were apparently reassured by Gladstone's speech. The *British Journal of Nursing* announced that Gladstone guaranteed the public that the 'government had no intention of putting an end to the occupation of women on licensed premises.'[46]

The *New York Times* reported with glee that 'the English barmaid is safe. At least she will not be legislated out of existence by the present Liberal Government.'[47] However, Gore-Booth's prediction was to become reality within weeks. The Licensing Bill was drafted in February 1908. Gore-Booth secured a copy of the printed bill on 27 February. The detailed document consists of forty pages outlining amendments to the Licensing Acts, 1828 to 1906. The main thrust of the proposed bill sought to dramatically reduce the number of public houses and transfer the remaining licenses from breweries to the government, effectively nationalising public houses. Almost hidden in part three of this document, under Clause 20, 'power to attach conditions to the renewal of a licence,' is a section which grants local magistrates the power to attach any condition which they see fit, including 'the employment of women or children on the licensed premises.'[48] Under this clause a local magistrate could refuse to issue or renew a public license unless a publican agreed not to hire any women for bar work. Gore-Booth was justified in her mistrust of a Cabinet Minister. Gladstone himself had ordered the proposed bill alongside Asquith, David Lloyd George and Herbert Samuel.

The clause was so far embedded into the document that in all likelihood the section pertaining to the employment of women may well have gone unnoticed without Gore-Booth's intervention. In response, she wrote a letter on behalf of the Barmaids' Political Defence League, which she circulated to all MPs. The letter dated 12 March pleaded for them to oppose Clause 20 of the Licensing Bill 1908:

> It will be seen that should this clause pass into law every one of the 100,000 Barmaids and women assistants at present employed on licensed premises will find her employment suddenly placed in an entirely precarious and insecure position, irrespective of any good conduct or misconduct on her part. The magistrates are in fact to be given absolute irresponsible power to do what 'they think fit' with regard to the means of livelihood of 100,000 people; they will judge, condemn, and punish without the necessity for a shred of evidence, a prosecution, or even so much as an accusation against the person whose livelihood is in question.[49]

The bill received a huge amount of interest from several quarters. Labour MP George Wyndham began a campaign in opposition. Wyndham was most concerned that revoking licenses would deprive publicans of incomes. Brewing companies lobbied against the proposal, contending that thousands of people would lose money invested in shares of breweries. Churchmen welcomed proposals to close public houses on Sundays and temperance suffragists hoped that the new proposals would reduce alcohol consumption. In all of these debates Clause 20 and the plight of barmaids was generally ignored or overlooked.[50]

The furore regarding the Licensing Bill would reach an all-time high after a dramatic cabinet re-shuffle over the coming months. By the time that Gore-Booth first met with Gladstone, Prime Minister Campbell-Bannerman was very ill. After his wife died on 30 August 1906, Campbell-Bannerman's own health deteriorated rapidly. By November 1907 he had experienced four heart attacks and although his state of health was kept hidden from the public, he could not remain in such a high profile political position. He formally resigned on 4 April 1908. Henry Asquith left the position of Chancellor of the Exchequer to become Prime Minister on 12 April. Asquith promoted Lloyd George to the position of Chancellor of the Exchequer and Winston Churchill to President of the Board of Trade on 16 April. Churchill entered cabinet at the young age of thirty-three. Campbell-Bannerman had held out until the bitter end, dying on 22 April while still in residence at 10 Downing Street.

Under the law of the time, a newly appointed cabinet minister had to resign his seat and stand for re-election. On his appointment, Churchill was forced to resign as MP for Manchester North-West and stand for re-election in the same constituency. It was common practice that a newly appointed cabinet minister would be returned unopposed at such by-elections. The election was viewed by many as mere formality. However, this was not the case in 1908. By then Churchill had become a central figure in the barmaid issue. He promised to impose further restrictions on women's right to work, including a law which would make it illegal for all women to work after 8pm. The employment of women became a controversial point in the Manchester by-election. Literary historian Katherine Mullin suggests that ultimately the election 'functioned as a referendum on the [barmaid] issue.'[51] Churchill expected an easy victory in this election. He had secured a majority of 62 per cent over the Conservative candidate, William Joynson-Hicks, in the same constituency at the 1906 general election. However, this was not to be the case and the election was later described by author Ronald Blythe as 'the most brilliant, entertaining and hilarious electoral fight of the century.'[52]

Churchill arranged to address the public in the Coal Exchange building in Manchester two days before the election. Irish nationalist Patrick Hickey entertained the crowd until Churchill's arrival. Churchill was supported by Irish nationalists who believed that the Liberal Party would bring about justice for Ireland.[53] The Exchange building had a capacity for hundreds, an unprecedented crowd of thousands arrived. People were lined along the side of the road when a cortege of black cars donned with the red rosettes and flags of the Liberal Party pulled up outside. Churchill was accompanied by Lloyd George, who spoke in support of his Liberal candidate. Churchill appeared confident of victory, announcing 'men of Manchester, we shall win.'[54] When a person in the audience shouted, 'you are bound to win,' Churchill responded that 'yes from information I have at my disposal I know that at last we have the upper hand. At every point that we have disputed we have forced our opponents from the field. They are hopelessly beaten.'[55] He continued by ridiculing his Conservative opponent Joynson-Hicks and departed from the crowd in high spirits.

Gore-Booth had launched an intense campaign in opposition to Churchill. She invited her sister, Markievicz, to Manchester to help with electioneering. The Barmaids' Defence League backed the Conservative candidate William Joynson-Hicks in the by-election. Gore-Booth was faced with no other choice but to support him because the Labour Party chose not to contest the election. However, Joynson-Hicks appears to be a rather unlikely candidate for Gore-Booth to support, he was staunchly evangelical and the *Manchester Catholic Herald* accused him of being anti-Catholic and anti-Irish.[56] Indeed, the Irish Nationalist Party deplored Conservative policies and actively campaigned against Joynson-Hicks. He did, however, support female suffrage and opposed the Licensing Bill, which was Gore-Booth's main concern in this by-election.

Gore-Booth organised a rather striking coach, drawn by four white horses, to be driven around Manchester on the day that Churchill held his meeting at the Coal Exchange. Markievicz was at the whip and she drove to Stevenson Square. On their arrival, Gore-Booth and Roper took to the roof of the coach and made a rousing address about Clause 20 of the Licensing Bill. The women explained how the clause would restrict, or possibly eradicate, the employment of barmaids. Roper appealed for a vote against Churchill in the by-election on the grounds that the 'Home Secretary had been induced to insert this clause in the bill by a number of rich persons who had attacked the moral charters of barmaids as a class.'[57] Gore-Booth exclaimed that a vote against Churchill would prove to the government that 'it was not a minor matter to take away the livelihood of 100,000 respectable, hard-working women.'[58] During the speeches, Markievicz and Reddish distributed leaflets advocating the work of the Barmaids' Political Defence League.

The following day Gore-Booth arranged a mass meeting in the Coal Exchange building in support of barmaids. This time Markievicz took the stand, announcing, 'I have come over from Ireland to help because I am a woman. I am not a Conservative – I am a Home Ruler – but I have come over here to ask everyone to vote for Mr. Joynson-Hicks because he, of the three candidates who are standing, is the only one who takes a straight and decent view of the barmaids' question.'[59] Stanislas recounted how Markievicz's quick wit and engaging oratory style easily won over the crowd, recalling how when his stepmother stood up to speak, 'she was heckled by a man in the crowd, with the inevitable male query, "Can you cook a dinner?" "Certainly" she replied, cracking her whip. "Can you drive a coach-and-four?"'[60] Markievicz relished the opportunity of being involved with her sister's political activities. Eva wrote to her brother Josslyn describing how 'we had a great show in the election and people got very enthusiastic about barmaids. Con was simply splendid driving four horses all day long and half the night. Nobody talked of anything but her beautiful driving.'[61] The excitement of being involved in such successful campaigns inspired Markievicz to become politically active in Ireland. That same year she joined the Irish Republican Party, Sinn Féin, and Maud Gonne's nationalist women's organisation, Inghinidhe na hÉireann (Daughters of Ireland).

The polling stations opened the next morning on 24 April. Unusually for the time of year, Manchester was immersed in snow and a bitter wind cut through the city.[62] Despite the dire weather conditions there was a large turnout, 10,681 people voted out of a total of 11,914 registered voters. Many volunteers in support of the Barmaids' Political Defence League and various suffrage organisations stood in the freezing cold outside polling stations pleading with voters not to support Churchill. Churchill spent most of the day driving through the streets of Manchester in an open topped car accompanied by his mother, Jennie, and Liberal Chairman Sir

Edward Donner. Similarly, Joynson-Hicks drove around the city accompanied by his wife, Grace, in a horse and carriage. At 9.30 that evening a blue flag waving outside of Manchester Town Hall signalled the end of the vote count and announcing the victory of the Conservative candidate Joynson-Hicks.[63] Winston Churchill was defeated by a margin of 529 votes. The by-election campaign was an immense victory for Gore-Booth and for the Women's Trades and Labour Council. Gore-Booth played a vital role in the defeat of Churchill. However, media reporting of the dramatic events focused not on Gore-Booth but on the fact that her sister, Countess Markievicz, drove a coach and four white horses in support of the barmaid campaign.[64]

Weeks later Churchill stood at a by-election in Dundee and was returned as MP in May; he remained in the Dundee constituency until 1922. Gore-Booth continued lobbying against the Licensing Bill. She wrote to *The Times* seeking financial help for the campaign. The letter signed by Gore-Booth and Roper explains that 'it was found simple enough to gain the sympathy and votes of the electors on the barmaid question,' at the Manchester by-election, however, 'those who wish to abolish barmaids are trying to work quietly and get the clause passed whilst no one realizes what is happening.'[65] The radical suffragists ensured that this would not happen. On 13 June 1908, the NUWSS organised another large suffrage procession from the Embankment to the Albert Hall in London. Gore-Booth and her group did not attend. Instead, they held a demonstration on behalf of Lancashire women workers in Trafalgar Square. The event was attended by over 2,000 people and numerous women's trade unions from Manchester travelled to the capital to take part. Gore-Booth addressed the issue on the 'serious displacement of women's labour by Act of Parliament involved in the attack on the barmaids trade.'[66] She delivered her speech from the foot of the Nelson column on the plinth, facing the fountains. After numerous speeches Markievicz took to the plinth, announcing how, 'they were told the bar was a bad place for a woman ("So it is"), but the Thames Embankment at night was far worse.'[67]

The barmaids' campaign drew the attention of Violet Douglas-Pennant, a remarkable philanthropist who worked mainly on behalf of disabled children and the unemployed in London. Douglas-Pennant was concerned that any move to ban the employment of barmaids would dramatically increase unemployment in London city. She organised a meeting in support of the barmaids at the luxurious Mayfair hotel, Claridge's, in London. Douglas-Pennant invited Gore-Booth to address the meeting, which was attended by an impressive list of influential people including Lord Sanderson, Lord Winterton MP, Wilfrid Ashley MP, Lady Emily Wyndham-Quin and Reverend Stewart Headlam. Lord Erroll, a Conservative politician and ex-government whip in the House of Lords, presided. This was a turning point in the barmaids' campaign. The attendees supported the overall essence of the Licensing Bill but now realised the negative implications of Clause 20 to women's employment.[68]

Within months, the Barmaids' Political Defence League overwhelmingly won their campaign. 294 out of 355 MPs rejected the 1908 Licensing Bill's endorsement of the 'idea that it was a sort of moral leprosy for women to get behind a bar.'[69] During the debate in the Commons, Liberal MP Horatio Bottomley declared that under Clause 20 local magistrates 'would be able to say that no woman should be employed on licensed premises in any capacity whatever. The sub-section would reduce law to anarchy and legislation to a farce.'[70] Conservative MP Wilfrid Ashley questioned whether 'a body of men elected entirely by men had any moral right to prohibit the employment of women in a certain trade purely on sentimental grounds.'[71] The barmaids' campaign was an unqualified success and Prime Minister Asquith removed the entire sub-section relating to women and children from the Licensing Bill on 2 November 1908. In celebration Gore-Booth and Roper wrote to *The Times* thanking 'those friends in and out of the House of Commons who so effectually aided the Barmaids' Political Defence League in their successful campaign.'[72]

Throughout the intensive campaigning on behalf of barmaids, Gore-Booth continued working on other issues with the Women's Trade and Labour Council. In May 1908, she was approached by a group of waitresses from the Clydesdale Café. The women came out of work on strike in an attempt to improve their working conditions. Gore-Booth set about organising them into a union and established a monetary fund to assist them.[73] Under the guidance of Gore-Booth, the waitresses returned to work with improved conditions and their union thrived. In July she represented a group of flower sellers at Oxford Circus in London. The London council had made recommendations to ban flower sellers from the area on the instruction of the Public Health Committee who maintained that the women were obstructing traffic. Gore-Booth and Roper organised a successful meeting with the mayor, Alderman Fowler, at Marylebone Town Hall to resolve the situation.

Through her various activities Gore-Booth had alienated the temperance suffragists and she again faced opposition from the women's anti-suffrage movement. In February 1907, an article entitled 'Women and Politics,' written by Caroline E. Stephen, appeared in the *Nineteenth Century and After*.[74] Stephen, a paternal aunt to Virginia Woolf, adamantly opposed women obtaining a vote at general elections.[75] She wrote as a self-appointed speaker 'on behalf of a great though silent multitude of women.'[76] In her article, Stephen maintained that achieving suffrage for women would 'inflict ... a grave injustice,' onto millions of women who did not want to be responsible for electing Members of Parliament.[77] She made a plea for 'women to be consulted before the introduction of any measure so profoundly affecting their interests.'[78] Gore-Booth did not delay with her response; in the next edition of the journal she published a direct attack entitled simply, 'Women and Politics: A Reply.'[79] In her article, Gore-Booth notes that 'as a simple matter of justice, it does not seem fair, or even reasonable, that the height of one personal intellectual ambition should be enforced as the legal limit of another person's activity. It may be that "nuns fret not at their convents' narrow room;" but surely that is no reason why we should all be shut up in cells.'[80]

Within another year anti-suffragist women would become more vocal. In 1908, an article by Lady Lovat appeared in the *Nineteenth Century and After* asserting that 'women would lose infinitely more than they gain by parliamentary enfranchisement.'[81] In order to animate her argument Lovat rested on the words of John Ruskin from *Sesame and Lilies* to explain the innate differences between men and women:

> The man's power is active, progressive, defensive. He is eminently the doer, the creator, the discoverer, the defender. His intellect is for speculation and invention; his energy for adventure, for war, and for conquest wherever war is just, wherever conquest is necessary. But women's power is for rule, not for battle – and her intellect is not for invention or creation, but for sweet ordering, arrangement, and decision. She sees the quality of things, their claims and their places ... The man in his rough work in the open world must encounter all peril and trial ... But he must guard the woman from all

> this; within his house, as ruled by her, unless she herself has sought it, need enter no danger, no temptation, no cause of error or offense.[82]

As if in direct response, Mrs Humphry Ward published 'The Anti Suffragist' the next month in the same periodical.[83] Ward announced the formation of the National Women's Anti-Suffrage League under the presidency of the Countess of Jersey. The league was formed on 21 July 1908 at Westminster Palace Hotel, after acknowledging a crisis point in the battle against women's enfranchisement. The women at the helm of the Anti-Suffrage League were seriously concerned that the women's enfranchisement bill would be passed.[84]

In 1907, the signatures of 37,000 women against suffrage had been collected and now they had organised into a formal society. The manifesto for the new organisation was drawn up by Ward and the editor of *Nineteenth Century*, William Wray Skilbeck, showing the periodical's probable bias on the topic. The manifesto began with a call for women to join the league as 'it is time that the women who are opposed to the concession of the parliamentary franchise to women should make themselves fully and widely heard. The arguments on the other side have been put with great ability and earnestness, in season and out of season, and enforced by methods legitimate and illegitimate.'[85] Ward dedicated herself to the campaign against women's enfranchisement and her novels soon began to reflect the league's sentiment.[86]

Gore-Booth was outraged at the two articles and she sent an article to the editor of *Nineteenth Century*, entitled 'Women and the Suffrage: A Reply to Lady Lovat and Mrs. Humphry Ward.'[87] The article was published in August 1908 and in it Gore-Booth directly confronts the issue in class-related terms noting that:

> The truth is, the power of the few women of the upper classes who by their position and social influence are able to keep in touch with legislation is no comfort at all to the mass of the working women, who want to be governed by people who are responsible to them, and to whom it will therefore come as a matter of course to consider their interests and consult their intelligence, and the fact that men will anxiously consult distinguished and philanthropic ladies does not touch the point of issue.[88]

As philanthropists and members of aristocratic society, Lovat and Ward were afforded access to decision-making processes, access that was unavailable to working-class women. In her article Gore-Booth warns that working-class women should not be dependent on men or upper-class-women to legislate fair laws.

Meanwhile another of Gore-Booth's plays, *The Sorrowful Princess*, was published by Longmans Green & Co.[89] Gore-Booth was asked by two friends, Helen Neild and Amy Kemp, to write them a play for a school performance they were organising. She wrote a play based on the traditional tale of the patron saint of England, St George slaying the dragon. As with most of Gore-Booth's literature she manipulates the original version of the myth. Her story is set in an Egyptian mystical background. In the play the people of Egypt are blighted by famine because of the seemingly indestructible dragon that roams their land. Princess Sabra of Egypt sacrifices herself in order to save her people. Sabra is killed and through this action St George gains access to the underworld and the magic sword with which he slays the dragon. Once the dragon is conquered Sabra is resurrected to life.

The two girls performed the play, along with fifteen of their friends, in St George's Wood, Haslemere on 27 July 1907. The publication records the performance and lists the performer's names. Gore-Booth dedicated the publication to Helen Neild, Amy Kemp and Esther Roper. This play marks a change in Gore-Booth's writings. This is perhaps the first literary evidence of her involvement with New Age religions. In the opening scene Gore-Booth includes a footnote explaining that she used an extract from *The Book of the Dead*, which became a key text for the Hermetic Order of the Golden Dawn, of which Yeats was a member.[90] The significance of this would not be apparent until nearly ten years later when Gore-Booth officially joined the Theosophical Society.

Notes

1 EGB, 'On the Embankment,' *CE*, p. 408.

2 Liddington, *Rebel Girls*, p. 75.

3 People's History Museum, Manchester, LP/GC/9/368, letter from Roper and EGB to W. Henderson, 25 November 1906.

4 'The Huddersfield Election: Closing Scenes of a Short Campaign,' *Daily Graphic* 5290: LXVIII (28 November 1906), p. 833.

5 Crawford, *Women's Suffrage Movement*, p. 736.

6 *Slater's Manchester, Salford & Suburban Directory, 1909*. (Historical Directories, 1909). Gore-Booth is registered as a householder of Cringle

Brook, Park Crescent, Victoria Park, p. 955 and Roper is registered as a householder of the same property, p. 1316.

7 Marion Ledward was Roper's friend and fellow activist during her days at Owens College. UK census for 1901 confirms that Marion, her mother and the Ledward family lived at Cringle Brook.

8 Working Class Movement Library, Manchester, 331.88/ F4, Box 17, *Manchester & Salford Women's Trades and Labour Council: Third Annual Report 1907*, p. 4.

9 EGB, *CE*, p. 12.

10 Ibid.

11 Unfortunately no copies of the *Women's Labour News* appear to have survived.

12 EGB, *CE*, p. 12.

13 NLI, MS 44,619, 'Life of Constance de Markiewicz [sic]' by her stepson Stanislas Dun Markievicz, p. 133.

14 As cited in Crawford, Women's Suffrage Movement, p. 736.

15 Ibid, p. 720.

16 Lady Frances was married to Eustace Balfour, the younger brother of Arthur Balfour.

17 'Votes for Women: March through the Streets of London,' *MG* (11 February 1907), p. 7.

18 For further debate as to the significance of the Mud March see Lisa Tickner, *The Spectacle of Women: Imagery of the Suffrage Campaign 1907–14* (Chicago: University of Chicago Press, 1988).

19 'Titled Demonstrators,' *Observer* (10 February 1907), p. 7.

20 Christabel Pankhurst, 'The Enfranchisement of Women,' *MG* (15 February 1907), p. 7.

21 EGB, 'Women's Suffrage,' *MG* (18 February 1907), p. 5.

22 Evelyn Sharp, 'Women's Suffrage,' *MG* (22 February 1907), p. 12. Gore-Booth's response to Sharp in *MG* (23 February 1907), p. 6.

23 Evelyn Sharp, *Unfinished Adventure: Selected Reminiscences from an Englishwoman's Life* (The Bodley, 1933; London: Faber & Faber, 2008), p. 128. As cited in Angela V. John, *Evelyn Sharp: Rebel Woman, 1869–1955* (Manchester: Manchester University Press, 2009).

24 *Parliamentary Papers*, iv: bill 8, 1907.

25 See Homer Lawrence Morris, *Parliamentary Franchise Reform in England from 1885 to 1918* (New York: Longmans Green & Co, 1921), p. 42.

26 'Women in Trafalgar Square: Defence of Barmaids,' *MG* (4 March 1907), p. 13.

27 Esther Roper, Sarah Dickenson and Eva Gore-Booth, 'Women's Suffrage,' *MG* (5 March 1907), p. 10.

28 'Letters to the Editor: Woman Suffrage,' *The Times* (8 March 1907), p. 11.

29 Ibid.
30 Joint Committee on the Employment of Barmaids, *Women as Barmaids: With a Preface by the Lord Bishop of Southwark* (London: King & Son, 1905).
31 Phil Mellows, 'A Lesson from the Past,' *Publican* (15 December 2008), p. 16.
32 'Abolition of Barmaids: Important Memorial,' *MG* (13 December 1907), p. 7.
33 'Maids are up in Revolt: Will Protest to England's Home Secretary,' *Baltimore American* (31 March 1907), p. 23. The *Baltimore American* published regular updates about Gore-Booth's campaign in support of barmaids including; 'The Work of Women,' (4 August 1907), p. 41; 'The English Barmaid,' (13 December 1907), p. 8.
34 'Demonstration made by Barmaids in Protest against Hostile Laws,' *Washington Post* (31 March 1907), p. 9.
35 PRONI, Mic 590, Reel 10, L/13/99, Proposals for Barmaids' Political Defence League.
36 Ibid.
37 Several pamphlets on the employment of barmaids were published by the Barmaids' Political Defence League, such as 'Facts about Barmaids,' in 1907. London School of Economics, HD6/82, M Pamphlets, 188.
38 People's History Museum, Manchester, LP/GC/13/110, letter from Ramsay MacDonald to EGB, 25 March 1907.
39 'The Barmaid: A Protest against Legal Control,' *MG* (28 March 1907), p. 5.
40 'Licensing Bill: Barmaids Deputation to Gladstone,' *MG* (29 November 1907), p. 7.
41 Ibid.
42 Ibid.
43 Ibid.
44 Ibid.
45 Ibid.
46 'Outside the Gates,' *British Journal of Nursing* (14 December 1907), p. 478.
47 'I will not Disturb English Barmaids,' *New York Times* (1 December 1907).
48 1908 (133) Licensing. A Bill to amend the Licensing Acts, 1828 to 1906 (House of Commons Papers, 27 February 1908).
49 PRONI, Mic 590, Reel 10, L/13/101, Barmaids' Political Defence League open letter to MPs, 12 March 1908.
50 'The Licensing Bill,' *MG* (24 March 1908), p. 7.
51 Katherine Mullin, '"The Essence of Vulgarity": The Barmaid Controversy in the "Sirens" episode of James Joyce's *Ulysses*,' *Textual Practice* 18:4 (2004), 477.

52 Ronald Blythe, *The Age of Illusion: England in the Twenties and Thirties* (London: Hamish Hamilton, 1963), p. 25.
53 Irish leaders including Daniel Boyle spoke on behalf of Churchill before the by-election. 'Midnight Electioneering,' *MG* (23 April 1908), p. 10.
54 'The Election in N-W Manchester,' *MG* (23 April 1908), p. 7.
55 Ibid.
56 'Midnight Electioneering,' *MG* (23 April 1908), p.10.
57 Ibid.
58 Ibid.
59 'The Barmaid Cause,' *MG* (24 April 1908), p. 8.
60 Stanislas Dun Markievicz, 'Life of Constance de Markiewicz [sic],' p. 133.
61 PRONI, Mic 590, Reel 10, L/13/121, letter from EGB to Josslyn Gore-Booth, 29 April 1908.
62 'The Election in N-W Manchester,' *MG* (25 April 1908), p. 9.
63 Final results: Joynson-Hicks (Conservative) 5,417, Churchill (Liberal) 4,988 and Dan Irving (Socialist) 276.
64 *MG*, 22 April 1908, as cited in Liddington and Norris, *One Hand Tied behind Us*, p. 286.
65 'Barmaids Political Defence League,' *The Times* (1 May 1908), p. 2.
66 'Working Women in Trafalgar Square,' *The Times* (15 June 1908), p. 9.
67 Ibid.
68 'Barmaids and the Licensing Bill: A Meeting,' *The Times* (11 July 1908), p. 6.
69 *The Times* (3 November 1908), p. 4.
70 'House of Commons,' *MG* (3 November 1908), p. 10.
71 Ibid.
72 'To the Editor,' *The Times* (6 November 1908), p. 12.
73 Working Class Movement Library, Manchester, 331.88/F4 Box 17, *Manchester & Salford Women's Trades and Labour Council: Fourth Annual Report 1908*, p. 13.
74 Caroline E. Stephen, 'Women and Politics,' *Nineteenth Century and After*, 60 (February 1907), 227–36.
75 Her brother, Leslie Stephen, was father to Virginia Woolf. Caroline became a convert to Quakerism late in life. Mary Gould Ogilvie (ed.), *Caroline Stephen, Quaker Strongholds* (1951; Pennsylvania: Pendle Hill Publications, 2005).
76 Stephen, 'Women and Politics,' p. 227.
77 Ibid.
78 Ibid.
79 EGB, 'Women and Politics: A Reply,' *Nineteenth Century and After*, 61 (March 1907), pp. 472–6.
80 Ibid, p. 472.
81 A.M. Lovat, 'Women and Suffrage,' *Nineteenth Century and After* (July 1908), pp. 64–73.

82 Ibid, p. 67.
83 Mary A. Ward, 'The Anti Suffragist,' *Nineteenth Century and After* (August 1908), pp. 343–52.
84 Lucy Delap, 'Feminist and Anti-feminist Encounters in Edwardian Britain,' *Historical Research*, 87:201 (August 2005), 380.
85 Ibid, p. 345.
86 Maroula Joannou, 'Mary Augusta Ward (Mrs Humphry) and the Opposition to Women's Suffrage,' *Women's History Review*, 14:3 & 4 (2005), 561–80.
87 EGB, 'Women and the Suffrage: A reply to Lady Lovat and Mrs. Humphry Ward,' *Nineteenth Century and After* (August 1908), pp. 495–506.
88 Ibid, p. 505.
89 EGB, *The Sorrowful Princess* (London: Longmans Green & Co, 1907).
90 Ernest Wallis-Budge (trans.), *The Papyrus of Ani: The Egyptian Book of the Dead* (London: British Museum, 1885); Reprinted (New York: Dover Publications, 1967).

7

World War One: from trade unionism to peace movements

'Men have got their pomp and pride –
All the green world is on our side'[1]

An article appeared in *The Woman Worker* on 4 September 1908 criticising Gore-Booth and questioning the basis of her social reform work. The article, authored by J.J. Mallon, describes her 'among sweated Cradley Heath chain-makers, and wretched factory girls.'[2] Under an unmistakeably disapproving heading, 'Errors of judgement,' it is suggested that Gore-Booth is 'opposed to all protective legislation for women. In her view, such legislation hampers women as competitors for employment, and is like[ly] to keep them in subjection to men.'[3] Mallon concludes with a personal snipe, describing how the long struggle to achieve the vote for women has made Gore-Booth 'impatient, has left her bitter, and a little overwrought.'[4] The article signals a deep disagreement between the Women's Trade and Labour Council and the most unlikely of opponents, the Women's Trade Union League (WTUL). This rupture would spark much controversy within the women's trade union movement over the next two years. Mallon had deep links with the WTUL and like Gore-Booth, was committed to improving the welfare of working women. However, Mallon and Gore-Booth disagreed emphatically about what exactly was in the best interest of women workers.

Mallon was secretary of the recently formed Anti-Sweating League (ASL).The organisation was founded in 1906 by trade union organiser and secretary of the Women's Trade Union League, Mary MacArthur. MacArthur was one of 30,000 people who had attended the Sweated Industries Exhibition organised earlier that year by the chocolate manufacturer and owner of the *Daily News*, George

Cadbury. Cadbury was committed to exposing the extent of dangerous sweated employment, which was undertaken mainly by women in homes and dilapidated outhouses around the country. The exhibition, staged in the West End of London, comprised stalls where forty-five workers demonstrated their typical day's labour. The practices of women engaged in making products such as chains and nails was exposed as gruesome work which involved working with a hot forge and heavy anvils, generally while caring for their young children on the same unsafe premises. The exhibition was a high profile event opened by the King's sister, Princess Beatrice. Numerous influential people attended including Ramsay MacDonald and Irish author and Fabian Society member, George Bernard Shaw.

Cadbury's exhibition was a great success. The public were outraged to discover that such unacceptable work practices were conducted in Britain. Women's history curator, Lynn Sinclair, contends that people around the country 'were shocked to find that a dress could have been made by a reasonably paid seamstress in an airy workroom, while the buttons and trimmings were produced by a sweated worker, and that wedding cakes manufactured in hygienic conditions were likely to be packed in attractive boxes glued together in a disease-ridden tenement.'[5] After attending the exhibition MacArthur acknowledged that there was a pressing need to outlaw sweated industries and she established the Anti-Sweating League; J.J. Mallon was appointed as the first secretary. The ASL maintained a close connection with the WTUL.

Mallon and MacArthur welcomed any government intervention which would reduce women's working hours and improve health and safety standards for workers. In contrast, Gore-Booth was actively campaigning against such legislation believing that it restricted women's access to employment and ultimately threatened their income and job security. The main legislation of interest to both groups was the Factory and Workshop Acts. These progressive acts were enforced throughout the latter part of the nineteenth century as a measure of protection for workers. Various Factory Acts ensured the introduction of better sanitation and access to emergency escapes and regulated against overcrowding in factories and mills. These controls were welcome at a time when accidents and work-related illnesses were particularly common.

Gore-Booth was not opposed to the health and safety regulations implemented through legislation. She was opposed to sections in the

Factory Acts which set regulations for the employment of women. Through various legislation women's hours of work were curtailed to a maximum daily limit. The first act to be introduced in the twentieth century, the Factory and Workshop Act 1901, was implemented on 1 January 1902.[6] This act consolidated all previous related acts and raised the minimum work age to twelve. Female inspectors visited factories to ensure that the acts were being adhered to. Men were not affected by any of this employment legislation. The Factory Acts only affected men in relation to health and safety measures. This was the point which concerned Gore-Booth, who argued that the same restrictions should apply equally to men and women in order to protect everyone and ensure that competition for jobs was equal.

At first the legislation referred only to factories but eventually this was expanded to cover many other industries and careers. A case before Lord Chief Justice Darling in April 1907 tested the boundaries of the acts. Darling found that since a room at the back of a florist's shop was 'substantially and mainly used for the purposes of manual labour,' this constituted a workshop, the employment of florists' assistants therefore fell under the legislation of the Factory and Workshop Act.[7] Through a broad definition of what constituted a factory or a workshop many more women fell under the protective legislation which enforced a ban on women working after 8pm. Restricting women's working hours would particularly affect florists' assistants, who were often required to work late into the evening to put the finishing touches to a ballroom or other venue. Florists' assistants were not organised into unions and so they formed a group to petition the Home Secretary, Gladstone. The female florists sought an exemption to allow them to work between the hours of eight and ten in the evening. In this instance, Gladstone was understanding and almost instantly granted the women the exemption they requested.

Gladstone's decision was not welcomed by the Labour Party. Hardie had resigned as chairman of Labour in 1908 and was replaced by Arthur Henderson. In November 1908, Henderson requested that the exemption to the Factory and Workshop Act relating to florists' assistants be withdrawn. Appalled, Gore-Booth, Roper and Dickenson wrote to the *Manchester Guardian*. They stated emphatically that 'if the Labour Party depended on the votes of working women as well as men Mr. Henderson would not be attacking to-night the Home Secretary's wise and considerate measure.'[8] Henderson was granted his request. The exemption was removed making it once again illegal for female florists to work after eight in the evening. In response the florists' organised a meeting at Horticultural Hall in Westminster. At the meeting Gore-Booth was appointed as their representative.

Her first action as a representative of the florists was to produce a penny pamphlet, *Women's Right to Work*, published on behalf of the Women's Trade and Labour Council.[9] In it Gore-Booth examined how the Factory and Workshop Act was being extended to restrict more women in their work. She maintained that such legislation was being enforced to reduce male unemployment. She brought the plight of the florists into the public domain, representing their interests at a suffrage meeting in the Free Trade Hall at Manchester in March 1909. Addressing the crowd with an engaging speech Gore-Booth declared that 'the exemption granted to girls at work in flower shops to work late hours on certain occasions had been withdrawn simply because there was not a single man in the House of Commons who was keen enough in the interests of working women to make a row.'[10] The Labour Party, she said, claimed that they had ensured the withdrawal of the exemption 'in the interests of sweated workers, in preventing them from having to do home work.' As if, she added, 'you could take a ballroom home and decorate it in your bedroom.'[11]

The Labour Party had in fact taken this step in support of the WTUL, agreeing that women's work hours should be reduced. Labour MP David Shackleton was an outspoken champion of the league. The previous year he wrote the preface to *Women in Industry*, a compilation of articles written by the president of the WTUL, Gertrude Tuckwell, along with articles by MacArthur and other advocates of the league. Shackleton was unequivocal in his praise of the WTUL, stating that 'as one who knows the important work of the writers in forwarding the solution of such [trade] problems, I earnestly commend their papers to the careful consideration of a sympathetic public.'[12]

The controversy regarding the florists' assistants loomed on. In May 1909, Gladstone bowed to pressure and appointed a commissioner, Judge Ruegg, to examine the situation.[13] Employers in the industry were well represented at the inquiry by the Florists' Association and a petition was submitted from the master florists across Britain. A solicitor, Freke Palmer, was employed to represent the interests of employers in the industry. In representations made by Palmer only one florists' assistant was called to give evidence. Gore-Booth and Roper appeared at the inquiry to express the views of the florists' assistants. However, Ruegg dismissed their findings announcing that 'I am not inclined to attach much weight to the resolutions.'[14] The Women's Trade Union League was well represented at the inquiry, Tuckwell, MacArthur and Mallon all attended. The WTUL demanded that the restrictions be tightened and the number of hours women worked be reduced. Ruegg highly commended the league; in his report he noted that 'the objections to any relaxation of the Factory Acts in the interests of the workers were ably put forward and agued by . . . the Women's Trade Union League, a society with a membership of 170,000 working women throughout the country.'[15]

While the various trade union groups and politicians waited for the commissioner's decision, Gore-Booth continued to campaign against protective legislation. She published an article in the *Englishwoman* denigrating how the Factory Acts 'handicap women,' through the actions of 'innocent philanthropists.'[16] She warned that 'women, often enough, do not realise their miserable position as regards industrial legislation, nor how the livelihoods of many hundreds, or indeed thousands, can be swept away at the whim of a few officials.'[17] MacArthur was in attendance at a suffrage demonstration in Queen's Hall in London when Gore-Booth addressed the audience. MacArthur interrupted her speech, attempting to question Gore-Booth regarding the campaign for florists' assistants. Gore-Booth refused to discuss the matter publicly. MacArthur was furious, she wrote to the *Daily News* that the WTUL has 'toiled for more than a generation' for protective legislation and they would not allow Gore-Booth to reverse all that they had achieved. MacArthur made a serious allegation that women's enfranchisement would be delayed because of 'the propaganda of that small body, of which Miss Eva Gore-Booth and Miss Roper are the chief exponents.'[18] Gore-Booth responded through the pages of the *Manchester Guardian* saying that she could not discuss the case regarding florists' assistants in public, while the matter was under legal consideration. However, she did comment that her women's trade council will 'go even further than Miss MacArthur; we think nobody should work for very long hours, and we would gladly see the acts extended to men, which would entirely do away with the difficulties in their application at present caused by the competition between men and women.'[19]

Judge Ruegg announced his final decision in November 1909. The outcome was not a straightforward one. Ruegg appreciated the perishable nature of flowers and the seasonal aspects of the industry, and he therefore found that it was sometimes necessary for women to work overtime as florists' assistants. He made an allowance entitling female florists to work two hours overtime on a maximum of thirty days per year. Ruegg included a provision that whenever one woman worked overtime, this would count as overtime for all the women employed in that workshop. Ruegg included this provision to ensure that factory inspectors could easily monitor overtime rates.[20] Gore-Booth was disappointed with the outcome but she had no time to dwell on the case. The outcome of the florists' campaign was closely followed by the announcement that a general election was imminently pending.

The Liberal government were experiencing instability due to the 'people's budget,' introduced in April 1909 by the Chancellor of the Exchequer, Lloyd George. The budget had promised social reform through taxation of wealthy landowners. By the end of the year it was rejected in the House of Lords, whose members mainly comprised aristocratic landed gentry.[21] In support of the people's budget, Prime Minister Asquith challenged the power of the House of Lords, a move which eventually forced the Liberal Party to return to the people for a general election. As soon as the election date was set for January 1910, Gore-Booth declared in the *Common Cause* that the industrial women suffragists of Lancashire would run an independent candidate in the Rossendale constituency.[22]

Rossendale was chosen because of its location in the heart of the cotton industry. The fact that there were only two candidates running in this constituency was an added bonus. The sitting Liberal, Lewis Harcourt, was running against the Conservative candidate J. Kebty-Fletcher. The LCWTOWRC were intent on removing Harcourt from his position as MP because they viewed him as an ardent anti-suffragist. Gore-Booth testified in the *Manchester Guardian* that 'this committee had experience of Mr. Harcourt's strongly hostile attitude to women's suffrage when in 1906 we took a special petition to him signed by 8,000 of the men and women of Rossendale urging the immediate necessity for the enfranchisement of women. An enemy in so influential a position as Mr. Harcourt is, we think, the gravest danger to the cause of women's suffrage.'[23]

The Women's Representation Committee had been quite successful at the general election of 1906 and Gore-Booth was hopeful that they would achieve an even better result this time around. However, while they had the support of Labour in the Wigan constituency during the last election, this would not be the case at Rossendale. The area was staunchly Liberal. The Labour Party had no real connections in Rossendale and they did not even consider contesting the constituency themselves. There was also an unforeseen problem with contesting a candidate in this area. Rossendale was an area deeply committed to non-conformist temperance, the radical suffragists' recent victory on behalf of barmaids was not viewed in a positive light by voters in this area.

The LCWTOWRC joined forces with the Industrial and Professional Women's Suffrage Society to fund and form the Rossendale Suffrage Election Committee. J. Malcolm Mitchell was chosen as their candidate. Mitchell was a journalist with *The Times* and he was founder and honorary secretary of the Men's League for Women's Suffrage. He was dedicated and driven to the campaign for votes for women. Gore-Booth was convinced that 'if Mr. Mitchell should get in, the Women's Suffrage movement would obviously gain enormous advantages. Not least of these would be to have a representative of Mr. Mitchell's abilities and proved sincerity, who would put Women's Suffrage before all party considerations and work for it with a single mind.'[24] In a cruel reminder of the Wigan campaign, Mitchell withdrew from the election at the last minute. It was recorded in the press that he was obliged to 'desist from his proposed candidature … owing to purely private reasons.'[25] Gore-Booth announced the new suffrage candidate as Arthur Bulley at a public meeting in the Bacup Mechanic's Hall on 21 December.[26]

Unfortunately Bulley was an unsuitable candidate. He was the owner of S.M. Bulley & Son, a cotton brokers in Liverpool, a member of the Independent Labour Party and of the Fabian Society. Bulley was mainly known as a somewhat unconventional but highly successful gardener. He had no connections in the Rossendale community and was an unlikely type to convince loyal Liberal voters to support women's suffrage. The £500 necessary to run a candidate was scraped together through funds from the Women Textile Workers' Representation Committee, the Industrial and Professional

Women's Suffrage Society and from Bulley himself. Bulley contributed £150 to his own election fund, which may partly explain why Gore-Booth chose him as their candidate.

Days before the election began Asquith pledged that if returned to government, the Liberal Party would look favourably on women's enfranchisement. Suffrage groups were not convinced. However, this promise appears to have appeased the WSPU, who engaged in only limited campaigning during this election. In contrast, Gore-Booth and her established group of election campaigners including, Roper, Dickenson, Reddish, Rowton and Cooper arrived in Rossendale in December. A host of recent recruits joined the campaign, including Cissy Foley, Sarah Whittaker and Margaret Wroe, along with Constance Markievicz and Esther's brother, Reginald Roper. Regardless of how hard the group campaigned it was almost impossible to change the focus of the election. The central concern was undoubtedly the struggle for power between the people versus the peers – the House of Commons versus the House of Lords. The Liberal Party took advantage of this by pasting posters around Rossendale emblazoned with the message 'a vote for Bulley is a vote for the House of Lords.'[27] The results of the Rossendale ballot were announced on 21 January. A total of 13,217 votes were counted – the Liberal Party had an overwhelming majority. Harcourt received a total of 7,185 votes, Kebty-Fletcher received 4,695 and Bulley was decimated at the polls, with a dismal return of 639 votes.

The January 1910 election resulted in a hung parliament. The Liberal Party returned 275 seats, just two more than the Conservative Unionist Party. Labour increased their number of MPs to 40. The Irish Parliamentary Party, led by John Redmond, secured 71 seats, which meant that they held the balance of power at Westminster. The Liberal Party formed a new government under the leadership of Asquith, with the support of Labour and the Irish Parliamentary Party. The coalition government established a cross-party pro-suffrage Conciliation Committee. Shackleton took a leading role in the committee and through him the group introduced the Conciliation Bill 1910, which, if passed, would grant women the vote at general elections for the first time. The bill included strict property qualifications ensuring that only unmarried property owning women would be enfranchised. Gore-Booth spoke in support of the bill at a suffrage demonstration in July but the lack of passion in her speech was noted by the *Observer*.[28] The bill was doomed, the government fell within months and another general election was called in December 1910. The Liberal Party, with the support of Redmond and the Irish Parliamentary Party formed a government under the leadership of Asquith in 1911. A second Conciliation Bill was introduced later that year but was dropped by Asquith, while a third bill in 1912 lost by a slight margin of votes in the House of Commons.

While Gore-Booth may well have become dismayed with the lack of political progress during 1910, her literature was receiving much positive acclaim. Professor Max Myers of the Royal College of Music, Manchester, set more of her poetry to music. The Irish song cycle *Maeve* was first performed in public at the Royal College of Music, in February.[29] The performance received rave reviews in the *Manchester Guardian*. Three months later Gore-Booth was invited to Dublin as a special guest by the Dublin Corinthian Club. She attended a banquet at the Gresham Hotel in honour of esteemed Irish literary women, taking her place amongst Katherine Cecil Thurston, Edith Somerville, Jane Barlow, Lady Augusta Gregory and other distinguished writers.[30]

Thurston, an Irish woman from County Cork, had won acclaim after her novel, *John Chilcote MP*, sold over 200,000 copies.[31] Thurston was known as an engaging public speaker and she wrote fiction which often focused on Irish, feminist and gender issues.[32] She had just published the novel *Max* when she and Gore-Booth met at the Gresham Hotel banquet. Gore-Booth was enthralled by the fictitious story of Maxine, a Russian Princess who masqueraded as a boy in order to live independently in Paris and work as an artist. The novel reflects Gore-Booth's belief that women could do the same work as men if they were not restricted by the social expectations of their gender. This was a defining moment for Gore-Booth and she would later adopt a line from Thurston's novel to advocate for an ideal world beyond the confines of gender. She was moved by a statement uttered by the character Max to explain her gender masquerade, 'sex is only an accident, but the world has made man the independent creature – and I desired independence. Sex is only an accident.'[33]

Throughout her campaigns for employment equality, Gore-Booth stressed that sex difference should not be the cause of discrimination. Now she began to view masculine and feminine roles as controlling and restrictive categories. Her belief that gender performance was simply learnt behaviour is apparent in her final Manchester trade union campaign. In 1911 Gore-Booth championed yet another marginalised group of workers, pit brow women. With an increased demand for coal during the industrial revolution the number of women working at mines in the Lancashire area grew considerably.[34] Although an act was passed in 1842, banning women from working below ground in mines, tubshoving at the base of mines continued as an occupation for thousands of women, many of whom were Irish, well into the twentieth century. The arduous work involved in tubshoving is described in a history series publication by Patrick Rooke, 'with a belt round her waist, and a chain between her legs, a woman could spend twelve hours each day bent double, dragging the coal tubs along the mine shafts.'[35] It was generally believed that mines were unsuitable places for women to work partly because of the supposed immoral language of miners.

In August 1911, a select committee in the House of Commons proposed a bill to ban women working at coal mines altogether and the Miners' Federation supported the proposal. Gore-Booth rallied to the defence of these women. She organised a public meeting in London on 31 October. She wrote to the *Manchester Guardian* requesting twenty or thirty pit brow women to attend in order 'to remove false ideas about their dress and appearance.'[36] At a subsequent meeting in Manchester on 9 November the following resolution was adopted:

> That this meeting demands the deletion of the Clause in the Coal Mines Regulation Bill that abolishes women's work at the Pit Brow. It affirms that there is overwhelming evidence to prove that this work is neither too heavy nor in any way unsuitable, being done under good conditions, short hours (an eight hour day) and very much in the open air. It also protests most earnestly against the proposal to abolish women's labour in the process erroneously called 'tubshoving.'[37]

In order to prove that women could work at coal mines, Gore-Booth went to work as a pit brow lass. She spent several days working with women at a local mine. This was an exceptional move for a genteel aristocratic woman with severe respiratory problems. Gore-Booth later boasted that she could shove the coal tubs with one hand.[38]

By 1912 Gore-Booth had become disillusioned with well-meaning philanthropists inflicting legal disabilities onto women in the workplace. She sought new approaches to overcome sex discrimination and in her search she encountered a remarkable individual, Thomas Baty. Baty, a somewhat eccentric lawyer from London, established a revolutionary organisation called the Aëthnic Union. Gore-Booth and Roper joined the union in 1912. The organisation openly rejected all forms of sex difference; this is reflected in the title of the organisation, which is taken from the Greek – *a*, not – *ethnos*, physical distinction. The group were keen to influence the mainstream suffrage movement. Baty wrote to Millicent Fawcett requesting that the NUWSS 'adopt the elimination of gender distinctions as one of its aims.'[39] Fawcett declined. A flier advertising the existence of the union highlights the extremely radical nature of the group:

> Modern Suffragists, while anxious to remove the superficial disabilities which stand in the way of political influence and economic advantage, seem disposed to accept with considerable humility the far deeper hindrances to self-development imposed by the clumsy differentiation which divides the race into 'men and women.' Society has split perfection into two, and imposes on the individual spirit conformity to one of two warped ideals: the stern masculine and the trivial feminine ... Those who are anxious to maintain that the ideal is a single ideal, combining sweetness and independence, are invited to join in an association for mutual support, called the 'Aëthnic Union.'[40]

The Aëthnic Union's intention was clearly presented, to overcome all distinctions which were based on sex difference.

Unable to involve conventional suffrage movements with the work of the Aëthnic Union, the group turned instead to the weekly feminist paper the *Freewoman*. The editors of the *Freewoman*, Dora Marsden and Mary Gawthorpe, proved to be allies of the union.[41] The paper transmitted news of the controversial organisation. Baty published articles in the journal promoting the union and establishing it in opposition to the mainstream. In one such article he describes the organisation, which 'recognises that upon the fact of sex there has been built up a gigantic superstructure of artificial convention which urgently needs to be swept away.'[42] The group later decided to launch their own newsletter entitled the *Phœnix*. Each issue of the newsletter contained minutes of the union's meetings and a list of members in attendance. Unfortunately the first five issues of the paper do not appear to have survived. Issue six, dated November 1913, details a list of twenty-six members. Of this membership a group of five people, Gore-Booth, Roper, Baty, Dorothy Cornish and Jessey Wade, would become firm friends.[43]

Meetings of the Aëthnic Union were held in London and by 1913 Gore-Booth and Roper were living in the capital city permanently. The smog bound industrial quarters of Manchester had become too much for Gore-Booth's declining health to bear. Both women had also become disillusioned with local politics and began to mix with a new circle of radical thinkers. They moved to the cultural centre of London, renting out the top two floors of a large house, 33 Fitzroy Square in Bloomsbury. The majestic house was originally built in 1794, designed by Robert Adam and made of Portland Stone, making it architecturally unique in London. Gore-Booth wrote to Josslyn that 'we have a bedroom each / Esther and I / one spare room / we can have two visitors by our doubling up.'[44] The women rented out a bedroom and a sitting room to a friend. They had many visitors to this address which certainly dispels Gifford Lewis' insistence that they never entered each other's bedroom.

Downstairs at 33 Fitzroy Square was taken over by the influential artist and art critic Roger Fry.[45] The bottom three floors housed the Omega Workshops, which Fry established as a place where struggling young artists could produce and sell minor pieces of art. The workshop became central to the Bloomsbury group of artists. All of the artwork produced at the Omega was signed with the Greek symbol Ω and did not include the artist's name. Artists who worked at 33 Fitzroy Square included, Duncan Grant, Dora Carrington and Wyndham Lewis. Fitzroy Square acted as a studio and an art gallery. Every Thursday night, the Omega Workshop operated as a club. Members of the Thursday night club included Gore-Booth's old friends and literary contemporaries, Yeats and Shaw. Vanessa Bell, sister of Virginia Woolf, was a director of the Omega Workshop and produced art in the workshop. Numerous prestigious visitors often arrived at the house, including Pablo Picasso in 1914.

Gore-Booth was now surrounded by an eclectic mix of artists, philosophers and writers. One can imagine her bumping into Virginia Woolf or Pablo Picasso on the stairwell at Fitzroy Square. She was living amongst the Bloomsbury Group, who held progressive views regarding sexuality, feminism and pacifism. Roger Fry's biographer, Frances Spalding, describes how amongst all the activities at 33 Fitzroy Square, 'resided, undisturbed, Eva Gore-Booth who lived in the top flat with her friend Miss Roper. But then even the war left her relatively unmoved; being devoted to the women's cause, she was capable of typing energetically throughout an air-raid.'[46]

Indeed, Gore-Booth and Roper saw out the war together in the top floor flat at Fitzroy Square. Gore-Booth refused to return to the relative safety of rural Ireland. She was a devoted pacifist and remained in London where she could dedicate herself to peace work throughout the war years.

In July 1914, the Women's Freedom League under the leadership of Charlotte Despard, made a special petition to the King, noting 'serious concern that year after year the gracious list of Birthday and New Year Honours contains no mention whatsoever of the many noble and public spirited women subjects of your Majesty who render invaluable Imperial and social service throughout your Majesty's dominions.'[47] The league compiled a short list of women whom they noted as 'outstanding names of persons worthy of the greatest degree of public recognition.'[48] The list included women thought to deserve appreciation for their accomplishments in various categories including imperial services, social services, education, writers, science and art. Gore-Booth and Roper were both listed as women who should receive a Royal Honour for their work in social services. The petition gained international media attention, the *Washington Post* acknowledging that 'men have so far been the only ones to receive titles in the distribution of honours on the king's birthday.'[49] However, the inclusion of women in the King's honours list was not to be that year; war erupted days after the WFL sent their petition.

War was declared on 4 August 1914, after which the suffrage and suffragette movements broadly suspended their campaigns for women's enfranchisement. Three days after war was officially announced the Home Secretary, Reginald McKenna, declared that if suffragette prisoners agreed to refrain from militant anti-government activity they would be released from prison under an amnesty. McKenna was particularly severe in his dealings with suffragettes, he had introduced the controversial Discharge of Prisoners Act in 1913. The act became known as the Cat and Mouse Act because under this law a suffragette prisoner on hunger strike would be released when she became ill and re-arrested when she was fit enough to return to prison. However, McKenna now realised that it was simply not viable to imprison suffragettes during war time.

Within three days of his original announcement McKenna made a further statement that all suffragette prisoners would be released, regardless. Christabel Pankhurst, who had fled to Paris to evade arrest, returned to London shortly after the amnesty was called. She announced her support of Britain in the war effort, declaring 'an armistice with the government [the WSPU] suspended militancy for the duration of the war.'[50] Although not all members of the WSPU agreed with this decision, Pankhurst along with her mother and Annie Kenney launched a countrywide tour of Britain. The suffragette group promoted conscription for men, calling for a legal draft of young men to war and for women to operate munitions factories. The NUWSS, under the leadership of Mrs Fawcett, proved their commitment to the British war effort by establishing support facilities such as Red Cross centres and canteens for soldiers.

World War One vastly changed the face of both the militant and non-militant suffrage movements. Mainstream organisations joined forces with the government in support of the British war effort. The radical suffragists were not so accommodating, they continued crusading for women's enfranchisement, but now they also organised anti-war campaigns. Gore-Booth refused to support any side, steadfastly objecting to violent warfare. Adopting a pacifist stance in England at this time was a particularly defiant act. Gore-Booth was no doubt considered unpatriotic.

German people living in Britain after the outbreak of war were viewed with extreme suspicion. The government opened camps and interned German men of fighting age. German women, children and older men did not face internment, however they must surely have experienced extreme distress at their circumstances. From September 1914 Gore-Booth undertook a relief scheme to aid any German citizen who had been trapped in England after the war began. Various agencies did provide financial support for these victims of war but Gore-Booth and Roper visited German citizens regularly, offering emotional support and friendship in their time of need. The government eventually arranged for German citizens in England to be returned to their homeland.

Gore-Booth was at risk of being labelled as a German sympathiser and as suffrage historian Sybil Oldfield stresses, 'to dissent from Britain's war-fever ... was the hardest and most vital act of moral courage any citizen could then undertake, and it was particularly difficult for women to seem ungrateful towards the men then volunteering for mutilation and death.'[51] Yet, from the onset Gore-Booth was prepared to make public anti-war statements. She signed an open Christmas letter addressed to the women of Germany and

Austria during Christmas 1914. Emily Hobhouse, a dedicated pacifist and social reformer, wrote the letter, which begins:

> Sisters,
> Some of us wish to send you a word at this Christmastide though we can but speak through the press. The Christmas message sounds like mockery to a world at war, but those of us who wished and still wish for peace may surely offer a solemn greeting to such of you who feel as we do. Do not let us forget that our very anguish unites us, that we are passing together through the same experiences of pain and grief ... Though our sons are sent to slay each other, and our hearts are torn by the cruelty of this fate ... We will let no bitterness enter into this tragedy, made sacred by the life-blood of our best, nor mar with hate the heroism of their sacrifice.[52]

The letter was signed by 101 British and Irish pacifist women including, Gore-Booth, Roper, Louie Bennett, Margaret Ashton, Sylvia Pankhurst, Margaret Llewelyn Davies and Helena Swanwick. The letter was a public call for peace and it was published in the monthly suffrage journal *Jus Suffragii*. Suffrage pacifist Mary Sheepshanks edited *Jus Suffragii* during the war years, in order to sustain international suffrage links.[53] Within two months, 155 German and Austrian women responded. The group included a number of high profile suffragists such as Anita Augspurg, Minna Cauer, Ida Jens and Helene Stocker. Their letter, also published in *Jus Suffragii*, was addressed 'to our English sisters, sisters of the same race.' The women 'express in the name of many German women our warm and heartfelt thanks for their Christmas greetings, which we only heard of lately.'[54]

By the end of 1914 Gore-Booth began to speak about what she termed, 'the intolerable and squalid horror of war.'[55] She gave her first anti-war talk, *Whence Come Wars?* in London at a meeting of the National Industrial and Professional Women's Suffrage Society on 12 December 1914. The speech is a frank and lucid depiction of the horrible consequences of war. The text was later published as a penny pamphlet. In it Gore-Booth provides a vivid account of the appalling suffering inflicted on soldiers at the front, describing:

> Brave people of all countries shot dead or mutilated for life ... the cold and wet, and the unbearable filth of the trenches, and the frightful illness caused by privation and suffering, the brain affection that is the result of staying for days with your feet in water, the tetanus that comes from poisonous conditions, the pneumonia and fevers, and the

thousand and one cases of mental and nervous collapse that must be the result of the unnatural and hideous conditions of life.[56]

Gore-Booth is clear that it is male politicians who are to blame for the outbreak of the Great War. In her conclusion she connects pacifism and women's suffrage, pointing out that successive governments have told women '"we can do quite well without you, thanks; men can manage the affairs of the world; we have no need of your assistance"... men have had it all their own way. And now look what they have brought the world to.'[57]

Other female pacifists agreed with Gore-Booth's analysis. A Dutch suffrage organisation believed that women were the key to successfully resolving the armed conflict and ending the war. Aletta Jacobs, Holland's first female doctor and a champion of birth control, called for an International Congress of Women to be held at The Hague in the Netherlands. Jacobs cabled suffrage organisations and individuals across the world asserting, 'we feel strongly that at a time when there is so much hatred among nations, we, women, must show that we can retain our solidarity.'[58] Within weeks the idea of an international congress gained momentum and a date was set for women from both sides of the conflict to meet in April 1915. The congress was organised with two main objectives in mind, 'to demand that international disputes shall in future be settled by some other means than war [and] to claim that women should have a voice in the affairs of the nations.'[59] Thousands of women signed up to attend the congress, now often referred to as the Women's Peace Congress.

Gore-Booth was one of the first on the list of attendees, amongst hundreds of supporters from across North America and Europe, including Britain, Germany, Hungary, Italy, Poland and Belgium.[60] Gore-Booth, Roper, Dickenson and their friends Beatrice Collins and Helen Neild, were part of a large group who wished to represent Great Britain and Ireland at the peace talks. The list of proposed delegates includes prominent suffragists Hanna Sheehy-Skeffington, Louie Bennett, Charlotte Despard, Evelyn Sharp, Marie Stopes and Sylvia Pankhurst. In total 180 women applied for exit permits to travel from Britain and Ireland across the Channel to neutral Holland. On 17 April, Catherine Marshall wrote to the British Home Secretary with the full list of women requesting travel permits. McKenna denied the request of most of the women. On 28 April, days before the congress was due to meet, the British Admiralty closed the North Sea to passenger shipping and none of the delegates from Britain were allowed to travel to The Hague. Nearly 1,300 women did attend the Congress – only three delegates were from Britain. Kathleen Courtney and Chrystal Macmillan were already staying in Holland and therefore could easily attend. Emmeline Pethick-Lawrence had been visiting in New York and travelled to the congress with the American suffragist Jane Addams.

At the close of the Women's Congress on 1 May 1915, the resolutions were announced. It was ultimately decided that women should be granted a vote at general elections, since women were the strongest force for the prevention of war.[61] Various resolutions were printed and distributed to heads of state in countries at war, with little outcome. The most significant result of the congress was the establishment of the Women's Peace Party, which in 1919 became the Women's International League for Peace and Freedom (WILPF) in America. The WILPF continues as the oldest surviving active peace organisation. From the outset Gore-Booth actively supported the organisation. When Pethick-Lawrence returned to London, Gore-Booth organised a special meeting of the National Industrial and Professional Women's Suffrage Society, at the YMCA in London. The meeting, over which Gore-Booth presided, was organised so that Pethick-Lawrence could provide a full account of the events, proceedings and outcomes of the congress at The Hague. Roper spoke about the unacceptable nature of war and Thomas Baty addressed the audience with his paper on War and International Law. The sudden and devastating onset of war had changed the shape of Gore-Booth's political campaigns. She continued to campaign for women's enfranchisement but her main focus was now on achieving peace.

Notes

1 EGB, 'Women's Rights,' *The Egyptian Pillar* (Dublin: Maunsel, 1907), p. 30.

2 J.J. Mallon, 'The Portrait Gallery: Miss Eva Gore-Booth,' *Woman Worker* (4 September 1908), p. 347. A copy of this article was kindly given to the author by Michael Herbert.

3 Ibid.

4 Ibid.

5 Lynn Sinclair and Barbara Harris, *Women Chainmakers: Be Anvil or Hammer* (Dudley: Black Country Living Museum Trust Ltd, 2009), p. 7.

6 'The Factory and Workshop Act 1901,' *The British Medical Journal* (28 December 1901), p. 1871.
7 'Kings Bench Division, Hoare v. Robert Green Limited,' *The Times* (29 April 1907), p. 3.
8 'The Home Office and Florists' Work Hours,' *MG* (23 November 1908), p. 5.
9 EGB, *Women's Right to Work* (Manchester: William Morris Press, c.1909). This pamphlet is undated, however scholars have attributed various dates from 1906 onwards, without explaining why. It is possible to identify the year of publication as 1909; in the introduction Gore-Booth refers to the recent victory against the abolition of barmaids and the introduction of a clause regarding florists' assistants to the Factory and Workshop Act.
10 'Women and the Vote,' *MG* (18 March 1909), p. 9.
11 Ibid.
12 Gertrude Tuckwell, Constance Smith, Mary MacArthur, May Tennant, Nettie Adler, Adelaide Anderson and Clementina Black, *Women in Industry: From Seven Points of View* (London: Duckworth & Co, 1908), p. xiv.
13 Judge Ruegg, K.C, 'Report as to the Application of the Factory and Workshop Act, 1901, to Florists' Workshops,' *House of Commons Parliamentary Papers* (London: His Majesty's Stationery Office, 1909).
14 Ibid, p. 3.
15 Ruegg, 'Report as to the Application of the Factory and Workshop Act,' p. 3.
16 EGB, 'Women and the Nation, the Workers: No Trades for Women,' *Englishwoman*, 5:2 (June 1909), 507–17.
17 Ibid, p. 507.
18 *Daily News* (8 July 1909), as cited in Liddington and Norris, p. 241.
19 'Women Workers and the Vote,' *MG* (14 July 1909), p. 5.
20 Ruegg, 'Report as to the Application of the Factory and Workshop Act,' p. 4.
21 The budget was rejected by the House of Lords by 370 votes to 75 on 30 November 1909.
22 EGB, 'Running a Suffrage Candidate,' *Common Cause* (25 November 1909), p. 432.
23 'Mr. Harcourt's Opponent: The Women's Suffrage Candidate,' *MG* (6 December 1909), p. 9.
24 Ibid.
25 'Rossendale: Withdrawal of Mr. J.M. Mitchell,' *MG* (8 December 1909), p. 9.
26 'Women's Suffrage Candidate: Campaign opened in Rossendale,' *MG* (22 December 1909), p. 14.

27 *Common Cause* (27 January 1910) as cited in Liddington and Norris, p. 246.
28 'Trafalgar Square Demonstration,' *Observer* (10 July 1910), p. 12.
29 *Maeve* was sung by Annie Worsley and accompanied by Max Myers on piano. 'Mr. Max Myer's Irish Song Cycle,' *MG* (8 February 1910), p. 7.
30 'Dinners: Irish Literary Ladies,' *The Times* (3 May 1910), p. 13.
31 Katherine Cecil Thurston, *John Chilcote, M.P.* (Edinburgh: William Blackwood and Sons, 1904). The same novel was published in America under the title *The Masquerader*.
32 Three years earlier Thurston published *The Mystics*, a novel which features a fictional religious group who could be mistaken for the Theosophical Society: *The Mystics* (Edinburgh: William Blackwood, 1907).
33 Katherine Cecil Thurston, *Max* (New York & London: Harper & Brothers, 1910), p. 303.
34 Alan Davies, *The Pit Brow Women of the Wigan Coalfield* (Manchester: Tempus Publishing Ltd, 2006).
35 Patrick Rooke, *Women's Rights* (London: Wayland, 1972), p. 60.
36 'Pit-brow Women,' *MG* (5 October 1911), p. 12.
37 Resolution of Pit Brow Women's Protest Meeting, Memorial Hall, Manchester, 9 November 1911.
38 Angela V. John, *By the Sweat of their Brow: Women Workers at Victorian Coal Mines* (Boston: Routledge & Kegan Paul, 1983), p. 154.
39 Fawcett Library, Metropolitan University, London, Fawcett collection, Box 295, Folder 4, letter from Thomas Baty to Millicent Garret Fawcett, 1911.
40 Ibid, Aëthnic Union flier, undated.
41 Emily Hamer, *Britannia's Glory: A History of Twentieth-Century Lesbians* (London: Cassell, 1996), p. 265.
42 T. Baty, 'The Aëthnic Union,' *Freewoman*, 1:14 (February 1912), 278.
43 *Phœnix*, 6 (November 1913).
44 PRONI, Mic 590, Reel 9, L/12:27, letter from EGB to Josslyn Gore-Booth, 1913.
45 A blue plaque signifying a site of English heritage was placed at 33 Fitzroy Square on 20 May 2010 in honour of Roger Fry and commemorating the house as the centre of the Bloomsbury group of artists.
46 Frances Spalding, *Roger Fry: Art and Life* (Berkeley: University of California Press, *c* 1980), p. 193.
47 'A Women's Honours List: A Suggestion to the King,' *MG* (3 July 1914), p. 9.
48 Ibid.
49 'Titles for Fair Sex,' *The Washington Post* (26 July 1914), p. 12.
50 Christabel Pankhurst, *Unshackled*, p. 288.
51 Sybil Oldfield, 'England's Cassandras in World War One,' in Sybil Oldfield

(ed.), *This Working Day World: Women's Lives and Culture(s) in Britain, 1914–1945* (London: Taylor & Francis, 2005), p. 90.

52 *Jus Suffragii*, 9:4 (1 January 1915), 228–9.

53 Sybil Oldfield, 'Mary Sheepshanks Edits an International Suffrage Monthly in Wartime: *Jus Suffragii* 1914–19,' *Women's History Review*, 12:1 (2003), 119–34.

54 Sybil Oldfield (ed.), *International Woman Suffrage: Jus Suffragii, 1913–1920*, Vol. 2, (London: Routledge, 2003), p. 67.

55 EGB, *Whence Come Wars?* (London: Women's Printing Society Ltd, 1914).

56 Ibid, p. 3.

57 Ibid, p. 12.

58 Oldfield, 'England's Cassandras in World War One,' p. 89.

59 Ibid.

60 For further information on the International Congress of Women see: Gertrude Bussey & Margaret Tims, *Pioneers for Peace: Women's International League for Peace and Freedom 1915–1965* (London: Women's International League for Peace and Freedom, 1980).

61 Jane Addams, Emily Balch and Alice Hamilton, *Women at The Hague: The International Congress of Women and its Results* (Chicago: University of Illinois Press, 2003).

8

Conscientious objectors and revolution: world war and an Irish rebellion

'Buried the broken dreams of Ireland lie'[1]

The British restriction placed on passenger shipping in the North Sea in 1914 was a timely reminder that war was escalating across Europe with dire consequences. In February 1915, the German government issued a declaration of more aggressive naval warfare. On 22 April, the German Embassy in Washington released a statement which was duly published in newspapers across America:

> Notice!
>
> Travellers intending to embark on the Atlantic voyage are reminded that a state of war exists between Germany and her allies and Great Britain and her allies; that the zone of war includes the waters adjacent to the British Isles; that, in accordance with formal notice given by the Imperial German Government, vessels flying the flag of Great Britain, or any of her Allies, are liable to destruction in those waters and that travellers sailing in the war zone on ships of Great Britain or her allies do so at their own risk.
>
> Imperial German Embassy Washington, D.C.[2]

As people read the notice in the *New York Times* a passenger ship, the Cunard Line's *Lusitania*, was pulling out of New York harbour. The ship bound for Liverpool was carrying nearly 2,000 passengers and crew. Charles Sumner, an agent for the Cunard Shipping Company, simply dismissed the threat.

At 3.25pm on 7 May 1915, a telegram arrived in the Cunard Liverpool office, which read, 'Lusitania torpedoed off Kinsale. Has sunk.'[3] The great liner was attacked by a German U-boat and sank just off the Irish coast. Over the coming days the entire extent of the disaster became evident. Nearly 1,200 people had lost their lives. Gore-Booth was devastated by the news and was even more shocked when she learnt that Hugh Lane was on board. Lane, a nephew of arts patron Lady Augusta Gregory had been engaged to Gore-Booth's close friend Lady Clare Annesley.[4] Lane had been an intrinsic part of Irish cultural development; he organised exhibitions showcasing Irish art and patronised many striving young artists including Jack B. Yeats and William Orpen. Lane was particularly inspired by Sarah Purser and he had become a notable art collector. In 1912 he donated a large collection of his paintings to Dublin on the understanding that a permanent gallery would be built to house them. A suitable gallery did not materialise and in desperation Lane removed a number of his paintings from Dublin in 1913. He lent the collection, including works by Degas, Renoir, Monet and Manet, to the National Gallery in London. Later in 1913 he made a will bequeathing these works to the London gallery on his death.

Lane did not survive the German attack and his body was never recovered. Shortly after his death a codicil to his will was discovered in his desk at the National Gallery of Ireland. Lane had written the codicil in 1914, reversing his decision to grant any paintings to London and instead granted his entire collection to the city of Dublin. The codicil was signed by Lane but because it was not witnessed it was deemed invalid under British law. The collection housed at the gallery in London remained there. A group of Irish artists and writers established the Lane Pictures Committee to contest the decision. Gore-Booth instantly gave her support. When Beatrix Duncan, secretary of the organisation, arranged a petition calling for the British government to recognise Lane's codicil, Gore-Booth was one of the 150 signatories. The group sent the petition directly to the Prime Minister on 29 January 1917 pleading their case:

> These pictures were originally hung in the Dublin Municipal Art Gallery as a gift contingent on the erection of a suitable gallery, and remained there for some years, pending the fulfilment of the conditions. Owing to circumstances into which we need not here enter it was not found possible to fulfil the necessary conditions within the specified time. Sir Hugh Lane then removed the pictures from Dublin to exhibit them as a loan collection in London, in order that their merits might be more widely known, and while there he devised them in a duly executed will to the National Gallery of England.

> Subsequently, however, Sir Hugh Lane reverted to his original intention, as expressed in a previous will, and bequeathing the pictures by the codicil to which we have alluded, to the City of Dublin.[5]

The appeal was not granted and a large portion of Hugh Lane's paintings remained at the London gallery. A dispute over ownership of the collection would rage between the galleries in Dublin and London until 1959, when it was agreed to alternate the collection between the two galleries.

The controversy regarding Lane's art was only a minor consequence of the sinking of the *Lusitania*. The tragedy had a profound effect on American popular opinion of what had, until then, been considered a European war. President Woodrow Wilson had so far managed to keep America neutral. The attack on the *Lusitania* is thought to have been the catalyst which eventually impelled America to join the war; 124 American citizens were among those killed. German authorities maintained that the *Lusitania* was carrying weapons and was therefore a legitimate target. British authorities depicted the sinking of the *Lusitania* as a savage attack on civilians. The tragedy was used to incite anti-German feelings and became a prominent feature in military recruitment campaigns. The British Council for Recruiting in Ireland printed graphic depictions of women and children drowning off the coast of Ireland (see Figure 11 calling for Irishmen to avenge the *Lusitania)*.

Gore-Booth was disturbed by the huge loss of life and the possibility that war would spread across Europe to America. She attended the Pacifist Philosophy of Life Conference at Caxton Hall in London on 8 and 9 July 1915. She spoke on the topic of 'Religious Aspects of Non-Resistance,' describing the Great War as the most destructive conflict that humanity had ever witnessed.[6] The pacifist conference was a great success; the official organ of the anti-war ILP, the *Labour Leader*, reported that 400 attendees were 'keenly attentive and sympathetic' and the papers were of the most 'high intellectual quality.'[7] The conference resulted in the formation of the League of Peace and Freedom, an organisation with which Gore-Booth instantly became involved. Her paper was later published as a pamphlet on behalf of the league.[8] At the conference she became acquainted with the academic and political agitator, Bertrand Russell, whose own address to the gathering was applauded as a brave and insightful view of war.[9]

11 'Join an Irish Regiment Today,' a military recruitment poster produced by the Central Council for the Organisation of Recruiting in Ireland in 1915

Gore-Booth also befriended Fenner Brockway, editor of the *Labour Leader* and a prominent ILP activist. Brockway founded the No Conscription Fellowship (NCF) in 1914 as protection for men who refused to take up arms on moral, religious or political grounds. Initially only men who volunteered for active service were sent to war, although Winston Churchill had been advocating for a form of conscription from as early as 1914. At the suggestion of his wife, Lilla, Brockway published an appeal for Conscientious Objectors (COs) to contact him in the autumn of 1914. There was a huge response and the NCF was established. By the beginning of 1915, membership of the organisation had grown so large that they opened an office in London at 8 Merton House, in a vibrant central location on Fleet Street. By the time that Gore-Booth met Brockway in July 1915 the NCF was a thriving and active organisation.

The Great War had now been raging for just one year and already it had claimed an enormous loss of life. The numbers of British soldiers at the front was declining rapidly. Not enough men were volunteering for service and those killed or maimed were simply not being replaced. One week after the pacifist conference was held at Caxton Hall, Prime Minister Asquith proposed a national registry to record the details of everyone living in England between the ages of fifteen and sixty-five.[10] The compulsory registry was quickly authorised and on 15 August the results revealed that two million eligible men had not yet volunteered for war service. The results compounded the argument for compulsory military service. Gore-Booth wrote to the *Manchester Guardian* warning about the danger of introducing conscription, she highlighted the detrimental effect of enforced war service for the individual, the nation and for liberty.[11] The fact that Britain was now suffering huge losses at the front meant that conscription was inevitable. Campaigning by individuals and the Independent Labour Party's attempt to halt a conscription bill were futile.

In an attempt to spread the ideals of peace and pacifism, Gore-Booth published a small volume of poetry, *The Perilous Light*, in 1915. The volume includes twenty-one poems all of which were previously published in other volumes. The book was published by Erskine Macdonald in London. She was advised by William Galloway Kyle to submit her manuscript to Erskine Macdonald for publication. As founder of a London poetry society, Kyle was a respected literary authority. He was also aware of the abundance of aspiring war poets.

Kyle took advantage of this new literary market by advising many poets and writers to publish their work with the publisher Erskine Macdonald. In fact, Macdonald was not an established publisher as Kyle claimed, but was an imprint established by him in order to earn sales commission. After the war was over, the publishing house of Erskine Macdonald was uncovered as a literary scam.[12]

Shortly after publication of *The Perilous Light* the Military Service Bill was brought into the House of Commons. Conscription came into effect in Britain on 2 March 1916. Unmarried men between the ages of eighteen and forty-one were automatically drafted into the army. Within four months the act was revised to include married men but men in Ireland remained exempt. The act contained a section allowing for individual exemptions due to conscientious objection, however the process for gaining an exemption would prove to be particularly challenging. The national register of 1915 was used to define registration districts. Each district established a local tribunal to decide on individual cases where exemption was sought. Over 2,000 local tribunals and seventy appeal tribunals were established across the country.[13] Local authorities elected people to serve on the tribunal boards. Tribunal members were generally male, middle class and middle aged. The work was unpaid and seemed to attract enthusiastic supporters of war. In his research of the NCF, historian Thomas Kennedy discovered that many members of tribunals in the Derby area owed their seats to their 'prominence in local recruiting activities.'[14] To add to this possible bias, at least one military representative appointed by the War Office was present at all tribunals.

During the first half of 1916 over 750,000 men officially filed for exemption to war service.[15] If, in the unlikely event, a man was granted an exemption he would be assigned a non-combatant post in the war service. Often the roles allocated to COs involved extreme danger, such as that of stretcher bearer in the firing line at the front. If a man failed to gain an exemption from the tribunal and still refused to go to war he would face a court-martial and ultimately a prison sentence. The law did not exclude the possibility of a death sentence for men refusing to take up arms. Appalled by this legislation Gore-Booth wrote again to the *Manchester Guardian*:

> With regard to the refusal of the Government to eliminate the possibility of the death sentence from the Compulsion Bill, may I point out

> that, as the bill now stands, if a man fails to convince a committee nominated by the local authority not only that he is a bona-fide conscientious objector, but also that a conscientious objector ought to be exempted, he may pay with his life for the private militarist views of members of his district council. For the district council is not bound to exempt conscientious objectors; it is allowed to do so if its members approve such exemptions.[16]

Although a number of absolute objectors were sentenced to death none were ever executed. Many COs did, however, commit suicide, unable to bear the stigma of being labelled as cowards and the death rate due to incarceration with hard labour was particularly high.[17] It is estimated that 16,000 men refused to fight and NCF records confirm that 6,312 of these men were arrested. Seventy-three men died after being incarcerated and a further forty suffered a mental breakdown.[18]

The NCF ran a highly organised press department to expose the injustice and brutality of how COs were treated. As part of their propaganda campaign the fellowship launched a weekly newspaper, the *Tribunal*, on 8 March 1916. Initially the journal was printed by the National Labour Press, the same printers of the *Labour Leader*. The NCF monitored all of the activities of local and appeal tribunals. Hundreds of people associated with the NCF attended tribunals across the country, performing the role of 'watcher.' Watchers recorded personal details of conscientious objectors, remarks made by tribunal members, any perceived illegal activities, the outcome of cases, which prison camp they were held in and even kept a record of the appearance of individual COs. These fastidious details were published in the *Tribunal* on a weekly basis.[19] Gore-Booth volunteered as a watcher and travelled across the country attending as many tribunals as possible. She dramatised a day watching tribunals and the stark story was published by the National Labour Press as a penny pamphlet. Her account provides a rare glimpse into the oppressive process involved in seeking an exemption from war service.

Gore-Booth's account, originally entitled 'At the military tribunal' was published simply as *The Tribunal*.[20] The pamphlet includes her poem 'Conscientious Objectors' on the cover. The poem which she submitted separately to the Labour Party's paper the *Herald* is particularly scathing of the tribunal process, concluding:

Before six ignorant men and blind,
Reckless they rent aside
The vail of Isis in the mind . . .
Men say they shirked and lied.[21]

The Tribunal opens with an emotional description of an elderly man seeking an exemption from military service for his son. The man has already lost the majority of his family through the war and he pleads for his one remaining son to be left at home. After the man pleads his case, the tribunal chairman simply looks up and points at his young son saying, '"we want that man," and in a moment the chairman was pronouncing his strange formula, "the Tribunal have carefully considered your case, and feel they cannot grant you an exemption."'[22] In the pamphlet Gore-Booth describes case after case being refused exemptions. She portrays members of the tribunal board harassing a young conscientious objector, when one board member, a clergyman, aggressively demands to know if 'your mother was attacked by a German with a bayonet, would you not kill him to save your mother's life?'[23]

The Tribunal was a blatant condemnation of the government's war policy and of the tribunal system, during the height of pro-war propaganda. It was a brave move for Gore-Booth to identify herself as author of such a contentious pamphlet. In June 1916, Bertrand Russell was arrested for authorship of a similar pamphlet. Russell was charged and fined £100 plus £10 costs or face 61 days imprisonment.[24] In his leaflet Russell discussed the case of Mr Everett, a teacher who was sentenced to two years hard labour for refusing war service. The leaflet was distributed by members of the NCF. Six men were arrested and sentenced to two years hard labour for simply distributing the material. Russell wrote to *The Times* identifying himself as the author and accepting full responsibility for the contentious leaflet.[25] Russell's sentence had serious implications for his career. He was dismissed from his lectureship post at Trinity College, Cambridge. He had been due to take a visiting lectureship at Harvard University but due to his sentence, he was denied a passport to travel to America.[26] Expressing anti-war opinions often had dire consequences.

In 1918 Russell was imprisoned for an article he published in *The Tribune*, alleging that American troops in Britain would be used to control and break up labour strikes. While in prison Gore-Booth sent Russell handwritten poems to lift his spirit.[27] Various members of the NCF were arrested and imprisoned for their activities against military conscription. Brockway himself was imprisoned four times during the course of the war. During his last incarceration in Lincoln Prison he befriended Irish political prisoners, most notably Éamon de Valera, who later became the leader of the first Irish Free State Government, Dáil Éireann. Through his friendship with Gore-Booth and his association with Irish political prisoners, Brockway became an adamant supporter of the Irish nationalist struggle for independence.

While Gore-Booth was immersed in the anti-conscription campaign in Britain she had overlooked the escalating political instability in her own country. Concern was growing that conscription would be introduced in Ireland. Since the onset of World War One, the recruitment of Irish men into the British army was a contentious issue. John Redmond and the Irish Parliamentary Party had gained real ground at Westminster. Home Rule for Ireland became law in 1914 but due to the outbreak of war, implementation of the bill was postponed. The Ulster Volunteer Force (UVF), a group formed to provide military opposition to Home Rule, offered their full support to the Imperial war effort. Members of the UVF formed a division of the British army, later known as the 36th Ulster Division. The issue was not so clear cut for the nationalist group, the Irish Volunteers. Redmond pledged that members of the Irish Volunteers would join the British army. He seemed assured that the British government would implement Home Rule once they received Irish support in the war effort, and this belief split the volunteers. The majority of the organisation, numbering nearly 170,000 men, supported Redmond and regrouped as the Irish National Volunteers. A minority of members, approximately 12,000 men, remained loyal to the leader of the Irish Volunteers, Eoin MacNeill, and the director of the organisation, Padraig Pearse.

Redmond made his pledge to support the British war effort in the House of Commons and thousands of Irish men responded by enlisting in Irish regiments of the British army. In response, Gore-Booth's friend Francis Sheehy Skeffington began organising anti-military meetings in Dublin attesting that Redmond simply 'sold Irish people to the British army for nothing.'[28] Skeffington conducted anti-recruitment meetings on a regular basis at Beresford Place in Dublin. At one such meeting on 23 May 1915 he declared that 'we are not in this war of our own free will. What interest have we in fighting England's domination of the seas? Anything that smashes and weakens England's domination of the seas is good for Ireland. Germany has never done us any harm. The only power that has ever done us any harm is England; the only power that is doing us any harm now is England.'[29] An undercover Royal Irish Constable, Patrick McCarthy, attended the meeting and made a complete report of Skeffington's speech to British military intelligence. Skeffington was arrested under the Defence of the Realm Act (DORA). His speech was deemed to cause 'disaffection and to prejudice recruiting.'[30] He was sentenced to six months imprisonment with hard labour and bail of £50.

On his release from prison Skeffington travelled to New York where he stepped up his campaign against Ireland's inclusion in the Imperial war effort. He made speeches and wrote several articles for American newspapers vilifying Redmond's decision. By October 1915 headlines in the *New York Times* declared that 'Redmond Committed His Country to the War for Nothing.'[31] While Skeffington fought against Irish inclusion in the war effort, Pearse and others viewed the European war as an ideal opportunity to strike a blow for Irish freedom, evoking Daniel O'Connell's declaration that England's difficulty is Ireland's opportunity. Pearse announced that the conflict 'has brought about a crisis which may contain, as yet hidden within it, the moment for which generations have been waiting.'[32]

The constant delay with introducing Home Rule coupled with the possibility that conscription would be introduced in Ireland increased the likelihood of an Irish rebellion. A group of executive committee members of the Irish Volunteers including Pearse, Thomas MacDonagh and Joseph Plunkett joined a secret organisation called the Irish Republican Brotherhood (IRB). Plunkett became the principal strategist in organising a rebellion in Ireland. In March 1915 he travelled to Berlin where he met with Roger Casement, who was seeking German support for an Irish rebellion. Plunkett received assurances from German forces that they would send small arms and ammunition to aid an Irish rebellion due to take place some time in the spring of 1916. Plunkett travelled on to New York to meet with Clan na Gael leader John Devoy.

Devoy, originally a member of the IRB in Ireland, was released from prison in England under the condition that he would not reside in British territory. He went to America in 1871 and became involved with Irish republican movements there. Devoy played a significant role in planning an Irish rebellion. It was he who sponsored Casement's trip to Berlin. Thomas Clarke joined Clan na Gael when he emigrated to New York and he became Devoy's private secretary. When Clarke returned to Ireland in 1907 he had Devoy's plan for an Irish rebellion clearly in mind.

The wheels were now in motion for a military strike against British rule in Ireland. Yet, Gore-Booth was unaware that her own sister was involved in a scheme to free Ireland by force. She and Markievicz remained particularly close throughout their lives. The sisters visited each other regularly and wrote often. During visits to Dublin, Gore-Booth and Roper stayed with Markievicz, often at Surrey House in the Rathmines suburb of Dublin. The house acted as a base for Markievicz's political activities. It was in these premises that the labour leader James Larkin hid out in August 1913 to evade arrest. The illegal newspaper founded by socialist James Connolly, the *Workers' Republic*, was also printed at this address for a time.

Gore-Booth met both Larkin and Connolly on her visits to Dublin. She shared ideas and friendship with the two men. Connolly had become involved with the ILP when he lived in Edinburgh during the 1890s and he had befriended Gore-Booth's ally Keir Hardie. The two men remained close after Connolly moved to Ireland and Hardie funded Connolly's news-sheet the *Workers' Republic*. Gore-Booth especially admired Connolly, whom she described as a 'a man who had that quality, rare indeed among politicians, that however absorbed he might be in fighting for a cause, he did not forget to answer the appeal of individual suffering.'[33] Connolly was an inspiring socialist whose campaign for reform incorporated equality between the sexes as a central goal. He viewed the 're-establishment of the Irish State' as useless unless it embodied the 'emancipation of womanhood.'[34] Gore-Booth did not associate Connolly or Markievicz with an armed rebellion. Indeed, Roper testified that Connolly 'was not a militarist.'[35] However, through his many union campaigns, Connolly rationalised that the only way to improve the rights of the working classes in Ireland was to achieve total independence from British oppression.

On a visit to Markievicz in 1915, Gore-Booth and Roper saw the Irish Volunteers marching through the streets of Dublin. Witnessing this event convinced the two women that an armed rebellion would not take place in Ireland. Roper recalls how both she and Gore-Booth sat in the window of a Dublin house:

> Watching the march past of men and women of the Citizen Army and Volunteers, Fianna boys, women of Cuman na mBan, and a crowd of sympathizers on their way to visit the grave of some Irish hero of the past. There were few uniforms, though Padraic Pearse, their leader, was in full uniform. When it was over I remember thinking with admiration of all the gifted people in those ranks, I said with relief to Eva, 'Well, thank goodness, they simply can't be planning a rising now, not with such a tiny force.'[36]

It is almost certain that Gore-Booth and Roper were witnessing Pearse as he led the Irish Volunteers to the graveside of O'Donovan Rossa, who was buried on 1 August 1915 at Glasnevin cemetery in Dublin. Rossa was a convicted Fenian who in 1871 was among a group released from prison in England under condition that they leave the country for the period of their sentences. He had sailed to New York with John Devoy and there he founded the republican paper, the *United Irishmen*.

When Rossa died in New York in June 1915, Devoy arranged to have his body shipped back to Ireland for burial. The funeral became a momentous occasion for Irish nationalists, which resulted in a huge propaganda exercise. His funeral was organised by a committee comprising over 100 of the most active republican figures, including Thomas McDonagh, Con Colbert and James Connolly. Members of Cumann na mBan, a female auxiliary force to the Irish Volunteers, played an active role organising the event. Sub-committees arranged every minor detail from publicity to transportation. Pearse gave the graveside oration uttering the now legendary words, 'they have left us our Fenian dead, and while Ireland holds these graves, Ireland unfree shall never be at peace.'[37]

Gore-Booth was unaware that Markievicz was on the organising committee for Rossa's funeral. Also unknown to Gore-Booth, Markievicz had played an intrinsic role in many republican organisations. As early as 1908 she had joined the Irish political party, Sinn Féin, which was founded by Arthur Griffith. That same year she became an active member of Maud Gonne's nationalist women's organisation, Inghinidhe na hÉireann. Shortly afterwards Markievicz helped found the first nationalist women's newspaper, *Bean na hÉireann*. She contributed articles and drawings to the women's paper as well as overseeing an entertaining and politically controversial gardening column. By 1909 Markievicz was devoting herself almost entirely to the nationalist cause. Her daughter, Maeve, went to live with her own mother at Lissadell House. Her stepson, Stanislas, was sent to boarding school and her marriage to Casimir became even less conventional. He spent much of his time away from their home and rumours circulated that Casimir was having affairs with other women.[38] Whether or not Casimir was involved in extra-marital affairs is impossible to determine but it is clear that the couple began to drift from each other after 1909. Casimir had no interest in political affairs and Constance's life was now taken over by politics. He left Ireland altogether in December 1913.

Along with the assistance of Sinn Féin member Bulmer Hobson, Markievicz established an alternative to the British Boy Scout movement in 1909.[39] She named the youth movement, Na Fianna Éireann, after the mythical warriors who defended the high king of Ireland. Members were trained in basic military methods and pledged that they would never join the British army. Markievicz's band of military trained youth would later play a vital role in the Irish rebellion of 1916. Gore-Booth and Roper often saw Fianna boys at Markievicz's house but she was careful not to speak to the two women about 'the revolutionary side of her life.'[40] Gore-Booth was undoubtedly aware that her sister had been arrested in 1911 for protesting against the royal visit of recently crowned British King, George V, to Dublin. However, Gore-Booth possibly assumed that the majority of Markievicz's political activities related to trade unionism and social reform.

From its formation in 1911, Markievicz had supported the Irish Women's Workers' Union (IWWU), a branch of the Irish Transport and General Workers' Union (ITGWU). Larkin was president of the women's union and his sister, Delia, was secretary. Markievicz had gained invaluable experience from Gore-Booth's many trade union campaigns. She spoke at one of the first ever meetings of the IWWU and remained a dedicated supporter for a number of years. The main objective of the union was to 'improve the wages and conditions of the women workers of Ireland, and to help the men workers to raise the whole status of labour and industry.'[41] This was an objective welcomed by Gore-Booth. However, the development of trade unionism in Ireland would become intrinsically linked with the nationalist cause.

In 1913 the ITGWU actively recruited thousands of unskilled Dublin labourers to its ranks. The owner of the *Irish Independent* newspaper and controller of the Dublin United Tramways Company,

William Martin Murphy, was concerned that one large union would provide labourers with too much power. In August, Murphy gave workers in the dispatch centre of the *Irish Independent* newspaper a choice, their jobs or membership of the union. When workers insisted on maintaining their membership of the ITGWU, Murphy dismissed them. Larkin refused to accept such a despicable act and launched a counter attack ordering a tram strike by ITGWU members. In a battle of wits, Murphy sought support from other employers in the capital city, who in turn locked out any employees who would not reject the union.

By the end of September 1913 20,000 already struggling labourers were out of work in an event which became known simply as the Dublin Lock-Out. Markievicz and Delia Larkin took over a welfare operation in the ITGWU head office at Liberty Hall in Dublin. The women organised soup kitchens and milk depots to feed starving locked out workers and their children. Markievicz spent six months fundraising, buying and cooking food and calling to workers' homes offering assistance. She recruited helpers including Francis Sheehy Skeffington. The situation in Dublin escalated when Larkin arrived on Sackville Street to address a group of union supporters on 31 August 1913. The meeting had been banned by the authorities and the Dublin Metropolitan Police launched a violent attack on the gathered crowd. The police charged into the unarmed group with batons, resulting in two deaths and hundreds of injuries. Realising the importance of defending workers' rights to demonstrate, Larkin, Connolly and Jack White founded the Irish Citizen Army (ICA) in November 1913 and Markievicz became honorary treasurer. Larkin sought support from British unions and toured Britain addressing huge audiences across the country. Connolly left his base in Belfast and now took control over the Dublin trade union movement.

On 9 December 1913, the British Trade Union Congress voted overwhelmingly against any action to support the Dublin workers. Larkin was devastated and in January 1914 he returned to Dublin where he appealed for workers to return to work. After six months of hostile dispute the Dublin Lock-Out was over.[42] Connolly later testified that the dispute highlighted 'in a very striking manner the terrible nature of the conditions under which women and girls labour in the capital city, the shocking insanitary conditions of the workshops, the grinding tyranny of those in charge, and the alarmingly low vitality which resulted from the inability to procure proper food and clothes with the meagre wages paid.'[43] Frustrated with the intolerable working conditions Irish people experienced under British rule, Larkin and Connolly decided on a military course. Roper provides an apt summary of the reasoning behind Connolly's eventual decision for military action; 'England's treatment of the Home Rule act and the recruiting in Ireland filled him [Connolly] with indignation, and he came to think that the moment had come for armed rebellion, perhaps Ireland's only chance. Not that he imagined that the small force of which he was one of the leaders could beat the English Army and Navy . . . but he believed this to be the only way to prove Ireland's determination to be free.'[44]

On Easter Monday, 24 April 1916, Padraig Pearse stood at the front steps of the General Post Office (GPO) on Sackville Street, (now O'Connell Street) in the centre of Dublin city and announced the Republic of Ireland, Poblacht na hÉireann. With the inspiring words Pearse began the Proclamation:

> IRISHMEN AND IRISHWOMEN: in the name of God and the dead generations from which she receives her old traditions of nationhood, Ireland, through us, summons her children to her flag and strikes for her freedom. Having organised and trained her manhood through her secret revolutionary organisation, the Irish Republican Brotherhood, and through her open military organisation, the Irish Volunteers, and the Irish Citizen Army, having patiently perfected her discipline, having resolutely waited for the right moment to reveal itself, she now seizes that moment, and, supported by her exiled children in America and by gallant allies in Europe, but relying in the first on her own strength, she strikes in full confidence of victory. We declare the right of the people of Ireland to the ownership of Ireland.[45]

A provisional government of Ireland had been formed. The flag of the Republic was raised and so began an armed rebellion against British forces, now referred to as the Easter Rising. The proclamation was signed by members of the provisional government of Ireland, Thomas Clarke, Sean MacDiarmada, Padraig Pearse, James Connolly, Thomas MacDonagh, Eamonn Ceannt and Joseph Plunkett.

The two main forces involved were the Irish Volunteers and the Irish Citizen Army. The strategy behind the Rising was to seize control of key buildings and areas across Dublin. Once key sites were secured the nationalists would hold out until Irish Volunteers across the country rose in support. Due to confusion over order and countermanded order a mass uprising of Volunteers throughout the country never occurred. The rebels in Dublin were, more or less, left to their own devices. There was speculation that Germany would assist with naval support or create a diversion by attacking British troops in Europe. The 'gallant allies' sent 20,000 rifles to arm the Irish rebels. However, the weapons and ammunition were scuttled with the German ship, the *Aud*, before Easter. The Irish rebellion was deemed as treason by British authorities. The British public were horrified that Irish people would plan a rebellion at a time when thousands of British soldiers were being killed in the war against Germany and her allies. Many Irish people were against the rebellion, viewing it as a reckless act destined for failure.

The GPO acted as the headquarters of the provisional government.[46] Five signatories of the proclamation were based there, Pearse, Connolly, Clarke, Plunkett and MacDiarmada. Connolly was appointed Commandant General of the new Irish army and he directed activities throughout the city. A relatively small band of 1,400 poorly armed Irish rebels held their posts across Dublin city. A company of ICA troops led by Seán Connolly seized City Hall, which adjoined Dublin Castle, the centre of British intelligence in Ireland. Helena Moloney and Kathleen Lynn were amongst the group who occupied the Hall and surrounding buildings. City Hall was subjected to intense gun fire almost immediately and Connolly was killed shortly after occupying the building. Commandant Edward Daly seized the law courts, known as the Four Courts. Occupation of the large building on the north of the River Liffey was of strategic importance; positioned between the GPO and the main British military barracks. As such Daly's battalion was involved in some of the heaviest fighting, especially in the North King Street area of the city. Daly also seized control of two other British positions in the area, the Bridewell Police Station and Linenhall Barracks.

In order to take control of the Four Courts Captain Seán Heuston and his battalion seized a large building near the Royal Barracks. They occupied the Mendicity Institution in order to shield Daly and his troops until they had established full control of the area. The Mendicity Institute was surrounded by soldiers armed with machine guns and Heuston was forced to surrender on Wednesday. Commandant Eamonn Ceannt and his battalion occupied an old workhouse, the South Dublin Union, located on the south side of the River Liffey about two miles from the GPO. Ceannt established three outposts in this area. Captain Séamus Murphy took over Jameson's Distillery at Marrowbone Lane, Captain Con Colbert seized Watkin's brewery, Ardee Street and Captain Thomas McCarthy occupied Roe's Distillery in Mount Brown.

Commandant Thomas MacDonagh, with Major John MacBride second in command and Michael O'Hanrahan next in command, seized Jacob's biscuit factory on Bishop Street. The building incorporated two tall towers which provided a clear sight over the city and enabled the second battalion to snipe at British soldiers coming from Portobello Barracks. The position of the snipers in the towers meant that Camden Street and Wexford Street were effectively closed off to British troops attempting to reach Dublin Castle.

Commandant Éamon de Valera and his troops occupied Boland's Mill. The Mill was a crucial site as it overlooked the railway line from Kingstown (now Dun Laoghaire) into Dublin City. It was agreed to occupy this building in order to prevent reinforcement British troops accessing Dublin city. Troops arriving from England would enter the port of Kingstown and mainly travel by train into the city. Volunteers stationed in this area ripped up sections of railway line preventing British troops from getting too close to the city. De Valera posted troops along the route from Kingstown to the city. Small bands of men took up positions along Northumberland Road. When battalions of British troops attempted to make their way down Northumberland Road, their progress was hampered by shots from various positions along the road. When British troops finally made their way to Mount Street Bridge, huge numbers of them were shot down from insurgents based in Clanwilliam House. Over 200 British troops were killed or injured at Mount Street Bridge, marking this as one of the primary sites of military engagement during the Rising. Clanwilliam was occupied by only seven Irish men, three of the men were killed and four escaped after the house went on fire.

Markievicz was centrally involved in the rebellion and took up arms as second in command to Commandant Michael Mallin. Markievicz and Mallin along with their troop of ICA combatants were based in St Stephen's Green. The twenty acre public park is based on the south side of Dublin city, near to Jacob's factory and about one mile south of the GPO. Mallin ordered his troops to occupy buildings overlooking the Green and to dig trenches in front of the numerous entrances to the park. There were not enough troops to occupy every building and within hours British snipers took up position in buildings overlooking the Green and troops on the roof of the Shelbourne Hotel directed machine gun fire into the park. It was impossible for the combatants to maintain their position. On Tuesday Mallin, Markievicz and their troops relocated to the enclosed premises of the College of Surgeons nearby.

Within days Dublin city was in ruins and numerous unarmed civilians, as well as many rebels and British soldiers were killed or wounded. Over 16,000 British soldiers were now in position fighting against the Irish insurgents. Machine guns placed at Trinity College blasted O'Connell Street and a patrol vessel, the *Helga*, was shelling buildings from the River Liffey. Under heavy fire Irish insurgents retreated from the GPO. Five members of the provisional government of Ireland convened a meeting at 16 Moore Street, in Hanlon's fish shop. The group agreed to surrender on Saturday 29 April. At 12.45pm Cumann na mBan member Nurse Elizabeth O'Farrell was sent to inform General Lowe that Pearse would negotiate a surrender. Pearse later surrendered unconditionally, 'in order to prevent the further slaughter of Dublin citizens, and in the hope of saving the lives of our followers now surrounded and hopelessly outnumbered, the members of the Provisional Government present at Head Quarters have agreed to an unconditional surrender.'[47] O'Farrell was instructed to deliver the notice to each Irish battalion around Dublin city. It took until the next day, under heavy gun fire, to reach each of the posts. The Irish rebels had managed to hold out for six days against the large heavily armed British military force.

Gore-Booth first learnt about the rebellion from newspaper reports in London. At first little information was passed through to England. The lines of communication had been severed by the republicans who controlled the General Post Office, and telegraph poles had been badly damaged during fighting. On Sunday morning, the final day of the Rising, Gore-Booth read an account in *Lloyd's Weekly Newspaper* that Markievicz's body had been discovered in St Stephen's Green. She was distraught and ran the length and breadth of London city attempting to find out more information about her sister.[48] Gore-Booth discovered that the report was not true. Markievicz was unhurt but had been arrested after the surrender. Later when the British authorities sought their revenge on the Irish rebels, Eva, fearful of what might happen to her sister almost wished that Constance had been killed in action. In a speech to a London society, she explained that it would be far worse for her sister to be 'executed coldly and deliberately at a certain hour by the clock than to be killed in the hurry and excitement of battle.'[49]

The city and county of Dublin had been placed under martial law with General John Maxwell appointed as Commander-in-chief of Ireland. He had full power as military governor to do everything necessary to restore order to the country. Once the rebels surrendered, Maxwell immediately began extracting what he considered to be justice. He organised closed court-martial trials for all the leaders of the Rising and those presumed to be leaders. Unlike civil trials, court-martials did not include a jury or allow legal counsel and sentencing could be more severe. In these trials the sentence for many was death. The executions began swiftly when Pearse, Clarke and MacDonagh were shot on Wednesday 3 May, only three days after fighting stopped. All of the executions took place by firing squad in Kilmainham Jail, Dublin. On the following Monday, Redmond warned Asquith in the House of Commons that 'the continuance of military executions in Ireland had caused rapidly increasing bitterness and exasperation among large sections of the population who had not the slightest sympathy with the insurrection.'[50] Redmond begged the Prime Minister to put a stop to the firing squads.

The majority of women who had been arrested for their part in the Rising were released shortly afterwards. Only six women, including Markievicz, remained in prison a week after the Rising.[51] Markievicz was taken to Kilmainham Gaol where she was court-martialled on 4 May under a charge that she 'did take part in an armed rebellion and in the waging of war against His Majesty the King, such act being of such a nature as to be calculated to be prejudicial to the Defence of the Realm and being done with the intention and for the purpose of assisting the enemy.'[52] Markievicz pleaded not guilty to the charge but guilty of attempting to 'cause disaffection among the civilian population of His Majesty.'[53] In her statement to the court she testified, 'I went out to fight for Ireland's freedom, and it doesn't matter what happens to me. I did what I thought was right and I stand by it.'[54] Under order of the convening officer, Maxwell and the court-martial president, Brig-General C.J. Blackader, Markievicz was sentenced to death by firing squad. Two days later Gore-Booth learnt from Asquith's secretary that this sentence was commuted to penal servitude for life.

A plea for mercy was inserted into Markievicz's charge sheet noting that 'the court recommend the prisoner to mercy solely and only on account of her sex.'[55] Other death sentences were later commuted to penal servitude, including those of Thomas Ashe and Éamon de Valera.[56] On hearing the news of Markievicz's sentence, Gore-Booth used all of her political contacts to secure special permission to travel to Dublin to visit her. Markievicz's stepson, Stanislas, explained that, 'although often separated for months, and even for years, the deep devotion of the sisters remained unchanged. Each was always ready to come to the assistance of the other, whether the crisis was an illness, a political campaign, or other emergency.'[57] On the night of 11 May, Gore-Booth and Roper set sail, arriving into Dublin the next morning aboard the *Leinster*.[58] That same day Asquith arrived in the city. The Prime Minister had taken responsibility as chief secretary for Ireland after Augustine Birrell resigned.[59] Asquith arrived into the city amid stories of British military atrocities. During the days after the rebellion, bodies were discovered buried in cellars and yards of buildings in the North King Street area of the city. It transpired that at least fourteen innocent civilians had been dragged from their homes and shot, supposedly by South Staffordshire Regiment soldiers.[60]

As Gore-Booth and Roper waited aboard the *Leinster* they were horrified at the scene that greeted them on the dock below. British soldiers had surrounded the gangway and were moving civilians in various directions. One soldier joked loudly to a group of descending passengers, 'if I let you go over there, I shall be court-martialled and shot at dawn!'[61] As Gore-Booth and Roper descended into the chaos they were greeted by a large banner announcing that James Connolly had been executed that very morning. Gore-Booth was sickened, recalling that her 'world turned black.'[62] She and Roper travelled by taxi to Mountjoy prison, where Markievicz was now being held. As they drove through the devastated Dublin streets, Gore-Booth thought that the area looked 'infinitely more tragic than the look one used to see in London on an air-raid night, just after the warning was given. As if everybody, even the very houses, were crouching down, hiding from something.'[63]

When Gore-Booth first saw Markievicz behind 'a sort of cage,' she worried about giving her the tragic news that Connolly had been executed earlier that day. Markievicz already knew about many of the executions, she had listened to the shots of firing parties for over a week. Gore-Booth wrote to Katharine Tynan 'what C[onstance] felt most the worst of all was her friends being shot every morning at Kilmainham outside her window while she was waiting for her sentence before she went to Mountjoy.'[64] Markievicz was concerned for the many Dublin families who were now left without husbands or fathers. She was most concerned for the wife of her commanding officer, Michael Mallin, who was executed four days earlier. Mallin and his wife, Agnes, had a young family; three sons and one daughter. Agnes was pregnant at the time of Mallin's execution and she went into hiding with her children. Markievicz pleaded with Gore-Booth to find Agnes and offer her financial and emotional support. Gore-Booth later wrote to Hanna Sheehy-Skeffington seeking help.[65] When Gore-Booth found Agnes she provided her with financial aid and introduced her to a local Inchicore priest, Father Ryan, who agreed to help protect the Mallin family.[66] Agnes gave birth to a baby girl four months after her husband was executed and she named her daughter Mary Constance in appreciation.

Gore-Booth spent the week in Dublin, helping destitute and grieving people in any practical way. She called to Markievicz's home at Surrey House, which had been seized by the British military and ransacked. The soldiers had crushed every one of Markievicz's lantern slides, ripped her clothes and dug up the garden. While Gore-Booth and Roper surveyed the house, a large crowd gathered outside. The resemblance between Gore-Booth and Markievicz was so striking that local people mistook her for the Countess, whom they thought had escaped from prison and returned home. The fact that Gore-Booth could easily be mistaken for her rebel sister caused serious concern that she would be shot in error. Gore-Booth was not deterred. She and Roper booked into the Hotel Pelletier on Harcourt Street in the centre of Dublin city.

Notes

1 EGB, 'Heroic Death, 1916,' *CE*, p. 508.
2 'German Embassy Issues Warning,' *New York Times* (1 May 1915).
3 'How the News Arrived,' *The Irish Times* (8 May 1915), p. 5.
4 The two were engaged for a short time in 1911.
5 National Archives, Kew, UK, Ref CAB/24/88, Image 0023, letter to Lloyd George, 29 January 1917.
6 Pennsylvania State University Libraries, Eva Gore-Booth Collection, box 1, folder 2: AX/B40/RBM/00139, handwritten paper 'Religious Aspects of Non-resistance,' by EGB.

7 *The Labour Leader* (15 July 1915), p. 13.
8 EGB, *Religious Aspects of Non-Resistance* (Bishopsgate: Headley Brothers Printers, 1915).
9 Russell was not a pacifist. He expressed the opinion that war was only ever justifiable if it furthered civilization. Ray Monk, 'Russell, Bertrand Arthur William, third Earl Russell (1872–1970,)' *Oxford Dictionary of National Biography* (Oxford: Oxford University Press, 2008).
10 Asquith made this proposal on 15 July 1915.
11 EGB, 'The Danger of Conscription,' *MG* (9 December 1915), p. 11.
12 For details of Erskine Macdonald and Galloway Kyle's activities see: Peter Brooker and Andrew Thacker (eds), *The Oxford Critical and Cultural History of Modernist Magazines: Volume 1* (Oxford: Oxford University Press, 2009), p. 178.
13 Thomas C. Kennedy, *The Hound of Conscience: A History of the No-Conscription Fellowship 1914–1919* (Fayetteville: University of Arkansas Press, 1981), p. 89.
14 Ibid, p. 90.
15 James. E. Edmonds, *Military Operations in France and Belgium 1916, Volume I: Sir Douglas Haig's Command to the 1st July: Battle of the Somme* (London: MacMillan, 1932), p. 152.
16 EGB, 'The Death Penalty,' *MG* (20 January 1916), p. 8.
17 Working Class Movement Library, Manchester, AG NCF Box 1, Folder F, Room 36, letter from Margaret Morgan Jones to Mr Burgess requesting details of men who have died, 13 November 1918.
18 See the No Conscription Fellowship papers held in the Working Class Movement Library, Manchester.
19 Working Class Movement Library, Manchester, ORG/NCF/1/C, Conscientious Objectors Information Bureau Reports, containing reports of arrests for resisting military, court-martials and details of COs in prisons, 1917–19.
20 Pennsylvania State University Libraries, Eva Gore-Booth Collection, box 1, folder 15: AX/B40/RBM/00139, original handwritten manuscript 'At the military tribunal,' by EGB.
21 EGB, 'Conscientious Objectors,' *Herald* (30 March 1916), p. 3.
22 EGB, *The Tribunal* (London: National Labour Press Ltd, 1916), p. 2.
23 Ibid, p. 7.
24 'Bertrand Russell Sentenced,' *The Tribunal*, 12:1 (8 June 1916).
25 'Adsum qui Feci' (trans. Here I am I did it), *The Times* (17 May 1916), p. 9.
26 Richard Rempel and Bernd Frohmann, (eds), *The Collected Papers of Bertrand Russell, Volume 13: Prophecy and Dissent, 1914–16* (London: Unwin Hyman, 1988).
27 McMaster University, Canada, Bertrand Russell Archives, poems by EGB

'Walls' and 'Where Great Waves Break' sent to Bertrand Russell, 1918.

28 National Archives, Kew, Colonial Office Record Series Vol 1, Dublin Castle Special Branch Files, CO 904/215/408, report on anti-militarist meeting held at Beresford Place by Patrick J. McCarthy Constable 36G, 23 May 1915. Many of these files have been published on CD by Eneclánn in 2006.

29 Ibid.

30 Ibid.

31 *The New York Times* (5 October 1915).

32 Padraig Pearse, *Collected Works of Pádraic H. Pearse: Political Writings and Speeches* (Dublin: Phoenix Press, 1916), p. 87.

33 Roper, (ed.), *Prison Letters*, p. 43.

34 James Connolly, *The Re-Conquest of Ireland* (Dublin: Maunsel, 1917), p. 243.

35 Roper, (ed.), *Prison Letters*, p. 16.

36 Ibid, p. 14.

37 Padraig Pearse, *Collected Works*, p. 137.

38 While researching for her biography of Countess Markievicz, Diana Norman was given the memoirs of Geraldine Plunkett Dillon, who knew Constance and Casimir. Dillion described Casimir as a blackguard regarding other women. Diana Norman, *Terrible Beauty: A Life of Constance Markievicz* (Dublin: Poolbeg Press, 1988), p. 61.

39 Marnie Hay, *Bulmer Hobson and the Nationalist Movement in Twentieth Century Ireland* (Manchester: Manchester University Press, 2009).

40 Roper, (ed.), *Prison Letters*, p. 13.

41 NLI, LOP 113/123, Irish Women's Workers' Union call for members, September 1911.

42 For a detailed history of the ITGWU see: Francis Devine, *SIPTU: Organising History* (Dublin: Gill and Macmillan Ltd, 2009).

43 James Connolly, *The Re-Conquest of Ireland*, p. 237.

44 Roper, (ed.), *Prison Letters*, pp. 16–17.

45 An original copy of the 1916 Poblacht na hÉireann is held in the ephemera department of the National Library of Ireland, Dublin. For an authoritative version see; *1916 Easter Rebellion Handbook* (Dublin: *Weekly Irish Times*, 1916; reprinted Dublin: Mourne River Press, 1998), p. ix.

46 For an interesting exploration of the events surrounding 1916 see: Clair Wills, *Dublin 1916: The Siege of the GPO* (Cambridge Mass: Harvard University Press, 2009).

47 NLI, MS 15,000 (2), Surrender notice signed by Pearse, Connolly and MacDonagh, 29 April 1916.

48 Roper, (ed.), *Prison Letters*, p. 48.

49 Ibid, p. 45.

50 'Mr. Redmond's Protest: Against more Executions,' *Southern Star* (13 May 1916), p. 3.
51 1,424 of the men were also released within a week of their arrest.
52 Roper, (ed.), *Prison Letters*, p. 24.
53 Ibid.
54 Ibid, p. 26.
55 Ibid.
56 'Mr. Asquith goes to Ireland,' *MG* (12 May 1916), p. 5.
57 Stanislas Dun Markievicz, 'Life of Constance de Markiewicz [sic],' p. 134.
58 A German U-Boat sank the *Leinster* two years later on 10 October 1918. outside Kingstown harbour (Dun Laoghaire). Roy Stokes, *Death in the Irish Sea: The Sinking of the R.M.S. Leinster* (Cork: Collins Press, 1998).
59 In his resignation speech to the House of Commons on 3 May 1916, Birrell accepted full responsibility for the outbreak of rebellion in Dublin. *Hansard* 5C, 82.31–5, 3 May 1916.
60 Roger McHugh (ed.), 'Statements Concerning Civilian deaths in the North King Street area of Dublin, between 6 p.m. April 28 and 10 a.m. April 29, 1916,' *Dublin 1916* (New York: Hawthorn Books, 1966), pp. 220–39.
61 Roper, (ed.), *Prison Letters*, p. 44.
62 Ibid.
63 Ibid, p. 46.
64 John Rylands Library, Manchester, Previous reference KTH1/330/2a, Box 3/39, letter from EGB to Katharine Tynan, undated.
65 NLI, MS 33,605 (4), letter from EGB at the Hotel Pelletier to Hanna Sheehy Skeffington, May 1916.
66 NLI, MS 13,777, letter from EGB to Fr. Ryan at Golden Bridge Chapel, Inchicore, Dublin, 22 May 1916.

9

Roger Casement and the aftermath of the Easter Rising

'I dream of the death that he died,
For the sake of God and Kathleen ni Houlighaun'[1]

In the weeks following the Easter Rising Gore-Booth described Dublin as a 'city of mourning and death.'[2] When the full severity of what happened began to take effect 'people broke down and wept for very little, even in the streets.'[3] Gore-Booth had lost many friends through the events of the rebellion, including Francis Sheehy Skeffington. While he supported the cause of Irish freedom, Sheehy Skeffington did not take up arms in the military uprising as he was a devoted pacifist. During the Rising, he attempted to keep order in Dublin city by preventing the looting of shops, enlisting the help of many priests and other civilians. On Tuesday 25 April 1916, he called a public meeting in the head office of the Irish Women's Franchise League at Westmorland Chambers, in the shadow of the fighting. At the meeting he organised the establishment of an interim Citizen's Defence Force to protect Dublin civilians and to maintain public order.

On his way home that evening, Sheehy Skeffington was arrested and questioned, he was unarmed and did not resist. Although he was not involved in the Rising, the Royal Irish Constabulary had been closely monitoring him since his anti-recruitment activities. By 1916 the Special Branch 'personality files' held at Dublin Castle contained a detailed account of Sheehy Skeffington's movements.[4] This time no charge was placed against him but he was taken to Portobello barracks where he was searched and questioned further. During the night the captain of the guard, J.C. Bowen-Colthurst, took Sheehy Skeffington out of the barracks with his hands bound behind his back. He was taken as a hostage, possibly to protect British soldiers during raids throughout the night. He was eventually returned to the barracks the next morning. Witness statements from other prisoners detail what happened next. Without any explanation Colthurst brought Sheehy Skeffington and two other unarmed civilian men into the yard of the barracks. On his order all three men were shot dead by a firing squad. Neither of the other two men, Thomas Dickson, editor of a loyalist paper, the *Eye-Opener*, and Patrick McIntyre, editor of the anti-Larkin paper the *Searchlight*, had any connection with the Rising either.

Once Gore-Booth learnt about the death of Sheehy Skeffington she wrote to his wife Hanna, 'I am so appalled and miserable about Sheehy Skeffington. Your suffering is too dreadful. The story is shocking and horrifying.'[5] When Gore-Booth first visited her sister in prison, Markievicz pleaded to know, 'why on earth did they shoot Skeffy? After all, he wasn't in it. He didn't even believe in fighting.'[6] After Gore-Booth left Mountjoy Prison that first day in Dublin she immediately went to visit Hanna Sheehy Skeffington at her home, 11 Grosvenor Place, near Markievicz's house. When Gore-Booth arrived she was horrified to see the recently widowed woman and her young son sitting in the front room of a dishevelled house with broken windows. Shortly after Sheehy Skeffington was killed, Colthurst had arrived at Grosvenor Place with a company of soldiers seeking evidence to justify the shooting. Gore-Booth wrote of the horror noting how Colthurst, 'raided his victims house, fired a volley into the window and kept the seven year old boy and his mother under arrest while he searched and [ran]sacked the house.'[7]

Hanna Sheehy Skeffington showed Gore-Booth a small package that she had recently received from Portobello barracks. The package included the final possessions of her murdered husband, his watch and collar and tie. The items were worthless and Gore-Booth realised how this package 'bore pathetic witness to the almost insane truth, – that those who did not scruple to steal human lives were yet most honourable and honest in their dealings with property.'[8] Gore-Booth was appalled at the details of Sheehy Skeffington's murder. She felt a special affinity with the man who, like James Connolly, she described as 'an enthusiast on the subject of the freedom of women.'[9] After listening to Hanna Sheehy Skeffington that day, Gore-Booth rationalised why 'Skeffy' had been shot, 'militarism had struck down its worst enemy – unarmed yet insurgent Idealism.'[10]

Hanna Sheehy Skeffington published and circulated a detailed statement describing her husband's unlawful execution and the harassment experienced by her and her family.[11] This statement was the first step in seeking a full inquiry into his murder. Gore-Booth described how Hanna Sheehy Skeffington 'pursued her relentless and irresistible way, disentangling the motives and circumstances of the murder, and bringing it home to the responsible authorities.'[12] Gore-Booth lobbied the Prime Minister's office on Sheehy Skeffington's behalf and she wrote to her brother, Josslyn, seeking assistance.[13] Josslyn had already lobbied his local Sligo MP, Charles O'Hara, on his sister's behalf and Gore-Booth hoped he would do the same in this instance. Eventually Asquith was compelled to grant an official inquiry into the death of Sheehy Skeffington.[14] In August 1916, Colthurst was tried by court-martial, found guilty of murder and declared insane.[15] He was sent to Broadmoor Criminal Asylum but later discharged and it was rumoured that he retired from service receiving half-pay.[16] Sheehy Skeffington epitomised the pacifist ideals expressed through the pages of National Labour Press publications and the press published details of *The Sheehy Skeffington Case*.[17]

Gore-Booth was motivated by the murder to publish a short play entitled *The Death of Fionavar*. The play consisted of the final three acts from *The Triumph of Maeve: a Romance*, a play that she had published eleven years earlier.[18] Gore-Booth describes it as an interpretation of the story of the high queen Maeve who is 'a symbol of the world-old struggle in the human mind between the forces of dominance and pity, of peace and war.'[19] She dedicated the volume 'to the Memory of the Dead. The Many who died for Freedom and the One [Francis Sheehy Skeffington] who died for Peace.' The dedication may well have been inspired by John Kells Ingram's poem 'The Memory of the Dead,' popularly referred to as 'Who Fears to Speak of Ninety-eight?'[20] While Kells Ingram's poem remembered the Irish rebellion of 1798, Gore-Booth's dedication honours the leaders of the 1916 Rising as apparent in the opening poem:

> Poets, Utopians, bravest of the brave,
> Pearse and MacDonagh, Plunkett, Connolly,
> Dreamers turned fighters but to find a grave,
> Glad for the dream's austerity to die.
>
> And my own sister, through wild hours of pain,
> Whilst murderous bombs were blotting out the stars,
> Little I thought to see you smile again
> As I did yesterday, through prison bars.

Gore-Booth asked Markievicz to illustrate the play. On the cover of the book, underneath the author's name, is proudly printed 'decorated by Constance Gore-Booth (Countess Markievicz)'. The opening page is adorned with Markievicz's sketches of winged horses flying gloriously free. The remaining eighty-five pages of text are bordered with Markievicz's drawings of flowers, sunsets and horses. The *Manchester Guardian* describes how the illustrations 'form a kind of continuous accompaniment to the poetry, each page being enclosed in a charming border sympathetically responsive to its moods and changes ... Gothic scrolls and flower patterns; but breaking out, at every hint of an occasion, into the mystic symbolism and visionary scenes of the Celt.'[21] The volume was published by Kyle's imprint of Erskine MacDonald press in England.[22] The play was marketed in America by Laurence James Gomme, a publisher and book collector in New York.

The *Manchester Guardian* hoped that 'the little volume may serve the cause of peace in Ireland and help to convince English people that the Irish movement was not in essence revolutionary.'[23] American reviewers were quick to note the obvious paradox. A play with a strong pacifist message was illustrated by a convicted armed rebel. Markievicz illustrated the play while being held in Mountjoy Prison, soon after the fighting in Dublin. Markievicz claims to have drawn the sketches using quills made from rooks' feathers that she found in the garden of the prison.[24] The *New York Times* dedicates an entire page to the wonder of this publication under the title 'Irish rebel illustrates non-resistance play.' The journalist concludes by noting that 'there is something ironical about the fact that the pages of this most passionately pacific work should be made by so convinced and practical a direct actionist as Countess Markiewicz [sic], the woman with the sword, who with her little band of fighting men helped hold the streets of Dublin for days and nights against the British machine guns.'[25]

On her return to London in May, Gore-Booth delivered one of the first Irish accounts of the Rising to a London society. Her talk provides a wonderfully detailed description of Dublin in the aftermath of the Easter rebellion. She begins with an emotional description of sailing into Dublin Bay, recording the 'beauty and delight' on that May morning with the eyes of an emigrant returning home. The pleasure at seeing her native land is disturbed by a harsh shriek of the boat's siren and the sight of a 'great mass of khaki-clad soldiers' on the docks. Gore-Booth's mystic literary style quickly changes to an account of how Ireland has been subjected to military oppression at the hands of British forces for generations:

> Soldiers of all times, of the same nationality and on the same quest. Soldiers in the queer bulky armour of the Middle Ages, soldiers in the gay colours of the Elizabethans, soldiers in Cromwell's drabs, soldiers in the stiff reds of the last century, and now soldiers in khaki. Soldiers with bows and arrows, soldiers with spears, soldiers with swords and muskets and all manner of old-fashioned weapons, soldiers with quaint and unwieldy cannon, and soldiers with rifles and revolvers and machine-guns. Soon there would be soldiers with tanks and aeroplanes. An endless procession of soldiers, with every kind of weapon, always on the same errand, always going, as they are going now, to conquer and hold down Ireland. And Ireland the Unconquerable suffering them helplessly, watching them land in their thousands.[26]

The repetitious use of the word soldier was almost certainly meant to evoke horror at the idea of Irish people being subjected to harsh military oppression for centuries. In this one short passage Gore-Booth creatively conjures up an image of British soldiers treading Irish soil from the Middle-Ages right up to the present day in 1916. She highlights the fact that all of these soldiers are of the same nationality, only their uniforms and weaponry change. Interestingly, Gore-Booth describes the Irish as passive, 'suffering' these weapons 'helplessly,' yet, the reason she went to Dublin was because of an armed rebellion by Irish forces.

In her account, Gore-Booth is careful not to mention the guns which the Irish rebels carried or the soldiers at which they shot. She announces to her English audience that Irish people should 'rejoice in the fact that once again in her long struggle for liberty Ireland had shown the world that she did not acquiesce in her age-long slavery.'[27] This section seems to refer directly to a line from the Proclamation announcing, 'in every generation the Irish people have asserted their right to national freedom and sovereignty, six times during the past three hundred years they have asserted it in arms.' Although the Proclamation was the result of joint authorship, this line is often attributed to Connolly, whom Gore-Booth especially admired. Her speech was most certainly an attempt to educate English people about the reality of British rule in Ireland, this is particularly evident when she concludes the piece with a story of her return journey from Dublin to London. After disembarking at Holyhead port,

Gore-Booth caught a train to London, a woman travelling in the same carriage talked loudly about the rebellion and declared, 'dreadful people the Irish ... so cowardly too, and ungrateful to stab us in the back like that, after all we've done for them!'[28] This story was recounted by Gore-Booth as a typical example of how people in England misunderstood the Irish pursuit for liberty and freedom.

By the time that Gore-Booth returned to England, the leaders of the Rising were becoming martyrs in Ireland. Iconic images of those arrested and executed began to appear in shop windows. Members of Cumann na mBan organised prayer meetings and masses in honour of those who died. General Maxwell was concerned that the imprisoned rebels would gain too much sympathy in their homeland and they were quickly moved to prisons in England. As the only female leader of the Rising, Markievicz was the last of the rebels to remain in Dublin. She was confined to a single cell and isolated from other prisoners in Mountjoy. Maxwell wrote to the Home Office advising, 'it appears to be desirable that the Countess Markievicz should be removed from Mountjoy Prison, Dublin to some prison in England. From censored letters it appears that sympathizers know how she is getting on in prison and that in some way information is leaking out.'[29]

Markievicz managed to get many letters out of Mountjoy. Maxwell suspected that the letters were being smuggled by visiting prison justices. This was an understandable assumption as the justices were elected by Dublin Corporation, an organisation in sympathy with Sinn Féin. However, Markievicz's biographer, Diana Norman, identifies the smuggler as an apprentice wardress, an Irishwoman from County Wexford.[30] The wardress managed to send Gore-Booth several 'unofficial letters' from her sister. When Markievicz supposed that she might be moved to a prison in England she wrote to her sister, 'I am alas! Going into exile. Make a point to try and get in to see me.'[31] The note was written on lavatory paper and smuggled out of the prison.[32] Markievicz reassured Gore-Booth that, 'I shall be quite amiable, and am not going to hunger-strike, as am advised by comrades not to. It would suit the Government very well to let me die quietly.'[33] Gore-Booth sent her sister a copy of the *Death of Fionavar*. Markievicz was delighted with the final version of the play, although she accused the printers of altering one of her sketches, placing a rose on its side inside a triangle, she wondered 'didn't I put it upright?'[34] She asked Gore-Booth to send a copy of 'our book' to the woman who was smuggling her letters out of prison and news and food into the prison, because 'she is taking awful risks for me.'[35]

Gore-Booth found it difficult to remain in London while Markievicz was imprisoned in Dublin. Since childhood the sisters believed that they had a telepathic connection and they attempted to commune with each other on a daily basis. One Sunday afternoon it was Roper who claimed to have a psychic experience. While talking about Markievicz and her fate, Roper felt an overwhelming urge to go to Euston station to meet the Irish mail train. Gore-Booth accompanied Roper to the station. While the women stood on the platform a train pulled in. Markievicz and her faithful cocker spaniel disembarked, flanked by numerous soldiers. In the midst of confusion at the station Markievicz managed to pass Gore-Booth a legal document which included details of her court-martial and the verdict, information which Gore-Booth had sought but been denied.[36] Recalling the strange event, Roper suggested 'by way of explanation, the fact that, as Markievicz told us later, when she had suddenly been taken from Mountjoy and put on the steamer and realized she was going to England, she was filled with an intense longing to see Eva.'[37]

Markievicz was transferred to Aylesbury Prison in Buckinghamshire. In her publication of Markievicz's prison letters, Roper dates this event as June 1916 and many of Markievicz's biographers have accepted this as the official date of her transfer to England.[38] Roper published her account eighteen years after the Rising and in all probability she did not remember the exact dates. Official records from Dublin Castle, released for public access in 1995, show that Markievicz remained in Mountjoy Prison until August 1916. [39] The matter of Markievicz's transfer to England was discussed in the House of Commons on 3 August and she was moved to Aylesbury Prison on 7 August 1916.[40] She wrote to Gore-Booth the day after her arrival in Aylesbury telling her sister that she missed Ireland, 'it's queer and lonely here, there was so much life in Mountjoy.'[41]

At first Markievicz was not allowed any visitors. Gore-Booth had not visited her sister since June but she had managed to keep herself particularly busy during this time. Gore-Booth became a central figure in the campaign for the reprieve of Sir Roger Casement. Casement had been arrested before the Easter Rising began. He was captured on Banna Strand, on the coast of County Kerry, where he landed from a German U-boat. The submarine was meant to rendezvous with the *Aud*, a German ship captained by Karl Spindler which was carrying a shipment of guns to arm the Irish Volunteers.[42] The *Aud* made it to the rendezvous point in Tralee Bay but failed to make contact with land agents. Three IRB men responsible for the land contact had crashed their car, driving off Ballykissane pier, the men were all drowned. Without any contact from land or from the U-boat, Spindler was forced to leave Tralee Bay. As the ship departed they were intercepted by a British naval boat. Before surrendering, the German crew set about scuttling the *Aud*. The boat, complete with its cargo of ammunition, sank off the Irish coast. The loss of the ammunition impacted dramatically on the rebellion and caused the Irish Volunteers in counties Cork, Kerry and further afield to stand down.

Meanwhile the U-boat on which Casement was travelling was unable to make it into Tralee Bay. Also on board were Robert Monteith, an Irish Volunteer enlisted by Tom Clarke to assist with the recruiting of Irish prisoners of war in Germany and Daniel Bailey, a prisoner of war who had been recruited. The three men set sail in a small dinghy. After the dinghy collapsed, Casement arrived on the coast, exhausted and ill. His companions set off for help but Casement was quickly found by British soldiers and arrested. He was brought to Dublin and from there he was sent to England and imprisoned in the Tower of London under a charge of treason. He was treated differently to the other leaders of the Rising as he had previously been employed by the British Foreign Service. In 1911, Casement had been knighted for his work in the Congo and Brazil. Through his investigations he exposed how the owners of rubber plantations were exploiting indigenous locals through a system akin to slavery. Casement's subsequent published reports exposed humanitarian abuses of floggings, rapes and mutilation.

As a former and a highly respected official of the British government, Casement's involvement with the Easter Rising caused a serious political scandal in England. On hearing of his arrest Casement's cousin, Gertrude Bannister, visited the Irish historian Alice Stopford Green to seek advice. Stopford Green had been a close friend of Casement's since 1904 when they both became involved in the Congo Reform Association. Casement inspired Stopford Green to become interested in Irish issues. In 1914 she became actively involved with the Irish Volunteers. In her capacity as chair of the

London Committee she coordinated a fund for the volunteers to which she personally contributed a large sum of money.[43] The fund enabled Casement to smuggle guns into Ireland through the port of Howth in July 1914. Stopford Green was well connected and introduced Bannister to George Gavan Duffy, a London solicitor who agreed to represent Casement. After a number of weeks imprisoned in the Tower of London, Casement was taken to Bow Street police station and an inquiry was heard which lasted for three days (see Fgure 12).

On 17 May, Casement was committed for trial under a charge of High Treason and he was transferred to Brixton Prison. Serjeant Sullivan was chosen to defend him in court. Bannister rallied support, requesting that Gore-Booth attend the trial. Gore-Booth had never met Casement and she did not relish the idea of attending. She replied to Bannister that she simply couldn't 'bear to go and look at him thus. It would seem like going to stare at his misfortune.'[44] When Bannister explained to her that 'the court will be full to overflowing with people hating Roger, looking for a sensation, anxious to be in at the death. Better that there should be some friends who can send him loving thoughts and try to sustain him,' Gore-Booth felt obliged to attend.[45]

Extraordinarily, when Casement first came into court and saw Gore-Booth sitting in the public gallery, he instantly smiled at her, she smiled back and he waved to her as if saluting an old friend. Bannister described it as a 'curious sort of affinity in their two characters. Both were mystics, Gore-Booth more so than Roger, both hated cruelty and deceit, both loved Ireland and idealised it – both worked in their several spheres to help the lot of the downtrodden – both incurred the enmity and cheap sneers of the worldly and materialistic.'[46] Gore-Booth later commented that she felt as if she had known Casement all of her life.[47]

On the fourth day of the trial, 29 June 1916, the jury of twelve men found Casement guilty of high treason. He remained calm listening to the verdict and then he asked to address the court. After a long and impassioned speech regarding the plight of Ireland under British rule, he dismissed Redmond's belief that Home Rule would be granted 'as a reward for the life blood shed in a cause which whoever else its success may benefit can surely not benefit Ireland.'[48] Casement thanked the jury for their verdict and apologised if his speech offended them. Concluding, 'I maintain that I have a natural

12 Roger Casement under arrest, seen here on the far right, arriving at Bow Street police station, 16 May 1916

right to be tried in that natural jurisdiction, Ireland, my own country.'[49] The Lord Chief Justice then passed a sentence of death. The day after the sentence Casement was stripped of his knighthood and transferred to Pentonville Prison to await execution by hanging.

Casement's solicitor, Gavan Duffy, submitted an appeal and Gore-Booth launched an intense lobbying campaign. She wrote first to the editor of the *Manchester Guardian*, C.P. Scott, on 4 July. In the detailed plea she requests that Scott contact Henry Asquith, stressing that the Prime Minister should be warned of the implications of following this course of action. While Asquith courted America to come to England's aid in the war, Gore-Booth asserted that executing Casement would seriously hamper this possibility, describing:

> The seething indignation in America and the fact that the stories of the Dublin executions is rapidly turning American sympathy against England. I have before me a resolution passed at a mass meeting at Boston, it is too long to quote but it is unmeasured in its condemnation of the barbarous and brutal crimes committed in Ireland 'the murders perpetrated in the streets etc etc.' And one hears of such resolutions being passed everywhere.[50]

Indeed, Casement's death sentence caused outrage in several quarters in America. This is understandable considering that in 1916 an estimated 20 million people in America were Irish by descent. At the national convention of the Ancient Order of Hibernians in Boston, the members, representing 250,000 Irish people in the United States, officially protested 'the hanging of Sir Roger Casement as an act of inhumanity that the Irish people can never forget and will never forget.'[51] The group later sent a telegram to Asquith testifying that 'the hanging of said Casement must be accepted by the Irish people as an act of hate and not of justice.'[52] In his research on American media coverage of the Easter Rising, Robert Schmuhl confirms that Casement quickly became the primary focus of American attention; he was a 'premier newsmaker' in the United States.[53] In her letter to Scott Gore-Booth highlights the American attention and continues by asserting:

> Surely when public opinion of a great continent is on the side of mercy statesmen might be wise to consider whether they are not injuring their committees good name by doing an action that rightly or wrongly will be considered an act of useless cruelty by a huge number of inhabitants of a neutral country. And here in England surely many

> people must feel that so many innocent people like Sheehy Skeffington were shot in Dublin, it would be an act of grace to give us one life of a rebel in return. When all is said many calm minded people feel sadly that England erred on the side of severity.[54]

Apparently inspired by Gore-Booth's appeal, Scott acted instantly. He wrote to Lloyd George, who had recently been appointed to the position of Secretary of State for War after the previous incumbent Lord Kitchener had drowned at sea. In the months after the Rising, Asquith faced condemnation for his handling of the rebellion and for the executions that followed. He asked Lloyd George to take over Irish affairs to help resolve the contentious issue of Home Rule. Rather than Asquith, Scott addressed Lloyd George, whom he considered to have a 'freer mind than anybody else.'[55] Scott declared that if it was 'politically possible to spare Casement's life? I think it would be in the highest degree politically expedient.'[56] In his correspondence he included a copy of Gore-Booth's plea, with the assurance that although she is 'personally connected with the Sinn Feiners, [Gore-Booth] is herself an ardent pacifist and condemns the whole bloody business of the insurrection.'[57]

When Gore-Booth learnt of Scott's appeal to Lloyd George, she wrote again to him, this time outlining what she described as 'the real story of Casement.'[58] In her account Gore-Booth claimed that while Casement was recovering from illness in a nursing home in Germany, he discovered through a spy's report, that a rising was planned in Ireland. Casement went to Berlin and secured a submarine to take him to Ireland. Gore-Booth was adamant that Casement's 'object in going [to Ireland] was to stop the rising which he considered a fatal mistake.'[59] Gore-Booth later clarified in the *Socialist Review* that 'Roger Casement was not against the Rising, only, knowing what he did, he feared that at the moment failure was inevitable. He was not able to get reliable information as to Irish events and hopes of success, and so came, at risk of his life, to warn his country people of the situation.'[60]

This argument was never actually put forward at his trial. Gore-Booth hoped that if she could prove that Casement was attempting to stop the rebellion, the charge of High Treason and therefore his death sentence would be dropped. However, many of Casement's activities even before his arrest at Banna strand qualified as High Treason. He had orchestrated the Howth gun running in 1914 bringing rifles from German sources aboard Erskine Childers yacht, the *Asgard*, to arm the Irish Volunteers. The time he spent in Germany attempting to raise a token force of soldiers to fight against the British was also clearly High Treason. Yet, despite the overwhelming circumstantial and other evidence, Gore-Booth persisted with a politically risky effort to save Casement's life.

To support her thesis, Gore-Booth sent Scott a transcript of a *Dublin Evening Mail* news report published on 20 May 1916. The article included an interview with Father Ryan, a Dominican priest at Tralee, whom Casement met after his arrest there. In the article Ryan recalls the conversation, testifying that Casement pleaded with him 'to tell the volunteers in the town and elsewhere to keep perfectly quiet. Tell them I am a prisoner and that the rebellion will be a dismal hopeless failure as the help they expect will not arrive.'[61] Ryan asserted that after he spoke with Casement he met with a volunteer leader in Tralee and relayed this message, which stopped the volunteers in County Kerry from taking any action during the rebellion. The fact that the ammunition meant to arm the volunteers had been destroyed was almost certainly the reason why they stood down, yet Scott was so impressed by Gore-Booth's account that he forwarded this letter directly to Lloyd George, imploring that this 'is an extraordinary story and ought to be explored and ought to be capable of verification.'[62]

In order to verify the story herself, Gore-Booth contacted Father Ryan in Tralee and received a signed statement from him testifying that 'Sir Roger Casement saw me in Tralee on the 21st of April and told me he had come to Ireland to stop the rebellion then impending. He asked me to conceal his identity as well as his object in coming until he should have left Tralee, lest any attempt should be made to rescue him. On the other hand he was very anxious that I should spread the news broadcast after he had left.'[63] Again copies of these items were forwarded to Lloyd George providing 'documentary evidence in regard to the Casement case.' Scott declared that 'it is pretty plain that his [Casement's] object in coming to Ireland was to stop the rebellion not to assist it. This is not to say that he is not an out–and–out rebel at heart, but it does put a very different complexion on his case.'[64] Gore-Booth also sent a copy of Father Ryan's testimony to Gavan Duffy's wife in the hope that the solicitor could use it as new evidence.[65]

On 17 July the Court of Criminal Appeal met to determine Casement's fate. The presiding officer was Justice Darling, who years earlier had tested Gore-Booth's wit over his decision to extend the Factory and Workshop Act to florists' premises. This time Darling was in a much more powerful position and in a spirit of self-importance, he contacted the artist Sir John Lavery. Darling asked Lavery to paint the scene at Casement's final appeal. Lavery accepted the commission but he could not hide his disdain for the proceedings.[66] Lavery sat in the jury box with his wife, Hazel, beside him, painting the portrait of what he later titled, 'the Court of Criminal Appeal.' Casement wrote to his cousin, Bannister, observing that 'the painter in the jury box ... came dangerously near "aiding and comforting" if not indeed "compassing" from the way he eyed Mr. Justice Darling delivering judgement.'[67] Lavery completed this painting after the court case finished and Gore-Booth takes pride of place in the final picture, seated in the public gallery.[68]

Casement's appeal was dismissed by Darling two days later but Gore-Booth refused to give up hope of his reprieve.[69] She wrote a public letter to the *Manchester Guardian*, pleading 'may I as an Irish woman appealing to the broad-mindedness of English people ask them to pause in the heat of their indignation against those who have rebelled against their rule.' She concluded with her personal insight that 'in England hanging is a "degrading punishment." But in Ireland to be hung by the English government is a crown of glory.'[70] Her campaign for Casement's appeal was relentless. She persistently lobbied the highest ranking politicians including Asquith; the Foreign Secretary, Sir Edward Grey; Liberal peer Lord James Bryce; director of the war trade department Lord Alfred Emmott and the Home Secretary, Herbert Samuel.

An inquiry was launched based on Gore-Booth's claims that Casement had arrived in Ireland to stop the Rising. A confidential report held in the British parliamentary papers confirms that the information sent by Gore-Booth, including the statement by Father Ryan, her letter of testimony and her own account of Casement's circumstances, was circulated to members of the British cabinet as late as 21 July. A letter by Gore-Booth was enclosed with the documents, in which she states:

> It seems to me quite clear from the priest's evidence that Casement really came to Ireland in a frantic attempt to dissuade the Sinn Fein leaders from what he considered the fatal mistake of the rising. It seems to me an intolerably ghastly idea that he should be hung as a result of this self-sacrificing and devoted effort, facing, as he did,

> almost certain death for the sake of preventing bloodshed and misery in Ireland on this matter. It would be impossible to exaggerate the feeling in Ireland on this matter, and the hopeless despair and bitterness with which the prospect of another execution is regarded – what they consider the deliberate and cold-blooded execution of a man who was not even in the rising.[71]

Legal adviser to the Home Office, Ernley Blackwell, was deeply concerned that Casement would be reprieved based on Gore-Booth's petition. Basil Thomson, head of the Criminal Investigation Department, noted in his diary how 'the waverers accepted the position that the law was to take its course, but on Thursday Lord Crewe circulated a letter from Eva Gore-Booth, Countess Markiewicz's [sic] sister, alleging that Casement's object in coming over was to stop the rebellion. Blackwell confessed he did not know, with such a weak Cabinet, what the result would be.'[72] Blackwell circulated his own memorandum refuting Gore-Booth's claim. He also included an extract from Casement's interrogation at Scotland Yard.

Casement did not receive a reprieve and the date for his execution was set for 3 August at Pentonville Prison. Blackwell was intent on ensuring that after his execution, Casement would not be made a martyr. He arranged for extracts from Casement's diaries to be copied and widely circulated. A set of diaries, which had been discovered during a search of Casement's home, described his homosexual activities in detail. Although not legally entered into his trial, pages were copied and circulated amongst journalists, politicians and anyone thought to have an interest in the Casement case. Blackwell further asserted, 'I see not the slightest objection to hanging Casement and afterwards giving as much publicity to the contents of his diary as decency permits, so that at any rate the public in America and elsewhere may know what sort of man they are inclined to make a martyr of.'[73]

When the American Ambassador to Britain, Walter Hines Page, informed Asquith that he had seen a copy of the diaries, Asquith remarked, 'excellent; and you need not be particular about keeping it to yourself.'[74] This certainly had the desired effect and Page warned American Secretary of State, Robert Lansing, not to become involved with a clemency plea for Casement because of the 'unspeakably filthy character' of his diaries.[75] Unfortunately Blackwell's plan was successful, beyond even his expectations. Debates over the contents and the authenticity of the diaries continue to cloud contemporary research about Casement.

Esther Roper was horrified by the way in which Casement's character was being attacked, commenting that 'relentless foes sat in seats of power and they poisoned the public mind by circulating lying stories (that had nothing to do with the case) against the personal character of Roger Casement. Only those that did not know him believed them, and it was a vile way of hunting a man to death.'[76] However, Gore-Booth did not venture her own opinion of Casement's so-called 'black diaries,' instead she remained focused on gaining a reprieve from his death sentence. The day before his execution date, along with Bannister, Stopford Green, Henry Nevinson and Philip Morel, she went to Buckingham Palace. The small group had an audience with King George V, whom they begged for a royal pardon. In his account of Gore-Booth's petition, Michael Begnal maintains that 'her appeal to the King was shunted through governmental channels and went for naught, since the monarch disclaimed all responsibility.'[77] The King claimed that the prerogative of mercy was the responsibility of his minister, the Home Secretary. Casement's biographer, Geoffrey De Parmiter, maintains that George V did contact the Home Secretary relaying the request.[78] All appeals were denied.

On the morning of 3 August 1916, shortly before his execution, Roger Casement was received into the Catholic Church. His confession was heard by the prison chaplain Father James McCarroll. Casement requested that his body be taken home to Ireland after the execution, imploring his cousin to 'go back to Ireland, and don't let me lie here in this dreadful place. Take my body back with you and let it lie in the old churchyard in Murlough Bay.'[79] Gore-Booth describes how at nine o'clock the priest walked Casement to the scaffold at Pentonville Prison. On his way 'Father McCarroll whispered to him: "now Roger for God and Kathleen Ní Houlihan." He answered, "Yes Father," and threw back his proud head with such a beautiful smile.'[80] At six minutes passed nine the prison bell announced the execution was over. The next day it was reported in various newspapers that a large crowd who had gathered outside of the prison 'began to cheer as soon as the first stroke of the bell was heard, and hats and handkerchiefs were waved by men and women.'[81] One week later Madame Tussauds, the famous London wax museum, announced that their exhibition now included a rather macabre new exhibit, a 'lifelike portrait model of Roger Casement.'[82]

After the execution, Gavan Duffy officially requested that Casement's body be released to his family for burial in Ireland. The Home Office denied the request, maintaining that Casement must be buried on the prison grounds at Pentonville. Gore-Booth signed a petition urging the Home Secretary to change his decision. It was all to no avail. She published a poem, aptly entitled 'heroic death, 1916,' lamenting Casement's fate:

> No cairn-shaped mound on a high windy hill
> With Irish earth the hero's heart enfolds
> But a burning grave at Pentonville
> The broken heart of Ireland holds.[83]

Casement's body remained in an unmarked grave at Pentonville for over fifty years, and when his body was finally repatriated in 1965 he received a state funeral.[84] Despite numerous requests to return his personal items, many of his possessions still remain in England. His diaries are held in the National Archives at Kew and his dress hat and sword were only returned to Ireland in March 2011.[85]

Immediately following his execution, the British government released an official statement, which included a repudiation of Gore-Booth's argument, 'the suggestion that Casement left Germany for the purpose of trying to stop the Irish rising was not raised at the trial, and is conclusively disproved not only by the facts there disclosed but by further evidence which has since become available.'[86] The conclusive evidence has never been divulged.

Gore-Booth later described her abhorrence of capital punishment in a speech to a London society, noting with horror how, 'the fore-knowledge of the exact minute of death is a form of mental torture entirely invented by human beings, in the fiendish ingenuity of vengeance sanctified by pious traditions. The world, as God made it, may be cruel in many things, but it is not cruel enough for that supreme and unnatural outrage.'[87] She published an emotional account of the 1916 executions entitled the 'Sinn Féin Rebellion.' The article was published in the August/September issue of the *Socialist Review*.[88] This periodical was committed to expressing pacifist ideals but Gore-Booth does not denigrate the armed rebellion anywhere in her article. In fact it is remarkable that the *Socialist Review* included her article at all. In the same issue the resolution of the Independent Labour Party's conference at Newcastle is printed, clarifying that the party refuse to support any war, against any government, even if that war is in defence of a nation,[89] and an editorial printed just pages before Gore-Booth's article, positions the *Socialist Review*'s stance that, 'in no degree do we approve the Sinn Fein rebellion. We do not approve armed rebellion at all, any more than any other form of militarism and war.'[90]

After establishing the leaders of the 1916 rebellion as people of good character, Gore-Booth provides an emotionally evocative description of how each man was executed in the most inhumane of ways. Recounting the execution of Padraig Pearse, whose 'unfaltering eyes ... he begged might be unbandaged that he might have his last look at Ireland seem to have unnerved the soldiers. Twice the order was given to fire, with no result.'[91] Gore-Booth's description of James Connolly's death emphasises the barbaric nature of the executions. Connolly was badly injured during fighting in the GPO and already 'dying in frightful agony, [he was] carried out on a stretcher and propped up to be shot, [he] could yet pray for the soldiers who formed the firing party.' Thomas MacDonagh 'thanked the court-martial who had just condemned him to death. He said: "It would not be seemly to go to my doom without trying to express, however inadequately, my sense of the high honour I enjoy in being one of those predestined to die in this generation for the cause of Irish freedom."' When John MacBride noticed a soldier in the firing party about to execute him show some emotion, he offered the soldier words of advice telling him, 'never let what you are doing to-day disturb you.'

Gore-Booth surmised that 'many thoughtful Englishmen must feel dubious of the wisdom of shooting a man who dies thanking you for the high honour you have done him in allowing so glorious a death.' Gore-Booth's article was reprinted in an Irish newspaper with the comment that 'whether viewed from a literary standpoint, or as an effort to get at the real genesis and facts of the rebellion, nothing has, in our opinion, so far been printed which can compare with it.'[92] In her private notes Gore-Booth expresses a rationalisation for the Easter Rising which is at odds with her publicly expressed ideal of pacifism. She writes that 'you cannot have liberty unless you imprison the enemies of liberty. You cannot have freedom without enslaving people. You cannot have peace unless you fight the militarists. You cannot have peace without war. In fact no perfect state can be established without the cruel and futile methods and machinery of the old order punishments, prisons, courts of justice and an army.'[93]

Her devotion to Roger Casement continued long after his execution. In 1918 Gore-Booth published a volume of poetry, *Broken Glory*, which is dedicated to the memory of August 3rd 1916, the date of Casement's execution.[94] The volume was published by Maunsel and fit naturally into their catalogue of Anglo-Irish literature; the twenty-seven poems focus specifically on the atrocities of the Easter Rising and the Great War. Her poem 'Government' equates the killing of Christ with the execution of Casement, 'Jesus Christ a thousand years ago ... And Roger Casement, just the other day.'[95] Similar religious imagery is evident in her poem 'Francis Sheehy Skeffington; Dublin, April 26, 1916,' comparing Sheehy Skeffington with Jesus, 'who in the Olive Garden agonized.'[96] This small volume is packed with strong political sentiments and includes a set of poems dedicated to Markievicz in prison.[97] The final poem in the volume is addressed to the Dublin poet Dora Sigerson Shorter, who died in 1918. The poem is subtitled, 'the sad years,' referring to Sigerson's final publication.[98] In her poem Gore-Booth clearly blames the atrocities of the Easter Rising for causing her death:

> You whom I never knew,
> Who lived remote, afar,
> Yet died of the grief that tore my heart.

David Gardiner remarks that the notion that Sigerson Shorter died of a broken heart following the 1916 executions became popularised through the writings of Gore-Booth and Katharine Tynan.[99]

In 1918 Gore-Booth published an article condemning Casement's execution in *The Catholic Bulletin*.[100] After the Rising British authorities established a new press censorship board and applied extreme controls regarding how the rebellion or its participants could be represented in the media. Brian Murphy's research on the *Catholic Bulletin* has uncovered how the journal's editor, J.J. O'Kelly, managed to by-pass these restrictions. O'Kelly 'was compelled to focus on the religious and social life of the men involved in the Rising,' and Murphy highlights how 'he did this in masterly fashion and to great effect. Simple and touching tributes to the leaders of the Rising gave way to accounts of the injured and imprisoned.'[101] Although Gore-Booth's article was published during a time of restrictive censorship rules, her article is hard-hitting. She employed Father McCarroll's final words to the condemned man for the title, 'For God and Kathleen Ni Houlihan.' In her conclusion Gore-Booth finally accepts the need for Casement to sacrifice himself for the greater cause of Irish freedom:

> Roger Casement was ready and willing to die, as he said, for the cause of Irish freedom. And indeed it might be said of him, that while many have died for their countries and for great causes in all ages, no man has ever in the annals of history done more than he did, by the manner of his dying, to exalt and glorify the country of his love. 'He died,' said one who was with him at the last, 'with all the faith of an Irish peasant woman . . . He marched to the scaffold with the dignity of a prince and towered straight as an arrow over all of us on the scaffold. He feared not death and prayed with me to the last. I have no doubt that he has gone to heaven.'[102]

Notes

1 EGB, 'Roger Casement,' *CE*, p. 511.
2 Roper, (ed.), *Prison Letters*, p. 53.
3 Ibid.
4 Dublin Castle Special Branch Files, CO 904/215/408.
5 NLI, MS 33,605 (1), letter from EGB to Hanna Sheehy Skeffington, May 1916.
6 Roper, (ed.), *Prison Letters*, p. 47.
7 NLI, MS 22, 654, article on Francis Sheehy Skeffington by EGB.
8 Roper, (ed.), *Prison Letters*, p. 51.
9 NLI, MS 22, 654, Francis Sheehy Skeffington.
10 Ibid.
11 Margaret Ward, *Hanna Sheehy Skeffington: A Life* (Cork: Attic Press, 1997), p. 161.
12 NLI, MS 22, 654, Francis Sheehy Skeffington.
13 NLI, MS 33,605 (5), letter from EGB to Hanna Sheehy Skeffington, May 1916.
14 Details of the inquiry were printed in *1916 Easter Rebellion Handbook* (Dublin: *Irish Times*, 1917).
15 Hanna Sheehy Skeffington, 'A Pacifist Dies,' in Roger McHugh (ed.), *Dublin 1916*, pp. 276–88.
16 Roper, (ed.), *Prison Letters*, p. 29.
17 Maude L. Deuchar, *The Sheehy Skeffington Case* (Manchester & London: National Labour Press, 1916). Deuchar normally wrote fiction and drama under the pseudonym Herbert Tremaine.
18 Eva Gore-Booth, *The Death of Fionavar from the Triumph of Maeve* (London: Erskine Macdonald, 1916).

19 Ibid, p. 11.

20 Kells Ingram, a Trinity College Dublin academic, published the ballad remembering the Irish rebellion of 1798 in *The Nation* (1 April 1843). The poem was revived in 1898, possibly inspiring Gore-Booth's dedication. Thank you to Ruán O'Donnell for pointing this out.

21 'New Books,' *MG* (9 October 1916), p. 3.

22 The book was supposedly printed by the highly esteemed William Morris Press in Albert Street, Manchester. This seems most unlikely since William Morris Press had offices in Albert Square, Manchester for a very short time, more than likely the printers closed there in 1884. Nicholas Salmon and David Taylor, 'Morris & Co. in Manchester,' *Journal of William Morris Studies*, 12:3 (Autumn 1997), 17–19.

23 'New Books,' *MG* (9 October 1916), p. 3.

24 Letter from Markievicz to EGB from Aylesbury Prison, 8 August 1916 in Roper, (ed.), *Prison Letters*, p. 150.

25 'Irish Rebel Illustrates Nonresistance Play,' *New York Times* (10 September 1916), p. 2.

26 NLI, MS 21,815, Holograph account of Dublin in the aftermath of the Easter Rising, by EGB.

27 Ibid.

28 EGB, *CE*, p. 53.

29 F.S.L. Lyons, 'From War to Civil War in Ireland,' in Brian Farrell (ed.), *The Irish Parliamentary Tradition*, p. 83.

30 Diana Norman, *A Life of Constance Markievicz*, p. 162.

31 Roper, (ed.), *Prison Letters*, p. 143.

32 Jacqueline Van Voris, *Constance de Markievicz in the Cause of Ireland* (Amherst: University of Massachusetts Press, 1967), p. 217.

33 Unofficial letter from Markievicz to EGB, in Roper, (ed.), *Prison Letters*, p. 143.

34 Ibid, p. 144. The image to which Markievicz refers is on page 15 of the *Death of Fionavar*.

35 Ibid.

36 Markievicz's dog reportedly rushed aboard the boat at Kingstown and none of the soldiers dared to touch him. He did not gain access to Holloway Prison with Markievicz, he was returned to Gore-Booth at her flat in Fitzroy Square.

37 Ibid, p. 66.

38 Including Van Voris, *Constance de Markievicz*, p. 217 and Anne Marreco, *The Rebel Countess* (Philadelphia: Chilton Books, 1967), p. 220.

39 Dublin Castle Special Branch Files, CO 904/209/297, report by Detective John Byrne – Constance Markievicz removed to H.M. Prison Aylesbury, 26 September 1916.

40 'In the House of Commons on 3rd August, Mr. Samuel, in reply to Mr. P. White, said all the other prisoners connected with the rebellion had

been removed to prisons in England, and it was intended to remove the Countess Markievicz also.' 'The Countess Markievicz,' the *The Irish Times* (12 August 1916), p.1. A further account of the same proceedings is also reported in the *Irish Independent* (3 August 1916), p. 3.

41 Letter from Markievicz to Gore-Booth, Aylesbury Prison, 8 August 1916 in Roper, (ed.), *Prison Letters*, p. 149.

42 See Spindler's own account: Karl Spindler, *Gun Running for Casement*, trans. W. Montgomery (London: W. Collins Sons & Co. Ltd, 1921).

43 See, Sonja Tiernan, 'Hidden in Plain Sight: Uncovering the History of Meath Women,' *Ríocht na Mídhe*: Meath Archaeological and Historical Society, XXI (2010), 93–109.

44 René MacColl, *Roger Casement: A New Judgment* (London: Hamish Hamilton, 1956), p. 249.

45 Ibid.

46 Ibid.

47 Geoffrey De Parmiter, *Roger Casement* (London: Arthur Barker Ltd, 1936), p. 331.

48 Ibid.

49 Ibid, p. 313.

50 Parliamentary Archives, Lloyd George Papers, LG/D/18/15/14, letter from EGB to C.P. Scott, 4 July 1916.

51 'Protest Hanging of Roger Casement,' *Boston Journal* (21 July 1916), p. 2.

52 Ibid.

53 Robert Schmuhl, 'Peering through the Fog: American Newspapers and the Easter Rising,' *Irish Communications Review* 12 (2010), 37.

54 Letter from EGB to C.P. Scott, 4 July 1916.

55 Lloyd George Papers, LG/D/18/15/14.

56 Ibid.

57 Ibid.

58 Lloyd George Papers, E/3/7/1, letter from EGB to C.P. Scott, 7 July 1916.

59 Ibid.

60 EGB, 'The Sinn Féin Rebellion,' *Socialist Review* (September 1916), p. 226.

61 Lloyd George Papers, E/3/7/2, transcript typed by EGB from *Dublin Evening Standard* (20 May 1916).

62 Lloyd George Papers, E/3/7/1.

63 Lloyd George Papers, E/3/7/3, letter from Fr. M. Ryan to Gavan Duffy, 12 July 1916.

64 Lloyd George Papers, E/3/7/3, letter from C.P. Scott to Lloyd George, 15 July 1916.

65 Pennsylvania State University Libraries, Eva Gore-Booth Collection, box 1, folder, 1, AX/B40/RBM/00139, letter from EGB to Mrs Gavan Duffy, 12 July 1916.

66 Sinéad McCoole, *Hazel: A Life of Lady Lavery 1880–1935* (Dublin: Lilliput Press, 1996), pp. 66–7.

67 John Lavery, *The Life of a Painter* (London: Casell and Co Ltd, 1940), p. 189.

68 Many thanks to Felix Larkin for alerting the author to this fact. Tate archive, London, 7245.1, letter from Margaret Gavan Duffy to John Lavery, 16 November 1916, as cited in Sinéad McCoole, *Passion and Politics: Sir John Lavery* (Dublin: Hugh Lane Gallery, 2010), p. 66.

69 For a transcript of the proceedings of the trial of Roger Casement for High Treason and his appeal to the court of criminal appeal see: George Knott (ed.), *Trial of Roger Casement* (Edinburgh: William Hodge & Company, 1917).

70 EGB, 'Correspondence: Roger Casement,' *MG* (29 July 1916), p. 4.

71 Lloyd George Papers, E/9/4/12, the case of Roger Casement; a confidential report, 21 July 1916.

72 Hansard Papers, Commons Sitting, HC Deb, vol. 552 cc749–60, 'the Roger Casement Papers,' 3 May 1956.

73 As cited in Lucy McDiarmid, *The Irish Art of Controversy* (Ithaca: Cornell University Press, 2005), p. 182.

74 Ibid.

75 Letter from Walter Hines Page to Robert Lansing, 3 July 1916, cited in Brian Lewis, 'The Queer Life and Afterlife of Roger Casement,' *Journal of the History of Sexuality* 14.4 (2005), 374.

76 Roper, (ed.), *Prison Letters*, p. 77.

77 Michael Begnal, 'Eva Gore-Booth on behalf of Roger Casement: An Unpublished Appeal,' *Éire-Ireland*, 6:1 (1971), 15.

78 De Parmiter, *Roger Casement*, p. 320.

79 B.L. Reid, *The Lives of Roger Casement* (London: The Yale Press, 1987), p. 434.

80 NLI, MS 40: 327/6, letter from EGB to R.M. Fox and Patricia Lynch, August 1916.

81 'Casement Hanged,' *MG* (4 August 1916), p. 12.

82 'Madame Tussaud's exhibition,' *The Observer* (13 August 1916), p. 5.

83 EGB, 'Heroic Death, 1916,' *CE*, pp. 508–9.

84 He is now buried in the republican plot at Glasnevin Cemetery in Dublin.

85 Casement wore his dress hat and sword for the ceremony of his knighthood in 1911. When his home was searched after his arrest in 1916, the items were amongst those removed by the Metropolitan Police. Many thanks to Mary O'Callaghan for alerting the author to the fact.

86 'The Refusal to Reprieve Casement: Official Statement,' *MG* (4 August 1916), p. 6.

87 NLI, MS 21,815, holograph account by EGB of her visit to Dublin in 1916.

88 EGB, 'The Sinn Féin Rebellion,' *Socialist Review* (September 1916), pp. 226–33.
89 *Socialist Review*, p. 287.
90 *Socialist Review*, p. 205. For further discussion see David Granville, a paper given at the 'Ripples of Freedom conference,' Dublin 13 May 2006, a text version is published in *Irish Democrat*, June/July 2006.
91 Ibid, p. 60.
92 Ibid, p. 56.
93 Pennsylvania State University Libraries, Eva Gore-Booth Collection, box 1, folder 17, AX/B40/RBM/00139, EGB notebook.
94 EGB, *Broken Glory* (Dublin: Maunsel, 1918).
95 Ibid, p. 7.
96 Ibid, p. 14.
97 Including, 'To Constance – in Prison,' and 'To C.M. on her Prison Birthday,' EGB, *Broken Glory*, pp. 10–11.
98 EGB, *Broken Glory*, p. 30. Dora Sigerson Shorter, *The Sad Years and Other Poems*, with memoir by Katharine Tynan (London: Constable, 1918).
99 David Gardiner, 'The Other Irish Renaissance: The Maunsel Poets,' p. 68.
100 EGB, 'For God and Kathleen Ni Houlihan,' *The Catholic Bulletin* (1918). The article was later republished by Roper in *Prison Letters*.
101 Brian Murphy, 'J.J. O'Kelly, 'The Catholic Bulletin and Contemporary Irish Cultural Historians,' *Archivium Hibernicum*, 44 (1989), 74–5.
102 Roper, (ed.), *Prison Letters*, p. 85.

10

Prison reform and military conscription in Ireland

'Outcast from joy and beauty, child of broken hopes forlorn'[1]

Markievicz was transferred to England on 8 August 1916, just days after Casement's execution. Gore-Booth and Roper were the first people granted a visit to see her at Aylesbury Prison. The women, dressed in their brightest clothes, finally saw Markievicz after months apart.[2] By now Gore-Booth and Markievicz were known to the authorities as women actively and publicly working against the British establishment. Not surprisingly the conversation between the two women was recorded by the prison matron, E.W. Sharp, who compiled a two page report. In the report, Sharp notes that Markievicz advised her sister to contact John Devoy if she required any assistance. Devoy acted as a key contact for Irish nationalists in America and he had established a channel of communication between the Irish rebels and forces in Germany. Markievicz may well have been concerned for her sister's safety. Devoy was a powerful ally who could have offered Gore-Booth an escape to America, if necessary. The fact that Devoy was a key orchestrator of the Rising and a central figure of the Irish revolutionary organisation Clan na Gael meant that any mention of Devoy was viewed as significant to British intelligence.

Sharp listed every detail discussed by the women, including people mentioned by Markievicz, such as 'Lucy Kenstone or Kempstone,' described as one of her chief messengers and a Dublin woman known as 'Prole.' Sharp notes that 'a short time before the Revolution Markievicz had promised to address a meeting. When the date of the meeting arrived, the leaders would not allow Markievicz to go as it was too near the time of the Revolution; she thereupon wrote a seditious speech, dressed Prole in some of her clothing and sent her to deliver the speech, and explain the reason of her absence.'[3] The report was sent by the Governor of Aylesbury Prison, W.H. Winder, to the under-secretary for Ireland, Robert Chalmers. Winder points out that 'the woman named Prole is identical with Prob – a person who is often referred to in letters written by the Irish Interned Prisoners.'[4] The woman was in fact Maria Perolz, a prominent member of the ICA and the IWWU as well as the registered owner of the nationalist magazine *Spark*, of which Markievicz was the editor. Winder was apparently oblivious to the fact that Perolz had been arrested for her part in the Rising and had been interned at Aylesbury Prison. She had only been released two weeks before Markievicz's arrival there.[5]

A full investigation into the meeting between Markievicz and Gore-Booth was launched. Edward O'Farrell, assistant to the recently appointed chief secretary of Ireland, Henry Duke, also received a copy of the report at his office in Dublin Castle.[6] O'Farrell welcomed the information and he implored Edward Troup, assistant under-secretary at the Home Office, to ensure that Markievicz and her sister be allowed to discuss the Rebellion at future prison visits as 'useful information may be obtained by inquiries on the lines suggested by the conversation, and in the case of future visits to this lady the Irish government would be glad that no obstacle be placed in the way of discussion of the Rebellion, it being understood that a similar report can be made of anything stated that might be of interest to the Government.'[7] The Special Branch of the Royal Irish Constabulary opened a personality file at Dublin Castle, the administrative centre of British intelligence in Ireland. Reports of Markievicz and Gore-Booth's activities were sent to the Castle and included in this file until 1921.

After Markievicz was transferred to England, Gore-Booth became concerned that hostile feelings towards her sister were increasing in that country. Immediately after the Rising rumours circulated that Markievicz was responsible for the death of a policeman, Constable Michael Lahiff of the Dublin Metropolitan Police, an officially unarmed force.[8] Lahiff was shot as he attempted to gain entry to Stephens Green. It was rumoured that Markievicz shot the man in the head and gloried in it. The story later appeared in one of the most popular narrative accounts of the Rising by Max Caulfield. Caulfield claimed that Markievicz 'took aim with her Mauser rifle-pistol. As she fired, two men beside her also shot. Lahiffe slumped to the ground, hit by three bullets. "I shot him!" shouted the Countess delightedly. "I shot him."'[9] This version of events has never been conclusively proved and Markievicz was not formally charged with shooting Lahiffe. However, versions of this story appeared in newspapers across the globe, including the *New York Times*, who announced on 30 April 1916, 'Countess Markievicz reported to have shot a Castle guard.'[10]

The idea that Markievicz shot an unarmed man and then celebrated as he dropped to the ground made her appear ruthless and vicious to people in England. Markievicz's biographer, Anne Haverty, is clear that 'whether she did it or not is surely academic. This was now a war situation and it was the duty of a good soldier on either side to shoot the enemy.'[11] However, after careful consideration, Haverty maintains that 'it would seem more characteristic of Con, if she were there, to take the constable prisoner.'[12] Gore-Booth did not believe that her sister took pleasure in shooting soldiers or policemen, she wrote to her friend Katharine Tynan describing how:

> Others have been strangely unsympathetic and misunderstanding about her, putting down to the absurd sentiments such as a mad desire to kill soldiers, which makes me laugh when I think of her universally friendly nature. In absolute want of any justice the accounts of her hob nobbing with her prisoners in Stephens Green are much more like her. She is incapable of thinking of individuals as enemies anyone who knows her knows that. She was fighting for a cause without anger and she told the Court-martial, 'it was the most glorious week of my life, Ireland was free for a week and now you can shoot me if you like.'[13]

In an attempt to sway opinion, Gore-Booth wrote to the *Daily Chronicle* 'with the forlorn hope of rousing a little sympathy and . . . in answer to an abusive one [letter] in the *Daily News* at the same time. I have tried to put clearly her love of the Irish country, the Irish people.'[14]

Gore-Booth became deeply concerned about her sister's welfare in prison, especially as Markievicz could associate only with convicted criminals. On 14 November 1916 the Home Secretary, Herbert Samuel, announced that the male Irish prisoners would be moved to Lewes Prison in East Sussex where they could associate together.[15] Roper described how Markievicz suffered because she was not allowed to associate with other political prisoners, 'her closest friends had been executed and she had been condemned to death, and then plunged into what was almost solitary confinement, as there was no one of her own mental level in the prison [Aylesbury] most of the time she was there.'[16] Five other Irishwomen had been sent to Aylesbury Prison for their part in the Rising, by November 1916 two of the women still remained there.[17] Winifred Carney had been arrested along with James Connolly at the makeshift headquarters in 16 Moore Street and Helena Moloney, a founder member of the ICA and president of the IWWU, was also interned for her part in the Rising.[18] Markievicz was not allowed contact with these women as they were held as internees in a different wing of the prison. Markievicz was placed in a criminal category as a 'star class' prisoner along with murderers and those charged with manslaughter.

In a personal plea to the Home Office, Carney offered to give up her privileges as an internee and to adopt a criminal status in order to provide Markievicz with companionship. Carney vowed that 'I will freely and gladly agree to live in the prison and conform to the rules with regard to food, work, hours of exercise and clothes if necessary,' adding her personal pledge 'not to make either now nor at any future date, political capital out of this arrangement.'[19] Her request was denied. In a letter to Tynan, Gore-Booth described how Markievicz 'has had worse suffering than any other Irish prisoner as she is the only one who is isolated (being the only woman convict) and forced to associate with people whose conversation is filthy.'[20] Gore-Booth arranged for a meeting with Captain Jack White, an ex-British army officer and a campaigner for Irish independence. White knew Markievicz through his involvement with the Irish labour movement. He had instigated the formation of the ICA by offering to drill the workers for their protection during the 1913 Dublin Lock-Out. White was concerned for Markievicz's emotional health, and he was aware of the stress of prison, having recently served three months for organising a Welsh miners' strike in protest at the execution of James Connolly. White, like Gore-Booth, was a free-thinking radical.

White instigated a meeting with the chief secretary of Ireland, Duke, to discuss the issue of Markievicz's imprisonment. After the meeting, Gore-Booth sent him a statement regarding her sister's prison conditions:

> Constance De Markievicz is the only one of the Irish Rebel convict prisoners who is not to receive the benefit of the most important of the

> late Home Secretary's concessions and this, notwithstanding the fact that she was on the list published by the Home Secretary of those who would benefit by these privileges. She is not to have the chief and most valuable privilege of association and conversation at stated intervals with other Irish prisoners, not because of any faulty conduct on her part, but because she is a woman. To overcome the practical difficulty may need a little commonsense adjustment on the part of the authorities, but surely in view of the suffering involved in the present state of things for this prisoner it is not too much to hope that the Home Office will make the necessary arrangements to carry out the Home Secretary's pledge.[21]

The statement concludes by describing Markievicz as living with 'the atmosphere and conversation of a brothel.'[22] White sent a copy of the statement to Duke explaining that, 'Countess Markievicz is one of my greatest friends and in many ways one of the finest women that ever breathed. It's horrible to think of her in the surroundings she is now, when but for her sex she would immediately have the privilege of associating with decent and sympathetic people.'[23] At Gore-Booth's request, White asked the Chief Secretary of Ireland to move Markievicz to Lewes Prison so that she could be with her fellow Irish political prisoners. The request was forwarded to the Home Secretary, George Cave, who had recently been appointed to the post. Cave denied the request.[24] An official at the Home Office responded that 'it is impossible to organize a "woman's side" at Lewes Prison to enable this prisoner to associate with the Irish male prisoners.'[25]

By the end of 1916 hundreds of Irish people remained in prison in England, most without any sentence. The Irish Parliamentary Party (IPP) MPs, especially John Dillon and John Redmond, consistently called for a general release of prisoners and for martial law in Ireland to be suspended. Although Asquith's party had a close association with the IPP, the Prime Minister refused all requests for leniency. The action of the British authorities to the Rising was now viewed by many as being what Charles Townsend describes as 'abnormally severe.'[26] The executions of most of the leadership and harsh sentences imposed on many more people after the Rising caused some political opponents to question Asquith's ability as leader. The Prime Minister had also overseen Britain's entry into the bloodiest battle of the Great War, just weeks after the Rising. When the Battle of the Somme finally ended in November 1916, Britain had suffered horrendous casualties of over 420,000 men. Asquith's own son,

Raymond, was killed during the battle. By December the media attack on him had escalated in the pages of the *Daily Mail* and *The Times* causing even Asquith's own party to question his ability to lead Britain through the Great War. He was forced to resign from the position of Prime Minister later that month.

Lloyd George had proved himself to be a capable secretary of state for war and he was viewed as resourceful in his dealings with Irish affairs, he was quickly nominated as Prime Minister. One of his first actions as parliamentary leader was to grant an amnesty for all those Irish interned at Frongoch Internment Camp and at Reading Gaol, as well as the two women, Carney and Molony, interned at Aylesbury. Lloyd George used these releases as a public relations campaign to help improve Irish feelings towards England. As legal historian Seán McConville observes, 'the Home Office was determined to maximise the political benefits of the releases, and to get all internees back to Ireland for Christmas.'[27] However, those prisoners held as convicted criminals, including Markievicz, remained in prison.

Gore-Booth continued to visit her sister, as well as numerous Conscientious Objectors in prison. She soon became aware of unsatisfactory conditions and unfair sentences. In a smuggled letter, Markievicz advised her sister how to approach prison reform, detailing a list of questions that all political prisoners should be asked:

> What do you weigh? What is your normal weight?
> What do you get to eat? Can you eat it?
> How much exercise do you get per day?
> How often do you get Underclothes?
> Are you constipated? Can you get medicine?
> What temperature is the room you work in?
> What is your task? How much do you do in a week?[28]

Gore-Booth regularly encountered prisoners whom she believed were 'quite unjustly convicted.'[29] While Markievicz was in Aylesbury, the socialist and anti-war campaigner Alice Wheeldon was sentenced to that prison for conspiring to assassinate Lloyd George.

Wheeldon, a member of the No Conscription Fellowship, established a network to support and shelter COs on the run. Wheeldon used her own house in Derby as a hideaway for men evading the military draft. She was targeted by an MI5 agent, Francis Vivian, who posed as a CO on the run. Through a complex undercover operation Wheeldon and three members of her family were arrested and charged with conspiracy to assassinate Lloyd George and Labour Party leader Arthur Henderson with poison darts.[30] Wheeldon was convicted mainly through the evidence of undercover agents who were not required to attend the trial. There was a public outcry as to the method of securing this conviction.[31] Gore-Booth was appalled but there was little action that she could take in this instance. The case inspired her to lobby on behalf of other female prisoners.

She became aware of another woman in prison with Markievicz, who was sentenced to seven years for shooting her lover. Roper describes how the woman 'was almost crazy with anger and fear when she did it, because she had just told him she was going to have a child and his reply was to inform her of his forthcoming marriage to another woman.'[32] While the man was virtually unharmed, the woman was imprisoned in Aylesbury and her child was placed in care when he reached the age of one. Gore-Booth contacted the suffragist Anne Cobden Sanderson, who had successfully campaigned on behalf of women imprisoned for refusing to pay tax. The women, members of the Women's Tax Resistance League, refused to pay tax until they received a vote at general elections.[33] Codben Sanderson was a close personal friend of George MacDonald, with whom Gore-Booth and Roper had stayed in Italy. After an intense campaign Cobden Sanderson secured the woman's release from prison. The woman and her child were reunited and left England to start a new life together in the colonies.

In March 1917, Gore-Booth was offered some hope for the release of her sister from prison. An Irish republican priest, Father Albert of the Capuchin order, was respected as the chaplain of the IRB Supreme Council. He wrote informing her that 'the Lord Mayor of Dublin called an informal meeting at the Mansion House to consider … the release of all our dear friends.'[34] While there was no immediate action taken to release Markievicz from prison, the Home Secretary granted Gore-Booth one extra visit per month to see her.[35] Within weeks the direction of the Great War shifted dramatically. In April 1917, America joined forces with Britain and her allies. The Irish question was again the focus of international attention and by June of that year Bonar Law announced a general amnesty for all Irish prisoners in England.

The amnesty was called for numerous reasons, partly to appease the large Irish American population but also in an attempt to placate Irish nationalists and to focus on ending the Great War. Following Redmond's suggestion, Lloyd George called for an Irish Convention, to include a panel of Irish representatives who would decide on the appropriate action to establish Home Rule. On 16 June, Bonar Law announced to the House of Commons that the Irish Convention was 'a great experiment . . . which would mark a new era in the relations of Ireland with the United Kingdom and the Empire, and it was desirable that the Convention should meet in an atmosphere of harmony and good will.'[36] In order to establish harmony it was necessary to release all of the Irish rebel prisoners. Within days of the announcement, a Home Office official called to Gore-Booth at her flat in London with the news that she could go to Aylesbury and accompany her sister home.

A group of women including Gore-Booth, Roper, Helena Moloney and Maria Perolz went to Aylesbury Prison. The women returned with Markievicz to Gore-Booth and Roper's flat at 33 Fitzroy Square. In the years after the Rising this flat had become a base for Irish nationalists in London, Hanna Sheehy Skeffington later described it as 'a home for all rebels.'[37] On 20 June 1917 Markievicz and Gore-Booth went to the House of Commons where they met with Jack White. In an act of defiance the group retired to the terrace of the House and ate strawberries and cream – the *Manchester Guardian* reported the event under the heading, 'strange times in the House.'[38]

Gore-Booth accompanied her sister back to Dublin onboard the *Munster* from Holyhead to the south Dublin port of Kingstown (Dun Laoghaire). A large crowd gathered on Carlisle Pier at Kingstown to welcome Markievicz. People lined the railway track for miles along the route to Dublin city, cheering as the train in which the Countess was travelling passed. Gore-Booth and Markievicz arrived in Westland Row train station in Dublin city to witness an extraordinary scene. Markievicz was the last of those imprisoned after the Rising to return to Ireland and thousands of people turned out to welcome her home. Kathleen Lynn drove the women along a route, passing Liberty Hall, the GPO, the College of Surgeons and Jacobs' factory, key places of rebel occupation during Easter week. The *Irish Independent* reported excitedly that 'the crowd cheered themselves hoarse.'[39] A London newspaper, the *Evening Standard*, announced their surprise that Gore-Booth was present, even though she 'had little or no sympathy with Sinn Féin.'[40] The *Irish Independent* was quick to clarify that 'although she is not a Sinn Feiner, she is an Irishwoman in sympathy with all who love liberty.'[41]

Markievicz had received instruction on Catholicism from the prison chaplain, Reverend Father McMahon, while imprisoned in Mountjoy. She was formally received into the Catholic Church through a baptism at Clonliffe College on 24 June, taking Anastasia as her baptism name. Shortly after Markievicz's release, Gore-Booth published a pamphlet entitled *Rhythms of Art*, for the League of Peace and Freedom.[42] In the article she discusses the importance of real beauty and art, as opposed to 'the rays of military glory,' concluding that 'at present the world seems bewitched by the malign powers of fear, cruelty and obedience; slowly, indeed, do we fight our way towards our far-off ideals of peace and freedom.'[43] Gore-Booth remained devoted to pacifist organisations and was quick to act when the government announced their intention to extend conscription.

In March 1918, the Irish Convention recommended the enactment of the Irish Home Rule Bill 1914. In a desperate effort to increase the number of soldiers fighting at the front, the British government agreed to enact Home Rule under the condition that conscription would be extended to Ireland. On 16 April 1918 the extension of the Military Service Bill, enforcing conscription in Ireland, was announced. This new legislation would ensure that all Irish men between the ages of eighteen and fifty would be called to join the British army. Roper describes the move as 'incredible to everyone connected with Ireland that England could really for a moment contemplate forcing men to fight for her who not two years before had risen against her, had seen their leaders executed and hundreds of their men and women imprisoned.'[44] Members of the IPP walked out of Westminster in protest. John Dillon and Joseph Devlin returned to Ireland to organise against conscription.

On 18 March, a meeting was held in the Lord Mayor of Dublin's residence at the Mansion House. The Lord Mayor, Lawrence O'Neill, hosted the meeting which saw the formation of the Irish Anti-Conscription Committee (IACC). The committee included members from all sections of Irish nationalist and trade organisations including Dillon and Devlin, Éamon de Valera and Arthur Griffith of Sinn Féin, Thomas Johnson and Michael Egan representing Irish labour and trade union movements and William O'Brien and Timothy Healy, from the political party the All-for-Ireland League

(AFIL). The Irish bishops were quick to support the anti-conscription movement and addressed the issue at their conference in Maynooth. The IACC developed an anti-conscription pledge, denying 'the right of the British government to enforce compulsory service in this country, we pledge ourselves solemnly to one another to resist conscription by the most effective means at our disposal.'[45] The Catholic bishops agreed that this pledge would be taken at the door of every church around the country before mass the following Sunday, 21 April.

Political instability in Ireland again intensified as anti-conscription activities increased, including a general workers' strike on 23 April. Esther Roper sent her brother, Reginald, to Dublin to ascertain details of the situation. Reginald Roper brought a copy of Gore-Booth's manuscript *Broken Glory* with him. He met with the Dublin publishers Maunsel Press and the pro-republican volume of poetry was surprisingly passed by the British censor and published by the press.[46] Among the verses dedicated to those who died during Easter week, was a poem entitled 'Government,' which clearly attacked British politicians, whom she described as 'savage and blind.'[47] The *Irish Independent* highlighted the volume as an expression of Gore-Booth's 'unswerving loyalty to native land, friends, and kindred.'[48] While in Dublin, Reginald Roper also met with Markievicz and brought up-to-date details of Irish activities back to Gore-Booth in London.

By the end of April, British Intelligence in Ireland claimed to have uncovered a Sinn Féin plot with Germany and they arrested seventy-three members of the organisation. Markievicz looked upon the idea of a German plot as a 'comic opera.'[49] She was among those arrested and deported to England without trial. She was imprisoned in Holloway Jail, however this time she was not on her own. She was imprisoned with Kathleen Clarke and Maud Gonne. Clarke, wife of the executed Rising leader, Tom Clarke, had established the Irish National Aid and Volunteer Dependants' Fund in order to grant financial assistance to the families of those killed or imprisoned as a result of the rebellion. Clarke employed the services of Michael Collins to organise and execute the fund, a position which helped him rise through nationalist ranks. Gonne, a prominent activist had, in 1900, established the first female political organisation since the Ladies Land League, Inghinidhe na hÉireann, which served to inspire a new generation of nationalist women.

Markievicz wrote to Gore-Booth from Holloway explaining that the imprisonments will 'rebound on our oppressors. Myself I think it is about the best thing that could have happened for Ireland, as there was so little to be done there, only propaganda, and our arrests carry so much further than speeches.'[50] The arrests seemed to inspire a more effective propaganda campaign. A full outline of the proceedings of the anti-conscription conference in the Mansion House was compiled by de Valera and addressed to Woodrow Wilson, then president of America. O'Neill arranged to personally meet with Wilson and give him the documents which were later published as a pamphlet by Maunsel Press, entitled simply *Ireland's Case against Conscription.*[51]

For her part in the propaganda campaign Gore-Booth wrote to British newspapers. Within days of her sister's arrest her letter 'The ruin preparing in Ireland' was published in the *Manchester Guardian* and received much attention. The letter opens with the determined assurance that in Dublin, 'special attention is drawn to the union of all classes in determined resistance to conscription, a resistance to the death which is being undertaken in a spirit of passionate revolt and religious faith which may turn Ireland into a nation of rebels and martyrs, but never into an army of conscripts.'[52] She detailed recent atrocities perpetrated by the British army in Ireland including a bayonet attack which killed one man and injured three others. On 29 March 1917, a group of British soldiers arrived to clear a public meeting room in Carrigaholt, County Clare. As people were walking out of the hall, the soldiers forced their bayonets into the backs of passers-by. The soldiers absurdly claimed that 'the people pressed on the bayonets.'[53] Thomas Russell, a local Irish language teacher, died from his injuries. Gore-Booth highlights the incident as 'provocation' against passive resistance.

In order to animate the determination of Irish people not to accept enforced conscription, Gore-Booth quotes an unnamed Irish woman landowner as saying:

> I am a farmer, I have farmed land all my life. Your government has demanded compulsory tillage and compulsory military service. That means that women must till the land. We will not do it. If my brother is taken he will not be taken alive, and I shall be left with farm and stock. I will do this. Neither crops nor cattle shall go to you. I will kill the stock; I will destroy the crop if I have to dig it up by the roots with my hands, and then I will take my rifle. I have used a rifle all my life, and I will take it and go out and fight and die.[54]

The letter concludes with the warning that although conflict between Ireland and England has been ongoing for centuries, the anti-conscription campaign was different because in this instance Ireland was 'the first time for many a year, united as a nation; the very policemen go about with no-conscription badges.'[55] Gore-Booth's campaign against the introduction of conscription in Ireland differs immensely from her previous campaigns against conscription in England. Her work there was based on ideals of pacifism and the promotion of choice for the individual. In her campaign against conscription in Ireland, Gore-Booth never mentions pacifist ideals but focuses instead on the fact that the introduction of conscription is yet another forced oppression of Irish people by British forces.

Gore-Booth's letter gained much attention – an article in the *Manchester Guardian* questioning the Vatican's support of the Irish Bishop's campaign quotes Miss Gore-Booth's 'remarkable letter.'[56] Days later Sidney Parry from Oxmead in Surrey wrote to the *Manchester Guardian* exclaiming how 'the striking letter of Miss Gore-Booth ... compels all thoughtful men and women to pause. We English people want above all things to win the war, and we ask ourselves whether the conscription of Ireland against her will is not the way to lose it. We may deplore Ireland's action, but we cannot ignore it.'[57]

Throughout these months campaigning, Gore-Booth was not allowed to visit Markievicz. Indeed, Markievicz was not allowed any visitors at all until August 1917, a fact which Gore-Booth informed the *Daily Express* about and which was subsequently reported on in the *New York Times*.[58] When Gore-Booth was finally granted access to see her sister, the visits were again recorded by prison officials. Reporting on the first visit the wardress, L.M. Grist, notes how Markievicz boasted about training her cocker spaniel dog, Poppet, 'to strafe everything English on the journey over.'[59] Despite British insistence, forced conscription of Irish men into the British army was never introduced. Markievicz wrote to Gore-Booth explaining that 'it wasn't talk blocked conscription: it was the astounding fact that the whole male population left at home and most of the women and kids would have died rather than fight for England, and they simply did not dare exterminate a nation.'[60]

Gore-Booth was moved to write another pacifist play. *The Sword of Justice* was the final one of her plays to be published during her lifetime.[61] In her introduction she alludes to the mistreatment of

Conscientious Objectors and the Irish rebel leaders, noting that, 'I have tried hard to give the devil more than his due, and his advocate a very favourable hearing. Forgiveness has not improved the murderer, it has merely increased his opportunities for evil. Everything has turned out for the worst in a way that might have been foreseen by the most bigoted of military tribunals.'[62] The play was performed in Tokyo in 1925, shortly before Gore-Booth's death.[63] Her friend from the Aëthnic Union, Thomas Baty, was then living there and it can be assumed that he oversaw production of the play.

The short prose play is based on the Christian story of Giovanni Gualberto who swore to avenge his brother's murder. The traditional tale concludes when Gualberto confronts the murderer on Good Friday at the church of San Miniato, and rather than seeking revenge he forgives the man. Gore-Booth based her play on the imagined events after Giovanni forgave his brother's murderer. This provides an interesting human dimension to the play as Gore-Booth strives to understand the difficulties and paradoxes of forgiveness. The main theme of the play emerges as a damnation of capital punishment. Gore-Booth shows that regardless of events, all actions must be worked out through the divine law of justice and even a murderer who commits the most hideous of crimes should not be executed. The *Occult Review* delighted with this message and in an appraisal of the play W.H. Cheeson observes that 'Miss Gore-Booth does not run the risk of dangerously exciting the reader who believes in capital punishment. Our poet asks, through one of her characters, "Can you wipe out a bloodstain by pouring more blood on it?"'[64]

Editor of Gore-Booth's plays, Frederick Lapisardi describes *The Sword of Justice* as the most perfectly constructed of her dramas. He notes how Yeats once drew a diagram to show how a play should be constructed. The diagram 'shows a wave-like line moving steadily upward. At the crest of each wave, Yeats penned the words: *climax, climax climax*.'[65] *The Sword of Justice* accomplishes just that as 'the action of the play moves in ever increasing intensity through a series of climaxes, each dependant on those before it, until the major climax / reversal / resolution is reached; then it ends abruptly leaving the audience to ponder the meaning of the story.'[66] The illegal journal the *Tribunal* also praised the publication, describing it as 'a play of intense dramatic power depicting the clash between pacifist and militarist ideals.'[67]

On 11 November 1918, an armistice was called. The Great War was finally over, but many COs remained in prison as did the Sinn Féin members who had been imprisoned for their support of a supposed German plot against Britain. Gore-Booth led a meeting at Essex Hall in London, demanding the immediate release of prisoners and for the abolition of conscription in Britain.[68] One month later a general election was announced to take place on 14 December. This was the first British general election since December 1910. Due to war, the election originally scheduled for 1915 did not occur. This was also the first general election to take place after the Representation of the People Act 1918 was introduced. The act vastly reformed the British electoral system by removing virtually all property qualifications, enabling men over twenty-one years of age to vote. Without electoral reform, millions of men who returned from fighting for their country would not have been entitled to a political franchise. Similarly millions of women who had actively supported the British war effort would also be excluded. Therefore, the act granted women over thirty years of age, who adhered to some property qualification, a vote at general elections. These two reform measures vastly increased the size of the Irish electorate and enabled women to vote in general elections for the first time. What should have been a victory celebration for Gore-Booth was overshadowed by the fact that her sister remained in prison and Ireland remained under British rule.

In Ireland the Sinn Féin Party were victorious at the election. The IPP, now under the leadership of John Dillon since Redmond's death earlier that year, was almost wiped out at the polls. Sinn Féin secured seventy-three seats out of a possible one hundred and five. The IPP won only six seats. Markievicz was returned as an MP for St Patrick's Division of Dublin and thus became the first woman ever to be elected to the British House of Commons. In line with Sinn Féin policy she refused to swear allegiance to the British Crown and thus rejected her seat at Westminster.[69] Significantly, out of seventeen female candidates who stood for election in 1918, Markievicz was the only one to be elected. She remained the only female candidate to be elected to the House of Commons on her own record for a number of years. The majority of female MPs received their seats through a process known as the widow's route, through which they occupied their husband's seat, often on his demise. In 1919 Lady Astor became the first woman to take her seat in the House of Commons through this very system. She was elected at a by-election, taking her husband's seat after he relinquished it to enter the House of Lords.[70]

Markievicz received a letter from Lloyd George at Holloway Prison inviting her to the House of Commons for the opening day of Sessions. Letters had been sent to each elected MP indiscriminately and Markievicz thoroughly enjoyed replying to it.[71] Markievicz's election was reported by Gore-Booth's friend, Thomas Baty, with glee. In an article by him he announced how she will not be bothered to attend Westminster. The mood of this article alters as Baty attacks the leader of the WSPU, noting how, 'Christabel Pankhurst nearly won: the most sedate publicists are to be found wishing she had quite won. They would like to have had the novel and inexpensive sensation of a lady member. Perhaps they were not without hope that Christabel would sooner or later do something wild which would set back the feminine clock.'[72]

Pankhurst ran for election in Smethwick but was defeated at the polls. Shortly after her defeat she moved to the United States and the WSPU disbanded. Gore-Booth made a public announcement in the *Daily Mail* regarding the election results, noting that 'women were not defeated as women. No special surprise of antagonism was aroused by their standing. Their failure is not attributed to their sex, but to the special conditions of the present election.'[73] The general election was won by a coalition of Conservatives, Liberals and a minority number of Labour and Independent MPs, forming a government led by Lloyd George.

The elected members of Sinn Féin formed the first Dáil Éireann on 21 January 1919. The members did not accept the title MP but took on the title TD (Teachatai Dala, Deputies of Parliament). The Dáil convened at the Round Room in the Lord Mayor of Dublin's residence, the Mansion House. The Declaration of Independence was formally adopted declaring Dáil Éireann the official Parliament of the Irish Republic. Only twenty-seven TDs were in attendance as the majority of those elected were still held in British prisons. The roll was called announcing the seventy-three names of TDs, the response on thirty-four occasions was simply Fe Glas ag Gallaibh (imprisoned abroad).[74] As the first Dáil met, two members of the RIC were killed by Irish Volunteers in County Tipperary. The Dáil supported the attack as an act of war against the foreign oppressor and acknowledged the Volunteers as the official army of the Irish Republic. The Volunteers later changed their name to the Irish Republican Army

(IRA). This marked the beginning of the Irish War of Independence, also known as the Anglo-Irish War.

In February 1919, Kathleen Clarke became ill in Holloway Prison and she was released into the care of Gore-Booth. Clarke stayed at Fitzroy Square until she was well enough to return home to Dublin.[75] Clarke later wrote that Gore-Booth 'was the essence of kindness to me, though I was a perfect stranger to her.[76] That same month Michael Collins orchestrated the escape of Irish political prisoners from English jails, most notably de Valera who escaped from Lincoln Jail with his help. Markievicz was released on 10 March and she went to stay with her sister in London for a number of days. Gore-Booth and Hanna Sheehy Skeffington immediately organised a public meeting calling for the release of the remaining Irish prisoners. The meeting took place at Essex Hall in London, adopting a resolution:

> (1) That Ireland is entitled to the right of self determination, and that the decision of her duly elected representatives in this matter must be respected and accepted. (2) That we demand the immediate release of all political prisoners both those who have been held for months without charge or trial and those who have been convicted and sentenced for political offences.[77]

The British government, fearful that the influenza pandemic of 1918–19 would spread through the prison population, released numerous Irish political prisoners that month.

While in London Gore-Booth arranged for Markievicz to meet with British trade union leaders and socialist activists to discuss economic matters. Markievicz could not resist a visit to the cloakroom of the House of Commons to see where her name had been etched over one of the coat pegs allotted to MPs.[78] She returned to Dublin in time for the Dáil to re-convene on 1 April 1919. De Valera was duly elected as the President, he nominated his cabinet; Eoin MacNeill – Industry, Michael Collins – Finance, Arthur Griffith – Home Affairs and Markievicz was elected as Minister for Labour. She became the first woman to be elected as a minister in cabinet. However, she did not remain free for very long, within months she was arrested again. In June 1919 Markievicz was charged with making a seditious speech in Newmarket, County Limerick and was imprisoned in Cork Jail. By September 1919 the British government officially proclaimed Sinn Féin an illegal organisation and Dáil Éireann an illegal assembly.

The political situation in Ireland rapidly deteriorated when in February 1920 Lloyd George approved the establishment of a special force of temporary constables for the RIC. The auxiliary force, known as the Black and Tans due to the colour of their uniforms, was meant to target the IRA but they inflicted untold horrors on the Irish population at large. Roper describes how, 'the English ex-soldiers recruited into the Royal Irish Constabulary and the ex-officers recruited as Auxiliaries at £1 a day with rations and uniform to assist the R.I.C., became violent at once. They were all armed, and began shooting people, burning villages and houses.'[79] Markievicz was released from Cork Jail in October 1919 and spent most of the next year on the run. She was in danger of arrest or attack by the Black and Tans. Gore-Booth became extremely anxious about the situation in Ireland and feared for her sister's safety. Due to consistent overwork and emotional stress she became quite ill. She and Roper moved from the centre of London, taking a house in the less polluted area of Hampstead at 14 Frognal Gardens. In order to gain some respite, she and Roper went to Italy where they would spend much of the year 1920–21.

The two women went first to stay with George and Margaret Gavan Duffy in Rome. Gore-Booth and Roper established a lasting friendship with the couple during the course of Casement's trial. After acting as Casement's solicitor, Gavan Duffy became deeply committed to the struggle for Irish independence. He and his wife moved to Ireland shortly after Casement was executed and he successfully stood as a Sinn Féin candidate for South County Dublin in the 1918 general election. In 1920 he and his wife moved to Rome. Gavan Duffy was fluent in Italian and he acted as an envoy for Sinn Féin, seeking international support for Ireland's freedom.

Although she was not Catholic, while she was staying in Rome, Gore-Booth attended a public audience with Pope Benedict XV at the Vatican. As the Pope passed amongst the gathered group, he gave individual blessings as each person kissed his ring. When it came to Gore-Booth's turn she began speaking to him rapidly in Italian. She told him of the current political situation in Ireland and of her sister's dangerous predicament in light of the new Black and Tan force. The Pope listened carefully. Roper looked on anxiously, later describing how the Pope's 'long pause appeared to alarm his attendants and some of them came hastily down the room.'[80] However, Benedict agreed to bless a set of rosary beads for Markievicz. The

Catholic religion had become deeply significant to her. Markievicz viewed it as the true religion of the Irish people. Sheehy Skeffington acknowledged that Markievicz was 'impressed by the great devotion of the boys of Fianna Na h-Éireann . . . Markievicz declared her desire to become a Catholic, to be with the boys in death.'[81] By the end of 1919 Markievicz had become concerned that British authorities were attempting to influence the Pope against Ireland. Gore-Booth's personal plea to Benedict was almost certainly an attempt to influence him to support the quest for Irish independence.[82]

After their stay in Rome, Gore-Booth and Roper travelled to Naples and Florence. Gore-Booth stayed in constant contact with her sister and was unaware that letters arriving from various prisons to her at Italian hotels caused some concern locally. On at least one occasion her hotel room was searched by police in Italy.[83] She also wrote of another incident to her friend, the human rights activist, T.P. Conwil-Evans, describing how, 'most mysterious people turned up yesterday, and very rough-looking men smoking large cigars, and lurking on the balcony, listening to our conversations about Con, etc. They had diplomatic passports, and if they weren't politicians doing themselves proud, they were Black and Tans on a peaceful mission, looking for trouble.'[84] Gore-Booth's health continued to deteriorate and she took solace visiting galleries and cathedrals throughout Italy. The two women ended their time in Italy with a visit to Bordighera where they had first met each other in 1896.

Notes

1 EGB, *Broken Glory* (Dublin: Maunsel, 1918), p. 10.

2 In a letter from Markievicz she implores Gore-Booth to, 'always visit criminals in your best clothes.' After this Roper and Gore-Booth 'used to borrow every bright thing our friends possessed to wear when we visited prisons.' Roper, (ed.), *Prison Letters*, p. 151.

3 Dublin Castle Special Branch Files, CO 904/209/297: 73–4, report from E.W. Sharp, Matron at HM Prison Aylesbury to W.H. Winder, Governor, 6 September 1916.

4 Dublin Castle Special Branch Files, CO 904/209/297: 72, letter from W.H. Winder to Edward Troup, 6 September 1916.

5 Lawrence William White notes that 'her incarceration so scandalised some members of her family, that they changed their surname to 'Prole' to avoid association with her.' Lawrence William White, 'Perolz, Mary Flanagan,' in *Dictionary of Irish Biography* (eds), James McGuire and

James Quinn (Cambridge: Cambridge University Press, 2009) http://dib.cambridge.org/viewReadPage.do?articleId=a7282 (Accessed 6 December 2010).

6 Duke was appointed to the role by Asquith on 31 July 1916. Lloyd George's announcement on 9 April 1918 regarding Irish conscription led Duke to resign in protest, formally made on 2 May 1918.

7 Dublin Castle Special Branch Files, CO 904/209/297: 70, letter from Edward O'Farrell to Edward Troup, 18 September 1916.

8 Lahiffe's death notice was posted along with a detailed list of those killed or wounded in the *Irish Times* (4 May 1916), p. 3.

9 Max Caulfield, *The Easter Rebellion: Dublin 1916* (New York: Holt, Rinehart & Winston, 1963) as cited in James, p. 165.

10 'Think Germans Sent Arms,' *New York Times* (30 April 1916), p. 2.

11 Anne Haverty, *Constance Markievicz: An Independent Life* (London: Pandora Press, 1988), p. 148.

12 Ibid.

13 John Rylands Library, Manchester, UK, KTH1/330/2a, letter from EGB to Katharine Tynan Hickson, November 1916.

14 Ibid.

15 Thomas Ashe, Éamon de Valera and Harry Boland were amongst the Irish rebel prisoners held at Lewes in 1916.

16 Roper, (ed.), *Prison Letters*, p. 70.

17 Marie Perolz, Brigid Foley and Nell Ryan were also held at Aylesbury Prison. Perolz and Foley were released before Markievicz was transferred there and Nell Ryan was released in September 1916 before the privileges were announced. See John McGuffin, *Internment* (Dublin: Anvil Books Ltd, 1973).

18 See Helga Woogan, *Silent Radical – Winifred Carney, 1887–1943: A Reconstruction of her Biography* (Dublin: Studies in Irish Labour History, 6, 2000).

19 National Archives, Kew, Home Office registered papers 144/1457/314179/8, petition of Winifred Carney, 1 December 1916.

20 John Rylands Library, Manchester, UK, KTH1/330/2a, letter from EGB to Katharine Tynan Hickson, November 1916.

21 Dublin Castle Special Branch Files, CO 904/209/297: 65, statement concerning prison conditions of Constance de Markievicz by EGB, undated.

22 Ibid.

23 Dublin Castle Special Branch Files, CO 904/209/297: 64, letter from Jack White to Henry Edward Duke, 21 December 1916.

24 Dublin Castle Special Branch Files, CO 904/209/297: 62, letter from Home Office signed by E. Blackwell, 8 January 1917.

25 Ibid.

26 Charles Townsend, 'Suppression of the Easter Rising,' *Bullán*, 1:1 (1994) 27–40.
27 Seán McConville, *Irish Political Prisoners, 1848–1922: Theatres of War* (London: Routledge, 2005), p. 507.
28 Roper, (ed.), *Prison Letters*, p. 145.
29 Ibid, p. 67.
30 Nicola Rippon, *The Plot to Kill Lloyd George: The Story of Alice Wheeldon and the Peartree Conspiracy* (London: Wharncliffe Books, 2009).
31 Numerous newspaper reports detail the scandalous nature of the trial, for example see: 'Poison Plot Trial: "Gordon's" Name: A Startling Suggestion Hint of the Line of Defence,' *MG* (7 March 1917), p. 5.
32 Roper, (ed.), *Prison Letters*, p. 68.
33 The minute books of the Women's Tax Resistance League are held at the Fawcett Library, London.
34 NLI, MS 5770 (5), letter from Fr Albert to EGB, 24 March 1917.
35 NLI, MS 41,934, letter from Home Secretary, George Cave to T.M. Healy, 6 March 1917.
36 'Irish Amnesty: Release of Rebel Prisoners,' *The Times* (16 June 1917), p. 7.
37 NLI, MS 41,189/5M, speech and notes for a radio talk on EGB by Hanna Sheehy Skeffington, undated.
38 'Strange Times in the House,' *MG* (21 June 1917), p. 4.
39 'Arrival at Kingstown,' *Irish Independent* (22 June 1917), p. 3.
40 'Miss Eva Gore-Booth and Sinn Féin,' *Irish Independent* (24 June 1917), p. 3.
41 Ibid.
42 EGB, *Rhythms of Art*, League of Peace and Freedom Pamphlet (London: The Pelican Press, 1917).
43 Ibid, p. 10.
44 Roper, (ed.), *Prison Letters*, p. 86.
45 Arthur Mitchell and Pádraig Ó Snodaigh (eds), *Irish Political Documents, 1916–1949* (Dublin: Irish Academic Press, 1985), p. 42.
46 Ibid, p. 88.
47 EGB, 'Government,' *CE*, p. 507.
48 'Miss Gore-Booth's New Poems,' *Irish Independent* (30 September 1918), p. 5.
49 Letter from Markievicz to EGB, 8 June 1918, in Roper, (ed.), *Prison Letters*, p. 179.
50 Ibid.
51 Éamon de Valera, *Ireland's Case against Conscription* (Dublin: Maunsel, 1918).
52 EGB, 'The Ruin Preparing in Ireland,' *MG* (26 April 1918), p. 8.
53 Ibid.

54 Ibid.
55 Ibid.
56 'The Vatican and Conscription in Ireland,' *MG* (26 April 1918), p. 4.
57 'Ireland and Conscription,' *MG* (1 May 1918), p. 3.
58 'Dublin's Calm Astonishes,' *New York Times* (22 May 1918), p. 4.
59 Dublin Castle Special Branch Files, CO 904/209/297/52, report from L.M. Grist to the Governor of Holloway Jail, Mr. Waller, 20 August 1918.
60 Letter from Markievicz to EGB, 14 February 1919, in Roper, (ed.), *Prison Letters*, p. 195.
61 EGB, *The Sword of Justice* (London: Headley Brothers, 1918).
62 Frederick S. Lapisardi (ed.), *The Plays of Eva Gore-Booth* (California: Mellen Research University Press, 1991), p. 131.
63 EGB, *CE*, p. 26.
64 W.H. Cheeson, '*The Sword of Justice*: A Review,' *Occult Review*, 29 (January 1919), p. 62.
65 Lapisardi, *Plays of Eva Gore-Booth*, p. 129.
66 Ibid.
67 *The Tribunal*, 132 (7 November 1918), 4.
68 'Release of C.O.'s Demanded,' *MG* (17 December 1917), p. 4.
69 Roper, (ed.), *Prison Letters*, p. 88.
70 Haverty, *Constance Markievicz*, pp. 186–7.
71 Roper, (ed.), *Prison Letters*, p. 88.
72 *Urania*, 13 (January/February 1919), p. 2.
73 EGB, 'Why Women M.P.s are Needed: A Reply to Arguments Against Them,' *Daily Mirror* (1 January 1919), p. 7.
74 Haverty, *Constance Markievicz*, p. 187.
75 'Mrs. Thos. Clarke's Release,' *Irish Independent* (14 February 1919), p. 3.
76 Kathleen Clarke, *Revolutionary Woman Kathleen Clarke 1878–1972: An Autobiography* (Dublin: O'Brien Press, 1991), p. 166.
77 'London Irish Demand,' *Irish Independent* (14 March 1919), p. 2.
78 Haverty, *Constance Markievicz*, p. 189.
79 Roper, (ed.), *Prison Letters*, p. 93.
80 Ibid, p. 104.
81 Ibid, p. 73.
82 Letter from Constance Markievicz to EGB, 1 October 1919 in Roper, (ed.), *Prison Letters*, p. 242.
83 Ibid, p. 105.
84 Letter from EGB to T.P. Conwil-Evans, Bordighera, 1921 in EGB, *CE*, p. 93.

11

Radical sexual politics and post-war religion

'In time the whole of things shall alter'[1]

Throughout this time of war and rebellion, Gore-Booth remained taken with the pursuit of gender equality. In 1916 she and Roper, along with three other members of the Aëthnic Union, Thomas Baty, Dorothy Cornish and Jessey Wade, advanced their campaign to overcome all distinctions based on sex.[2] The group, led by Gore-Booth, established a remarkable journal entitled *Urania*.[3] An unsigned article in the journal positions Gore-Booth as the inspiration behind its establishment, 'Eva Gore-Booth formulated a concise statement which we have adopted ... as the nearest and clearest expression of our views. It declared that sex was an accident and formed no essential part of an individual's nature.'[4] Gore-Booth, motivated by a line from Katherine Cecil Thurston's novel, *Max*, had established a journal which called for nothing less than the elimination of gender as a category of difference. The mission statement printed on every issue of *Urania* testifies to its unique subject matter:

> Urania denotes the company of those who are firmly determined to ignore the dual organisation of humanity in all its manifestations. They are convinced that this duality has resulted in the formation of the two warped and imperfect types. They are further convinced that in order to get rid of this state of things no measures of 'emancipation' or 'equality' will suffice, which do not begin by a complete refusal to recognise or tolerate the duality itself. If the world is to see sweetness and independence combined in the same individual, all recognition of that duality must be given up. For it inevitably brings in its train the suggestion of the conventional distortions of character which are based on it. There are no 'men' or 'women' in Urania.

The title *Urania* establishes the journal as advocating something beyond mainstream feminism of the time. Gore-Booth may well have been inspired by her interest in the occult, choosing to name the journal after the first temple of the Hermetic Order of the Golden Dawn, the Isis-Urania Temple.[5] However, the choice of Urania rather than Isis for the title indicates something quite revolutionary. The German sexologist Karl Heinrich Ulrichs first coined the term to describe homosexuality in a series of booklets published between 1864 and 1879.[6] The term was filtered into the English language by the socialist and campaigner for homosexual equality, Edward Carpenter, who applied uranian 'to indicate simply those whose lives and activities are inspired by genuine friendship or love for their own sex.'[7] The content of the journal reflects this bold choice of title.

The goal of *Urania* was to highlight how individuals could achieve their full potential if the constraints of gender restrictions were removed. The central message of the journal tied in with Gore-Booth's trade union campaigns, which highlighted sex difference as a cause of discrimination in the workplace. The editors of *Urania* launched a pioneering campaign, they reprinted articles from worldwide newspapers relating to cross-dressers, individuals who transgressed gender roles and in later issues, cases of transsexuality. Each issue follows a similar pattern. The journal usually opens with an editorial commentary, a letter section, book reviews, progress reports on co-educational schools and various reprinted articles from England, India and Japan. Most issues contain a 'star dust' section which records details of women who achieved success in male dominated areas, such as the first woman to receive a degree in science, the first female doctor in a speciality area and so on. Articles in this section do not simply list an increase of women in certain occupations, they are carefully chosen to highlight that innate differences do not exist between the sexes. One such article listed under 'athletics' exhibits the journal's unique approach.

The case of a nineteen year old girl, Mitsuko Sakamoto, who woke to discover a burglar in her room, is republished from the *Japan Advertiser*. The report notes how, 'with a deft twist of her soft hands [Sakamoto] took him off his feet and placed him on a quite unrelated part of his anatomy. Not caring for this pose, she tried him in another position, which brought his face into violent contact with the mat . . . Sakamoto, as the burglar now knows, has devoted much of her time to the study of jujutsu.'[8] Although a curious inclusion for an athletics section, the message is significant, women can achieve the positive aspects of masculinity, such as assertiveness and strength, while overcoming the negative feminine characteristics of passivity and weakness.

Gore-Booth and the other four editors arranged for the journal to be printed at their own expense, a huge financial burden especially during wartime. The journal survived for more than twenty-four years, spanning three decades. The editors privately printed and circulated eighty-two issues in total. This was a remarkable achievement considering that the contemporary journal, the *Freewoman*, was in existence for less than one year, that paper was discontinued due to lack of finances in 1912. The fact that the *Freewoman* was banned by booksellers, including W.H. Smith, was a sure indication that if *Urania* was offered for sale it most probably would have been excluded by mainstream booksellers. Instead the journal was offered free to any person who agreed with *Urania*'s ethos. A distributor's note printed after each mission statement exclaims that 'a register is kept of those who hold these principles, and all who are entered in it will receive this leaflet while funds admit.'[9] To date it has not been possible to secure a copy of the distribution register. Roper most probably kept this after Gore-Booth's death, while the journal was still in circulation. Gore-Booth's great-nephew, Josslyn, maintains that the Roper family destroyed all of her personal papers after her death, ultimately destroying vital information about the journal's readership.[10]

The journal boasted a circulation of over 250, and one article cites university libraries which subscribed to *Urania*, 'Girton, Newnham and Lady Margaret (Oxford) Colleges in Britain, and Vassar and Wellesley in America.'[11] These are impressive women's colleges. Girton and Newnham form part of Cambridge University, they were established during the late 1870s while Vassar was opened just north of New York City earlier in 1861, followed by Wellesley women's liberal arts college near Boston in 1875. The principles expressed in *Urania* thus reached hundreds of intellectuals with every issue.[12] The fact that students and staff at esteemed women's colleges were reading and possibly contributing articles to the journal, may lead one to surmise that it was a vehicle of current feminist discourse of the day. However, on close examination *Urania* offered a unique strand of thought that was not deemed suitable by all female intellects. An unnamed editor of the journal notes that, 'one or two of the Oxford "Ladies" colleges surprised us by declining what Cambridge willingly accepts. And we had one very peppery letter from an unmarried lady whose eagle – (or shall we say, vulturine?) – eye detected untold horrors in our refined pages.'[13]

The 'untold horrors' no doubt refer to the journal's unconventional views regarding sexuality and gender. Same-sex female life unions were presented in the journal as a preferable alternative to heterosexual marriage. Cultural historian Alison Oram comments that 'an integral part of *Urania's* feminist perspective was its strong rejection of both marriage and heterosexual sex. Marriage, it was claimed, inhibited individual development and spirituality, especially for women, since it enforced gender differentiation.'[14] The editors of *Urania* acknowledged that in order to dissolve the categories of male and female, the institution of marriage must be contested. This was a pioneering position to adopt as few feminists rejected the model of marriage in the early twentieth century. Lucy Bland observes that, 'despite seeing marriage as immoral, most feminists did not reject [it] *per se*. On the contrary, they wished for it to be radically reformed.'[15]

From the onset articles relating to marriage appear in *Urania;* one of the earliest recorded appears in a 1919 issue, one year after Marie Stopes published *Married Love*.[16] *Urania* reprints an article from the *London News*, 'do unmarried women miss the half of life?' The commentary argues that single women have a rounder, fuller life than their married counterparts because, 'it is the married woman who too often only sees one side of life – the domestic side. The single woman sees all the others, and she knows as much as she wants to know of the married woman's preserve . . . To very few single women love has not come with all its broadening education.'[17] This article offers a challenge to Stopes' book. In his introduction to a reprinted version of *Married Love*, Ross McKibbin notes that although the book was controversial at the time of publication, the morality expressed in it was conventional.[18] *Married Love* portrayed marriage as the ideal state for women and in turn 'marriage should be crowned by children.'[19] Articles in *Urania* challenge the notion that all women aspire to be married and that only those who are undesirable remain unmarried.

One article reprinted from the *Exchange* entitled 'Why we marry,' confronts the idea that due to a lack of prospective husbands, undesirable women remain unmarried against their will:

> Although there are 2,000,000 surplus women in England, do not let us run away with the idea that these are all spinsters against their wills. No. Some of the most-sought-after women never marry and some of the least-sought-after do. Among the women who have not married will be found some of the most charming, the most attractive, and the best-looking of their sex. There are naturally many and diverse reasons why women do not marry, just as there are many and diverse ones why they do.[20]

In an attempt to prove that marriage was becoming redundant the journal even records announcements of broken engagements. An article in a 1929 issue declared, 'the first publicly announced engagement to be broken in the New Year is announced as follows:– "The marriage arranged between Captain Geoffrey Fielden and Miss Jean Anderson will not take place."'[21] This announcement was first published in the *Cumberland News*, as it involved a high profile family. Captain Fielden was the son of Manchester Exchange MP Edward Brocklehurst Fielden. *Urania* reprints the news as a cause for celebration.

Urania occasionally printed stories portraying marriage as a joke. One such account is printed under the heading 'scraps,' the dialogue used suggests it has an Irish origin: 'a Bishop came to examine some children. "Tell me, Sean," said he to one of the boys, "what is matrimony?" "It is a period of punishment," said Sean, "to which souls are sentenced for their sins." "Sean," cried the parish priest, "think again, boy! What are you saying?" "Ah leave him alone," said the Bishop. "What do you and I know of it? Maybe the lad's right."'[22]

It is important to note that the term marriage is used in *Urania* in the conventional sense – that is, a union sanctioned by religion and state between a man and a woman. While *Urania* encouraged spinsterhood, the editors proposed female same-sex life unions, such as the relationship between Gore-Booth and Roper, as a superior alternative to heterosexual marriage. Accounts were published in the journal presenting love between women as pure, yet full of passion.[23] One such article is reprinted from *Twenty-five Years Reminiscences*, written by Gore-Booth's friend, Katharine Tynan. The story simply entitled 'an Irish school-girl,' depicts female love as natural and idyllic:

> We had our little passions, sometimes for a nun, sometimes for each other . . . Mine was a passion for an elder girl about to become a nun . . . I used to cry a great deal at night because she was going away, and she

> used to come and comfort me ... Once, on a dark winter morning, washing in cold water as was our custom, and groping my way by candle-light, I was told she had come back the night before ... In the dark corridor on the way to mass, as we passed the warm kitchen, delightful on a cold winter morning, she came behind me and kissed me. Oh, rapture! Oh, delight! Oh, ecstasy! Was there anything in more mature passions quite as good?[24]

Urania also published accounts of famous women in history who loved other women. One such article discusses Queen Christina of Sweden's love for various women throughout her life. The article comments that the Queen had an 'absorbing affection' for Countess Ebba Sparrë, who was just one of many women the Queen courted.[25] The article continues to note that Christina 'picked up a young girl of Lyons in 1656, kissed her "très amoureusement," and wanted to have her sleep with her ... Two years earlier, a chronicler ... relates how she fell in love with a Jew girl, "whom she allowed publicly to ride in her carriage, and with whom she occasionally slept on the journey."'[26] Queen Christina's love of women was put forward as a positive quality. The article concludes that she had 'accomplished a great deal. She had hammered, like another Thor, a milestone on the road of progress.'[27]

While an article describing the relationship between Countess Golovina with the Empress of Russia, Elizabeth Alexeievna, was placed under the iconic heading of 'An Exalted Love.' The article introduces the two women, noting that there are no letters remaining from the Countess Golvina but over twenty long letters remain from Elizabeth. Besides the comment that Elizabeth's letters began 'just a year after her marriage, on the 11th of August 1794,' there is no analysis of the content.[28] Extracts from the letters are simply reprinted in *Urania* detailing the depth of Elizabeth's love for the Countess, such as the following:

> My heart is too full, I cannot resist it, my thoughts are killing me ... Weeping and thinking of you is my occupation all day long. I have scarcely the strength to keep my tears back before other people when I see you or when I think of you ... My God! What a power you have over me! ... I adore you, yes, that is the only word for it. Would not anybody believe, reading this letter, that it was addressed to a lover?[29]

The journal also refers to the ancient Greek poet, Sappho of Myteline, on a number of occasions. Sappho lived on the island of

Lesbos in the seventh century BC. She was mentor and teacher to young unmarried women on the island and she wrote passionate poetry displaying her love of these women. The term Sapphic was thus used for centuries to refer to female same-sex relations. With the increasing popularity of sexological research in the late nineteenth century, the term lesbian (from the island of Lesbos) was appropriated to describe female same-sex behaviour. The term lesbian appears to have been originally used in a medical sense, often positioning female same-sex behaviour as deviant. Gore-Booth and Roper were amongst the first people in the twentieth century to present Sappho from a socially romantic context, attempting to overthrow the notion of female same-sex relationships as sexual deviancy. Their appropriation of Sappho was ahead of the modern-day trend to regard her as the original lesbian.[30]

A powerful piece published in a 1933 issue of *Urania* was written by an unnamed author in response to a 'recent work on Sappho.' Although the book in question is not named it clearly refers to *Sappho of Lesbos* by Arthur Weigall.[31] The article attacks the basis of the book and describes how Weigall 'has proceeded to weave a tissue story out of his own head, and to invent a life for Sappho of the kind that he would have her live.' The article continues by discounting the Phaeon myth as laughable. This myth maintains that Sappho fell in love with a boatman named Phaeon and when he refused to return her love, she threw herself off a cliff and drowned. *Urania* describes how 'it is difficult to refrain from laughing at such reasoning.'[32] The article concludes by stating, 'if anybody likes to believe that this passionate and possessive adorer of beauty and charm in women preferred in her latest days to die for the embraces of a masterful man, they are at perfect liberty to believe so.'[33] The inclusion of such an article is significant in relation to the quotation inscribed on Gore-Booth and Roper's headstone. Gore-Booth had died by the time this article appeared in *Urania* but Roper was listed as one of the editors for this issue. Roper chose an extract from Sappho's poetry for the headstone of what would become the joint grave of herself and Gore-Booth.

The editors of *Urania* also engaged in a campaign to expose gender as a masquerade by including accounts of cross-dressers in the journal. Cases reported primarily relate to women passing as, or reinventing themselves as men and often include a sympathetic account of same-sex relationships. Individual accounts showed that women could achieve anything if they were not constrained by social expectations and legal restrictions of the era.[34] The most detailed article relating to cross-dressing women is simply entitled 'Women as Men.' The article was written by Edwin Arnold and is reprinted from *The Weekly Scotsman*.[35] The article begins with an account of Irish born James Barry, who Arnold notes became 'Inspector-General of hospitals fighting several duels during his career, making love to women, bullying the War Office of the time, no one doubting that he was a masterful and high-spirited man until "he" died.'[36] After Barry died it was discovered when 'his' corpse was laid out, that 'he' in fact was biologically a woman.[37] In principle James Barry was the first female doctor in England, which alters the record of history as Elizabeth Garrett Anderson is listed as the first woman to graduate in medicine.[38] Anderson graduated in 1865, the same year that Barry died.[39]

As the journal progressed the contents became even more radical, reporting on actual changes of sex from the early 1930s. The details of these cases are often ambiguous, such as an account of a girl admitted to hospital in 1934 and discharged as a boy. The article entitled 'Another Change of Sex,' is taken from *Reynold's Newspaper* and simply states that 'Margaret Hutchinson who was admitted to hospital as a girl and [has been] discharged as a boy.'[40] The first ever recorded case of a medical sex reassignment surgery appeared in *Urania* in 1936, the journal's format was changed to allow for the following announcement to be placed centre on the front page, demonstrating its importance:

> AUTHENTIC CHANGE OF SEX.
> PRAGUE, December 3. – "Miss" Zdenke Koubkova,
> the famous Czechoslovak athlete and holder
> of the women's world 800–meter record established
> last year at London, will soon become "Mr." Zdenk Koubka.
> Doctors informed Miss Koubkova that she had
> The option of being either a man or a woman. She
> Decided to submit to a minor operation and Become a man.[41]

The central argument for the elimination of gender was consistent throughout every issue, challenging contemporary mainstream feminism, medical sexology and perceived norms of society.

The challenge to deconstruct gender, sexuality and biological sex are assumed to be part of a post-modern movement popularised in the late twentieth and early twenty-first century. However, Gore-Booth and the founders of *Urania* had begun this radical approach nearly 100 years previously in 1916. Through her trade union activities and political campaigns, Gore-Booth witnessed how politicians and philanthropists attempted to achieve gender equality by treating women differently to men. Mainstream feminism during the early twentieth century was working towards a goal of equality from within this mindset. Groups such as the Women's Trade Union League welcomed protective legislation for women, and temperance suffragists encouraged the ban on women working in public houses. These forms of equality were at odds with Gore-Booth's own beliefs. She established *Urania* to challenge the mainstream approach, declaring that 'no measures of emancipation or equality will suffice which do not begin by a complete refusal to recognise or tolerate the duality itself.'[42]

Although the contents of the journal clashed with many mainstream organisations, it was welcomed by alternative and new age groups, including the Theosophical Society. A 1919 issue of *Urania* announced that they received 'a most encouraging letter from one whose name is a house-hold word – Mrs Mona Caird.'[43] Caird was a member of the Theosophical Society and a regular contributor to an associated magazine, *Quest*.[44] *Urania* regularly paid homage to their Indian Friends, a term referring to members of the Theosophical Society at their headquarters in Adyar, India,[45] while two issues of the journal also noted that the Irish theosophist and writer James Cousins supported the work of *Urania*.[46] The basic principles of theosophy echoed Gore-Booth's radical views on sex and sexuality as expressed in the journal.

Theosophy is a New Age esoteric religion which combines science, eastern religions and spirituality. Helena Petrovna Blavatsky co-founded the Theosophical Society in 1875 with William Quan Judge and Henry Olcott. Annie Besant became president of the society in 1907 when Olcott died, a move that had significant feminist implications. Similar to Gore-Booth, Besant was a key player in the women's trade union movement. She published an article in *The Link*, exposing the dangerous working conditions and meagre pay of women employed in the match company, Bryant and May's. This move is credited with inspiring women to strike in what is infamously known as the match-girl strike of 1888. It is apparent from the membership records of the Theosophical Society that after Besant became president the English section of the society became dominated by women.[47] Gore-Booth formally joined the Hampstead branch of the Theosophical Society on 17 June 1919 (see Figure 13, Gore-Booth's membership certificate, which was personally signed by Besant).[48]

Women's politics and women's spirituality are rarely connected in feminist history. However, there is a deep association between theosophy and the first-wave suffrage movement. A study by Olive Banks identifies that from a representative list of prominent nineteenth- and early-twentieth-century feminists, almost ten percent joined the Theosophical Society at some stage.[49] Many more women engaged with some other form of unorthodox spirituality, indeed Christabel Pankhurst spent her later years writing and preaching on the Second Coming.[50] Mainstream religions were slow to endorse women's rights. Christian traditions such as Anglicanism and Catholicism presented women as subservient to men. Esoteric and occult religions were more amenable to feminist politics. Testimony to this was apparent when the first martyr of the suffrage movement, Emily Wilding Davison, died. The Occult Church of the Seers in Brighton, immediately announced 'a Requiem, with music, for the repose of the soul of Emily Davison.'[51]

Irish suffragist and president of the Women's Freedom League, Charlotte Despard, wrote a pamphlet entitled *Theosophy and the Women's Movement*, explaining the connection between the two. Despard highlighted the fact that in order to join the Theosophical Society people 'are required to take one pledge – and only one. It is the acceptance of the truth of Brotherhood – not theoretically alone, but practically. Our first object is "to form a nucleus of the universal brotherhood without distinction of race, creed, sex, caste or colour."'[52] A new age religion which overlooked difference based on sex was especially attractive to Gore-Booth and she became an active member of the society. Long before officially joining, she presented papers at theosophical lodges and contributed articles to their publications. Many of her poems and essays were published in the *Occult Review*, *Herald of the Star* and *Service*, three of the most distinguished theosophical journals of the time.[53] While in Italy she worked on a series of articles for *Herald of the Star*.[54]

The basic principles of theosophy, such as reincarnation and the law of karma, derived from Eastern religions but theosophists employed an avant-garde analysis of these doctrines to present

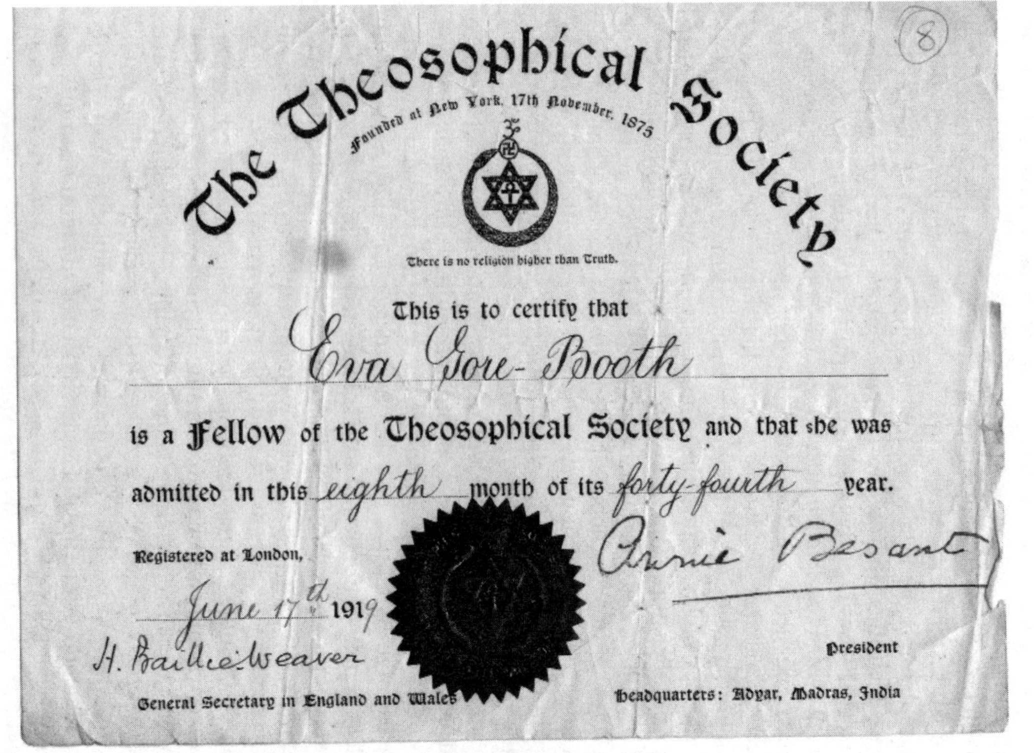

(8)

The Theosophical Society

Founded at New York, 17th November, 1875

There is no religion higher than Truth.

This is to certify that

Eva Gore-Booth

is a Fellow of the Theosophical Society and that she was admitted in this eighth month of its forty-fourth year.

Registered at London,

June 17th 1919

H. Baillie-Weaver

General Secretary in England and Wales

Annie Besant

President

Headquarters: Adyar, Madras, India

13 Theosophical Society Membership Certificate of Eva Gore-Booth, signed by then president of the society, Annie Besant

gender and sexuality as fluid. A soul, they argued, would not remain the same sex throughout multiple incarnations. Furthermore, the Theosophical Society explained that the division of society into male and female was only a provisional system. In an open letter to members of the society, Besant insisted that, 'the separation of humanity into two sexes ... is but a temporary device for the better development of complementary qualities, difficult of simultaneous evolution in the same person.'[55] Charles Lazenby, a leader of the Blavatsky Institute, coined the term Divine Hermaphrodite, to describe this androgynous ideal.[56]

Theosophy's principle of gender-bending reincarnation had deeper feminist significance when connected with the law of karma. In her groundbreaking research on the relationship between theosophy and feminism, Joy Dixon notes that this doctrine had a powerful effect on male attitudes to the first-wave suffrage movement because 'if men really believed that they might find themselves in female bodies in the next life, they would hesitate before perpetuating women's subordination.'[57]

Gore-Booth embraced the concept of gender changing reincarnation and presented this as a central story-line in her play 'the death of Deirdre.'[58] She rewrote the ancient Celtic myth of Deirdre of the Sorrows not only to elucidate her radical politics but also to explain the theosophical principles of reincarnation and the law of karma. A range of Irish authors had rewritten the Deirdre story, including Russell, Yeats, Synge and Douglas Hyde. Gore-Booth's play was distinctive.[59] The protagonist, Deirdre, in myth the most beautiful woman in Ireland, is, in Gore-Booth's version, the reincarnation of a male Irish King. In act one Deirdre admits to her foster mother, Lavarcam, 'I, whom you call a young and innocent maiden, was an old and jealous King. I too, had a deep grave dug in the forest, and slew my own heart's happiness because of the jealousy of love, and buried her whom I loved, in the deep grave under the oak trees.'[60]

Through this one short speech Gore-Booth successfully appropriates a traditional Celtic myth to establish the basic theosophical principles of gender-changing reincarnation. In the introduction to the play, she establishes a link between theosophical ideals and ancient Celtic religions, declaring that 'the idea of re-incarnation is not so exclusively an Eastern doctrine as many people think. Mr. Douglas Hyde, in his *Literary History of Ireland*, points out its place in Irish literature, and explains that it seems to have been part of

Druidic teaching. Whether this involves some ancient, little-known connection between East and West, it would be hard to say.'[61] To gain credence for her portrayal of reincarnation Gore-Booth refers to Hyde because he was a great authority on Gaelic language and culture and then the president of the Gaelic League. Hyde was to become the first President of Ireland in 1938.

As well as attracting radical feminist thinkers, the Theosophical Society attracted members of the Celtic Revival from Gore-Booth's literary circle, including her friends and contemporaries Yeats and Russell.[62] In turn the two men introduced James and Margaret Cousins to theosophy. Margaret Cousins co-founded the Irish Women's Franchise League in 1908. James was an active supporter of the league and he co-edited their weekly paper the *Irish Citizen*. The Cousins met and befriended Besant when they attended the convention of the Theosophical Society in London, in July 1907.[63] Besant maintained a deep connection with Ireland and although born in London, denied her Anglo-Saxon connections. In her autobiography Besant asserted that 'three-quarters of my blood and all my heart are Irish.'[64] Indeed, Besant was initiated into the Theosophical Society through her concern for Irish Independence. Not surprisingly Irish women writers, including Ella Young, were attracted to the society. Young joined the Dublin lodge of the Theosophical Society and later moved to a theosophical commune in California in 1936.

Gore-Booth actively engaged with other associated activities of the Theosophical Society, such as astrology. Madame Blavatsky had revived the study of astrology and theosophists were driven to establish an astrological lodge in London, in 1915. Gore-Booth drew her own astrological chart, using the time and place of her birth along with the position of the stars and planets to determine her future destiny. She calculated charts for her friends and relatives at their request, including Roper, Markievicz, Clare Annesley and Margaret Wroe. She completed charts for many other people that she knew including Yeats, Lloyd George, Churchill, Oscar Wilde and Emmeline Pankhurst, in order to determine what their futures would hold.[65] A detailed chart prepared by Gore-Booth for Ella Young indicated honour, money, fame and eminent friends for the writer (Figure 14 shows the intricacies of an astrological chart that she prepared for herself).[66]

While in Italy, Gore-Booth had begun a close reading of the fourth

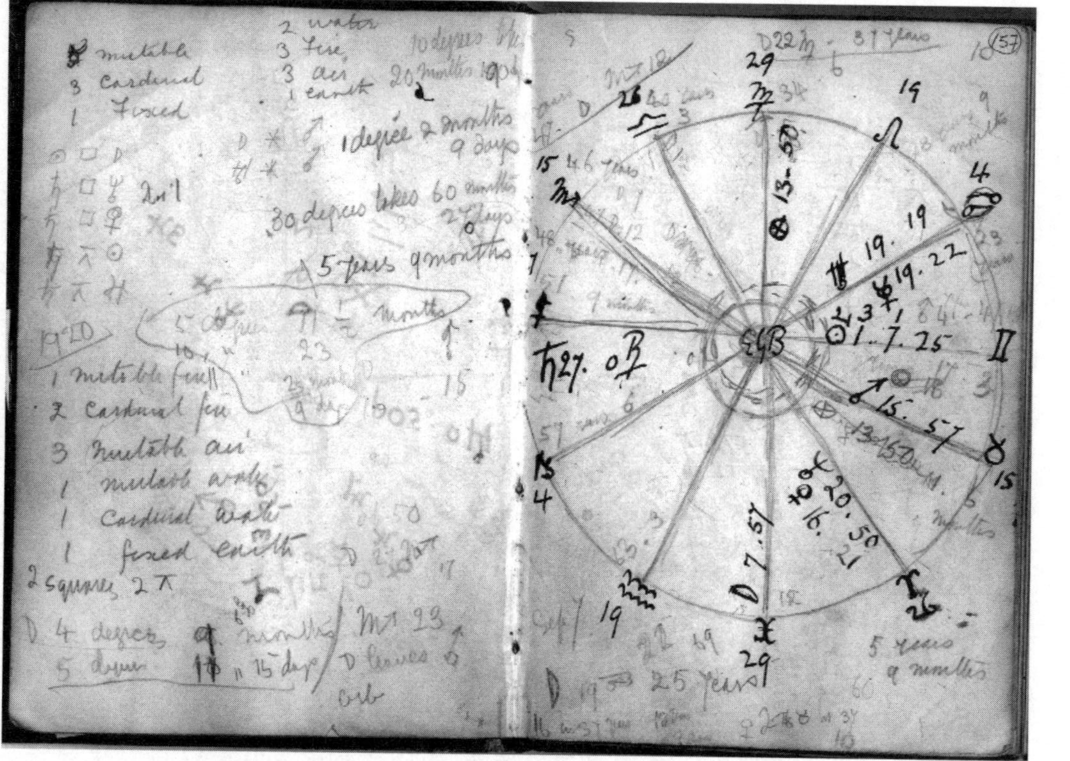

14 Astrological chart prepared by Eva Gore-Booth for herself

Gospel in an attempt to identify connections between Eastern religions and Christianity, from a specifically Irish feminist perspective. This research would culminate in her largest publication, *A Psychological and Poetic Approach to the Study of Christ in the Fourth Gospel*. It is a sizeable book, consisting of 363 pages of a detailed reading of St John's Gospel. The personal significance of the work to Gore-Booth can be seen by the original manuscript held in the Public Records Office of Northern Ireland. The handwritten text is carefully transcribed in a journal, leather bound and tied with a ribbon.[67] This is in stark contrast to Gore-Booth's other manuscripts, which are generally written, or sometimes typed, on individual sheets of paper or in copybooks, often bordered with chaotic notes and scribbles. Markievicz recognised that once she had completed this work, her sister's 'whole task in life was finished.'[68] Gore-Booth was absorbed in writing this prose work for over three years, learning Latin and Greek so that she could read the Bible in its original form.[69]

Her reading of the Gospel is pioneering. In her analysis she addresses three themes of feminist concern – the construction of gender, control of sexuality and desire, and patriarchal dominance and female exclusion from the hierarchies of the church. Gore-Booth highlighted how mistranslations and inaccuracies in the modern version of the Bible tarnished the role of women in the Christian church. Once the authenticity of a biblical text was confirmed, she explained that the text may have been altered for political or religious reasons. Aware of these complications, Gore-Booth presents the miracle at Cana as a prime example of a mistranslation that has been used to exclude women from the hierarchies of the church. In St John's description of the event, Mary approaches Jesus to inform him that the celebrations would come to an abrupt end because the wine is nearly finished. Gore-Booth focuses on a single phrase in this parable 'when Mary says, "They have no wine," Christ is supposed to answer her with the extraordinary words, "Woman, what have I to do with thee?"'[70]

She proposes that Brooke Foss Wescott in his *Gospel According to Saint John* interprets this line to prove, 'that Christ could not take a suggestion from a woman, even if that woman was his mother.'[71] Gore-Booth focuses on the ancient Greek language and interprets Jesus' statement in terms of a local idiom. Her analysis shows that a misreading such as Wescott's facilitates a 'deep subconscious justification in people's minds for the extraordinary exclusion of women from celebrating the Eucharist and preaching, an exclusion nonetheless materialistic and extraordinary because for many years unquestioned.'[72]

Gore-Booth's *Study of Christ* is a powerful feminist approach to the Bible and religious doctrine, which can now be read as a precursor to current feminist theological thought. Irish theologian Mary Condren applauds how Gore-Booth 'anticipated many themes only now being explored by contemporary feminist theory and theology regarding the politics of interpretation, the psychic underpinning of religion, the role of imagination, the critique of sacrifice, the ethic of non-violence.'[73] Indeed, Gore-Booth's research was more radical than the contemporary American egalitarian theology. *The Women's Bible* published between 1895–98, was written by a group of feminist scholars and theologians. The head of the revising committee, Elizabeth Cady Stanton, explained the object of their publication, 'to revise only those texts and chapters directly referring to women, and those also in which women are made prominent by exclusion. As all such passages combined form but one-tenth of the Scriptures.'[74] *The Women's Bible* sought to mitigate sexism in the Bible, in a feminist attempt to establish the genders as equal in Christianity. In contrast Gore-Booth analysed the actual text of the Bible, offering a reinterpretation of the language used, rather than re-reading the event as the American feminists did. The project to expose patriarchal dominance and female exclusion from the hierarchies of the church was paramount to Gore-Booth.

When she completed the manuscript of the *Study of Christ* in 1922, Gore-Booth sent it to Longmans for publication. The director of the publishing company, C.J. Longman, wrote to Gore-Booth with his apologies. He informed her that the publishing adviser did not recommend the manuscript for publication as he said 'the book is quite off the usual lines, and unlikely to appeal to the general public in sufficient numbers.'[75] Longman added that the adviser did recognise her earnestness in writing the book and acknowledged that it contained 'many beautiful thoughts and passages of real insight.' He offered to provide Gore-Booth with the opportunity of self publishing the book. A further letter from Longmans on 8 December 1922 confirms that Gore-Booth ordered 1,000 copies of the book to be printed, which she financed herself. The publisher allocated 260 copies to be distributed in the United States and they sent out seventy review copies (Figure 15 shows a photograph of Gore-Booth around this period).[76]

15 Eva Gore-Booth circa 1920

Reviews of the *Study of Christ* generally acknowledged the book as making a significant contribution to theological research. The celebrated theologian and mystic, Evelyn Underhill, reviewed it in *The Torch* in 1924, noting that 'Miss Gore-Booth's remarkable reinterpretation of the Fourth Gospel; in conjunction with her intensely poetic temperament enables her to bring out fresh meaning and value from this, the most poetic and most mystical document of the New Testament. Her book is one of those which must be lived with, if the full and vitalising meaning of its teaching is to be grasped; for it is the fruit, not merely of the study, but of life.'[77] This was significant praise as Underhill was a respected theologian who published extensively and became the first female visiting lecturer of religion at Oxford University in 1921.

Notes

1 EGB, 'Time,' *CE*, p. 545.
2 Dorothy Cornish was a Montessori educator and Jessey Wade was an animal rights campaigner.
3 For more details regarding the establishment of *Urania* see: Sonja Tiernan, '"No Measures of Emancipation or Equality Will Suffice:" Eva Gore-Booth's Radical Feminism in the journal *Urania*,' in Sarah O'Connor and Christopher C. Shepard (eds), *Women, Social and Cultural Change in Twentieth Century Ireland* (Newcastle: Cambridge Scholars Publishing, 2008), pp. 166–82.
4 *Urania*, 29 & 30 (September/December 1921), 1.
5 The temple opened in London in 1888. Robert Gilbert, *The Golden Dawn: Twilight of the Magicians* (London: Aquarian Press, 1983).
6 Karl Heinrich Ulrichs, *The Riddle of 'Man-Manly' Love: The Pioneering Work on Male Homosexuality*, trans. Michael A. Lombardi-Nash (Buffalo: Prometheus Books, 1994).
7 Edward Carpenter, *The Intermediate Sex* (London: George Allen & Unwin Ltd, 1916), p. 108. The term was further ascribed to a group of poets who celebrated man–boy love, 'Uranian poetry' is used to describe the works of poets such as William Johnson, Lord Alfred Douglas and John Addington Symonds.
8 *Japan Advertiser*, 22 March 1926 in *Urania* 57 & 58 (May/August 1926), 12.
9 For example: *Urania* issues numbers 69 & 70 (May/August 1928), 10.
10 'At a quick glance, there are no issues of *Urania* or pamphlets about the Aëthnic Union ... I believe Esther Roper's family destroyed her papers, so I am not sure what else to suggest.' PRONI, Mic 590, Reel 11:18, letter from Josslyn Gore-Booth to Angela Ingram, 9 March 1991.

11 *Urania*, 14 (March/April 1919), 3.
12 In the centenary issue, *Urania* claimed an average circulation for each issue of 'a little over two hundred, as a rule.' *Urania*, 101 & 102 (September/December 1933), 1.
13 Ibid.
14 Alison Oram, '"Sex is an Accident:" Feminism, Science and the Radical Sexual Theory of *Urania*, 1915–40,' in Lucy Bland and Laura Doan (eds), *Sexology in Culture: Labelling Bodies and Desires* (Cambridge: Polity Press, 1998), p. 215.
15 Lucy Bland, *Banishing the Beast: English Feminism and Sexual Morality* (London: Penguin, 1995), p. 133.
16 Marie Stopes, *Married Love* (1918: Oxford: Oxford University Press, 2004).
17 'Do Unmarried Women Miss the Half of Life, from A Single Woman,' *London Evening News*, *Urania*, 14 (March/April 1919), 6.
18 Ross McKibbin, introduction, *Married Love*, by Marie Stopes (Oxford: Oxford University Press, reprinted 2004), p. i.
19 Ibid.
20 'Why We Marry,' *Urania*, 51 & 52 (May/August 1925), 2.
21 'Engagements Dissolved,' *Urania*, 77 & 78 (September/December 1929), 11.
22 *Urania*, 129 & 130 (May/August 1938), 11.
23 For a complete assessment see: Sonja Tiernan, '"Engagements Dissolved:" Eva Gore-Booth, *Urania* and the Lesbian Challenge to Marriage' in Mary McAuliffe and Sonja Tiernan (eds), *Tribades, Tommies and Transgressives: Histories of Sexualities volume I* (Newcastle: Cambridge Scholars Publishing, 2008), pp. 128–44.
24 'An Irish School-Girl,' *Urania*, 31 & 32 (January/April 1922), 1.
25 *Urania*, 101 & 102 (September/December 1933), 2.
26 Ibid, pp. 3–4.
27 Ibid.
28 'An Exalted Love,' *Urania*, 139 & 140 (January/April 1940), 3.
29 Ibid.
30 Many thanks to Linda E. Mitchell for her comments on this aspect of Sappho.
31 A reference to 'Sez Weigall' makes it clear that the book is Arthur Weigall, *Sappho of Lesbos* (London: Thornton Butterworth, 1932).
32 'Sappho Up-To-Date,' *Urania*, 99 & 100 (May/August 1933), 1–2.
33 Ibid, p. 2.
34 Further information on the accounts of cross-dressing see: Sonja Tiernan, 'The Journal *Urania* (1916–40): An Alternative Archive of Radical Gender Masquerade' in Sharon Tighe-Mooney and Deirdre Quinn, (eds), *Essays in Irish Literary Criticism: Themes of Gender, Sexuality, and Corporeality* (New York: Edwin Mellen Press, 2008), 55–69.

35 Edwin Arnold, 'Women as Men,' *Urania*, 69 & 70 (May/August 1928), 4.
36 *Urania*, 69 & 70 (May/August 1928), 4–5.
37 A newspaper article details the case of Dr James Barry, 'thus it stands as an indisputable fact, that a woman was for 40 years an officer in the British service, and fought one duel and had sought many more, had pursued a legitimate medical education, and received a regular diploma, and had acquired almost a celebrity for skill as a surgical operator.' 'A Strange Story,' *MG* (21 August 1865), p. 3.
38 After Barry's death it was accepted that 'he' was a biological woman, more recent research disputes this and claims that Barry was in fact a hermaphrodite. Rachel Holmes, *Scanty Particulars: The Scandalous Life and Astonishing Secret of Queen Victoria's most Eminent Military Doctor* (New York: Random House, 2002).
39 No London newspaper carried her obituary, on 14 August 1865 a Dublin paper, *Saunder's News-Letter* and *Daily Advertiser*, published an account entitled 'a female army combatant.'
40 *Reynolds' Newspaper*, 25 March 1934 as cited in *Urania*, 103 & 104 (January/April 1934), 6.
41 *Urania*, 115 & 116 (January/April 1936), 1.
42 Mission statement printed on every issue of *Urania*.
43 *Urania*, 13 (Jan/February 1919), 3.
44 Joy Dixon, *Divine Feminine: Theosophy and Feminism in England* (Baltimore: John Hopkins University Press 2001), p. 152.
45 *Urania*, 71 & 72 (September/December 1928), 8.
46 *Urania*, 107 & 108 (September/December 1934), pp. 4–5; also 129 & 130 (May/August 1938), 6.
47 Figures based on Dixon's calculations, *Divine Feminine*, p. 68.
48 PRONI, Mic 590, Reel 5:41, Theosophical Society membership certificate of EGB, 19 June 1919.
49 Olive Banks, *Becoming a Feminist: The Social Origins of 'First Wave' Feminism* (Brighton: Harvester Wheatsheaf, 1990), pp. 168–70.
50 For example: Christabel Pankhurst, *'The Lord Cometh': The World Crisis Explained* (London: Morgan & Scott Ltd., 1923).
51 *Suffragette* (13 June 1913), p. 570.
52 Charlotte Despard, *Theosophy and the Women's Movement* (London: Theosophical Publishing Society, 1913), p. 7.
53 For a complete list see appendix with Eva Gore-Booth's major publications.
54 Letter from EGB to Margaret Wroe, Italy, 1920 in EGB, *CE*, p. 80.
55 Archives of the Theosophical Society in England, Box 3/46F, letter from Annie Besant to the members of the Theosophical Society, November, 1908. Cited in Joy Dixon, 'Sexology and the Occult: Sexuality and Subjectivity in Theosophy's New Age,' in Elizabeth A. Castelli (ed.), *Women, Gender, Religion: A Reader* (New York: Palgrave, 2001), p. 295.

56 'The reproduction of the species will be by the spiritual will of the Divine Hermaphrodite impregnating his own womb, and the children will be born instruments for loving human service,' Charles Lazenby, 'Sex III,' *The Path* (May 1911), p. 235.
57 Dixon, *Divine Feminine*, p. 158.
58 Pennsylvania State University Libraries, Eva Gore-Booth Collection, box 3, folder 2, AX/B40/RBM/00141A, manuscript *Buried life of Deirdre* by EGB, originally entitled 'the Death of Deirdre.'
59 Æ, *Deirdre: A Drama in Three Acts* (Dublin: Maunsel, 1907), W.B. Yeats, *Deirdre* (Stratford-Upon-Avon: Shakespeare Head Press, 1914), J.M. Synge, *Deirdre of the Sorrows* (Dublin: Maunsel and Company Ltd, 1911) and Douglas Hyde, *Déirdre the First of the 'Three Sorrows, or Pities, of Story-Telling'* (Dublin: Talbot Press, 1939).
60 Lapisardi (ed.), *Plays of Eva Gore-Booth*, p. 166.
61 Ibid, p. 152.
62 For further discussion of occult influences on the literary work of Yeats see Stephen Regan, 'W.B. Yeats and Irish Cultural Politics in the 1890s,' in Sally Ledger and Scott McCracken (eds), *Cultural Politics at the Fin de Siècle* (New York: Cambridge University Press, 1995).
63 Catherine Candy, 'The Occult Feminism of Margaret Cousins in Modern Ireland and India, 1878–1954,' PhD diss., Loyola University, 1996.
64 Besant's father, William Persse Wood, was born in Ireland and studied medicine at Trinity College, Dublin. Her mother, Emily Roche Morris, was from an Irish family. Annie Besant, *An Autobiography* (1893, Adyar: Theosophical Publishing House, 1983), pp. 3–4.
65 PRONI, Mic 590, Reel 9, L/7:149–226, notebook of astrological calculations.
66 PRONI, Mic 590, Reel 9, L/7:250, astrological chart for Eva Gore-Booth.
67 PRONI, Mic 590, Reel 5:51–52, EGB manuscript, *A Psychological and Poetic Approach to the Study of Christ in the Fourth Gospel.*
68 Letter from Markievicz to Roper, Dartry, 1926 in Roper, (ed.), *Prison Letters*, p. 311.
69 EGB, *CE*, p. 27.
70 EGB, *A Psychological and Poetic Approach to the Study of Christ in the Fourth Gospel* (London: Longmans Green & Co, 1923), p. 163.
71 Ibid, p. 169. The original reference to which Gore-Booth refers is Brooke Foss Westcott, *Gospel According to St John* (London: John Murray, 1898), Chapter II, Note 4, p. 82.
72 Ibid, pp. 169–70.
73 Mary Condren, 'Theology and Ethics: The Twentieth Century,' in Angela Bourke, Siobhan Kilfeather, Maria Luddy et al. (eds.), *The Field Day Anthology of Irish Writing, Volume IV Irish Women's Writing and Traditions* (Cork: Cork University Press, 2002), p. 655.

74 Elizabeth Cady Stanton, *The Women's Bible Part 1: Comments on Genesis, Exodus, Leviticus, Numbers and Deuteronomy* (New York: European Publishing Co, 1895). Elizabeth Cady Stanton, *The Women's Bible Part II: Comments on the Old and New Testament from Joshua to Revelation* (New York: European Publishing Co, 1898).

75 PRONI, Mic 590, Reel 5:41, letter from C.J. Longman of Longmans, Green & Co to EGB, 22 November 1922.

76 Pennsylvania State University Libraries, box 1, folder 1, AX/B40/RBM/0039, letter from Longmans, Green & Co to EGB, 8 December 1922.

77 Evelyn Underhill, *The Torch* (April 1924), p. vi. Publication details unknown, copy held in the PRONI, MIC 590, Reel 10:100.

12

Final years

'I am alive, alive, alive,
High tide and sunrise in my mind'[1]

Gore-Booth's religious writings were particularly inspired by her experiences in Italy. Much of her writings after 1920 reflect the time that she spent there. In July 1921, a short article entitled 'A Sketch in Florence,' appeared in *The Flame*, the official journal of the League of Peace and Freedom.[2] This anti-conscription article recounted a visit she made to the Uffizi Gallery in Florence. As she made her way through the streets of the city, Gore-Booth encountered a group of people gathered on the banks of the river Arno. She quickly discovered that the crowd were waiting for the body of a twenty-four year old man to be taken from the river. The man had drowned himself the day before, rather than be conscripted to military service. Gore-Booth recounted this story to illustrate what she termed 'the evil slavery of military life.'[3]

Her interest in Italian language, culture and history had also inspired her to write a novel, 'On Bloodstained Wings.' A work of historical fiction set in 400 AD Italy, which centred on the Barbarian invasion.[4] This is the only novel that she ever wrote. The text, however, is convoluted. The manuscript is handwritten and difficult to read. To date it has not been published.

While in Italy she also planned to write a series of articles for the theosophical journal the *Herald of the Star*. In a letter to her friend Margaret Wroe she explained that she wanted to examine 'fundamental religious instincts ... and analyse these ideas in the different religions.'[5] However, this series of articles never materialised and she returned to Hampstead in 1921.

Gore-Booth's interest in Irish affairs continued to be keen. On her return to England she became particularly aware of the Restoration of Order to Ireland Act, introduced in 1920. The act effectively replaced trial by jury for alleged IRA cases. Those suspected of republican activity would now be tried and sentenced by a military court-martial. Kevin Barry, a nineteen year old medical student from Dublin, was the first person to be sentenced and executed under this system. He had been convicted of killing three British soldiers. He was hanged in Mountjoy Prison on 1 November 1920. By December 1920 martial law had been proclaimed in Counties Kerry, Limerick, Cork and Tipperary. This was extended to cover Waterford and Clare in January 1921. Martial law dictated that all weapons and ammunition in these counties must be surrendered to the authorities. Anyone found in possession of arms would be arrested, tried by court-martial and could face a death sentence. Throughout 1921 the number of executions of Irish men rose at an alarming rate.[6]

In response, Gore-Booth and Roper became secretaries of the Committee for the Abolition of the Death Penalty. This committee was a branch of the League of Peace and Freedom (LPF). The two women sought volunteers to address meetings around England in the hope of pressurising the government to abolish the death penalty altogether. Gore-Booth addressed a meeting of the LPF explaining the basis of the organisation. She began by stating that, 'in the minds of many who have followed the course of events both in this country and in Ireland for the last eight years, new thoughts and questionings have arisen. Fundamental problems of human life have become urgent and imperative as never before.'[7]

Days after her public talk, on 14 June 1921, a young man named Patrick Casey was arrested by a British officer in County Cork. He was searched but no arms were found on his person. However, it was alleged that a Mauser pistol and ammunition found on a window sill nearby, belonged to him.[8] Despite his denial Casey was sentenced to death for possession of a weapon and ammunition. Together with her friend, Clare Annesley, Gore-Booth came to Casey's defence. Writing to the *Manchester Guardian* the women stressed:

> The evidence seems strangely inconclusive to anyone accustomed to the procedure of civil courts. In any case, to carry out a death sentence now for such a technical offence as the possession (not the use of) a weapon is to render futile any effort to bring about a state of feeling in which a peaceable settlement is possible. Surely if the military machine goes on acting without regard to any change in the moral

> atmosphere it is the duty of the civil Government of this country to interfere before is too late. If there is any chance of peace with Ireland all executions must stop.[9]

In this instance it appears that Casey was one of the lucky ones. Although it is not possible to trace what happened to him, it is certain that he was not executed.[10]

Gore-Booth's opposition to the death penalty was not confined to Ireland. By the beginning of 1923, capital punishment became a controversial focus of media attention in England. In January of that year the execution of a young attractive woman, Edith Thompson, generated public horror. Thompson was executed for colluding with her lover, Freddy Bywaters, to murder her husband. Thompson had played no part in the actual murder and she was heard by witnesses screaming 'oh don't' during the attack on her husband. She was, however, executed in Holloway Prison on 9 January 1923. Historian Victor Bailey observes that 'she was hanged for adultery as much as for murder.'[11] Rumours began to circulate that Thompson had a miscarriage on the gallows. She was carried to the scaffold almost unconscious and held over the trap door while the executioner, John Ellis, prepared the execution. Ellis, the same executioner who had conducted the hangings in Mountjoy Prison, was so disturbed by the Thompson case that he retired shortly afterwards and attempted suicide the following year.

A special meeting to consider the abolition of capital punishment was held in London in March 1923. Members of the LPF, the Committee for the Abolition of the Death Penalty and members of the Labour Party attended. Gore-Booth and Roper both addressed the gathering. In her talk entitled, 'The Victim's Friend,' Gore-Booth discussed her experiences as a friend and relative of those condemned to death. Discussing particular cases after the Easter Rising, she described her agony during the three months leading up to the execution of Roger Casement. She pleaded:

> We have done away with the rack and bodily torture, but I am perfectly certain mental torture is just as painful. I do not think anyone has the right to inflict that on another. I think we all ought to realise the extreme of pain that society is inflicting, and because of that we must stop it, not in two, three, four or five years. While we are talking about it, more people are going through this dreadful agony, and their relations and friends are also going through the extremes of agony.[12]

Service, the official organ of the theosophical order of service in Europe, published the proceedings of the meeting. The April issue of the journal was entirely devoted to the cause for the abolition of the death penalty. At their annual conference in June of that year, the Labour Party passed a resolution seeking to abolish capital punishment.[13] The increased focus on the issue led to the establishment of the National Council for the Abolition of the Death Penalty in 1925.

By now Gore-Booth's health was continuing to deteriorate. At the beginning of 1925 she was diagnosed with cancer of the colon. Obviously this news was devastating to Eva and Esther. They agreed not to tell anybody about the terminal illness and instead deal with the situation together. Gore-Booth's appearance seems to have caused some concern to her family and friends. Although she was only 54 years old, she now looked like a much older woman. Yeats visited her during her final illness and he was shocked when he saw her looking weak and old. This image of her was in stark contrast to his memory of that beautiful young woman, the gazelle to whom he had contemplated proposing marriage. Yeats, unaware of Gore-Booth's condition, blamed her demanding political activities for the demise of her beauty. He was later moved to write a poem in memory of the Gore-Booth sisters, describing Eva he pondered,

> I know not what the younger dreams –
> Some vague Utopia – and she seems,
> When withered old and skeleton-gaunt,
> An image of such politics.[14]

During the final eighteen months of her life, Gore-Booth devoted herself almost entirely to writing about religious topics and delivering talks to theosophical societies. She published *The Shepherd of Eternity and other Poems* in 1925. This was to be her last publication during her lifetime.[15] The volume of religious themed poetry includes a picture of a statue from the Lateran Museum in Rome, 'Christ as Hermes,' on the inside cover. The poetry reflects her religious prose work, evident from the titles of poems such as 'The Miracle at Cana,' and 'Eden and Gethsemane.' A poem of particular interest is 'In Praise of Life,' which is an elegy to Sappho. This poem was obviously significant to both Gore-Booth and Roper, an extract 'life that is love is God' from the conclusion, was chosen as the inscription for their joint headstone:

Sappho was right:
Life that is Love is God, and Mercy wise
Is that which never dies –
Life, Love and Light.[16]

During the early months of her illness, Gore-Booth was called to the Kings Bench at the High Court of Justices for jury service. Women had been excluded from jury service at criminal trials in England until January 1921. Reporting on the first day that women were called to serve, a woman juror described the occasion as 'an event of considerable importance in England's judicial history.'[17] However, out of twenty-four women called as jurors at the central criminal court on that first day, ten requested to be excused from service and one woman did not turn up.[18] Gore-Booth also refused to serve on the jury. Responding to her notice with a letter excusing herself on conscientious grounds. She insisted, 'I have a very strong religious objection that makes me unable to find in punishing either capital punishment or prison etc. I cannot take an oath to do something that would be wrong for me to carry out.'[19]

By now Gore-Booth had been a strict vegetarian for many years. For moral issues she did not eat meat. She also remained committed to animal welfare and anti-vivisection causes. She delivered a talk entitled 'The Cry of the Dumb,' to the Tunbridge Wells Theosophical Society during animal week in 1925. The United States had celebrated a 'be kind to animals week' on 13 April for a number of years previously. The decision to hold an animal welfare week in Ireland was announced in *The Irish Times* on 17 February 1925.[20] In May that year the first animal week was held in Dublin and in celebration Gore-Booth gave an address at Tunbridge Wells in Kent. Her talk presents a modern take on issues regarding animal cruelty. In her conclusion she asserts:

> Imagination alone will help people realize that the hunted animal knows the horror of fear, that vivisection is real agony, and that for the majority physical life is nourished on pain, terror and death of millions of creatures with nervous systems of like pattern, though less developed than our own. It is no excuse for us that these animals are cruel to one another. Of course animals are cruel, because they are wanting in that brain power that produces in man the wholly human quality of constructive imagination. Animals have hearts, they can feel. But they cannot think, therefore they do not know pity.[21]

In November 1925 she gave another talk to a Theosophical Society. This time she spoke on 'Re-incarnation and Transmutation in the New Testament,' to her local Hampstead branch. In a letter to her friend T.P. Conwil-Evans she explains that the reasoning behind the paper was to show connections between Christianity and Theosophy.[22] This is the last record of a public speech by Eva Gore-Booth. A few weeks later she became extremely ill and on New Year's Eve she came close to death. She survived and wrote an emotionally charged poem in celebration.

I have come forth from dark distress
Into the singing light again,
The ancient lilt of loveliness
Pours onward flooding through my brain.

A dweller in dim corridors
And caverns of a twilight land,
Now have I found the windy shores,
The living waves, the yellow sand.

Great treasure in my hand I hold,
A bright shell found in that dark cave,
Sea splendour built up fold on fold
By rushing tide and breaking wave.

I run, I sing, I swim, I dive,
I fly along the dawnlit wind,
I am alive, alive, alive,
High tide and sunrise in my mind.[23]

By January 1926 Eva was mainly bed-ridden and Esther nursed her full-time. The two women confided in Esther's brother, Reginald, as to the seriousness of her condition. Reginald had lived with the two women in Manchester when Eva first moved there. He had maintained a close relationship with his sister and Eva over the past twenty-five years. He regularly supported the women with their many political campaigns. Now he moved into their home in Hampstead and helped to nurse Eva. Reginald had never married. He trained as a physical educator and worked for a number of years at Mostyn House Boys School at Parkgate in Chester. He was interested in alternative medicine and had written several books on physical welfare.[24] Reginald provided much needed emotional and practical support for Esther. He was devoted to caring for Eva and alleviated her discomfort through massage.

In possibly the only emotional account ever written by Esther, she describes how after suffering terribly for two days, death came suddenly to Eva. Esther was by her bedside until the end. Eva suddenly looked up at her 'with that exquisite smile that always lighted up her face when she saw one she loved, then closed her eyes and was at peace.'[25] Eva died in the home that she shared with Esther on 30 June 1926. She had just turned 56 years of age the month before.

Constance was unaware of the nature of her sister's illness and she went into shock when a telegraph arrived in Dublin with the news that Eva had died. Grief stricken, she did not attend the funeral, in a letter of condolence to Esther she admitted, 'I simply could not face it all. I want to keep my last memory of her so happy and peaceful.'[26] She sent a wreath of Eva's favourite white and blue flowers.

Reginald witnessed the death certificate on 1 July 1926 at their home, 14 Frognal Gardens, Hampstead. Although Eva described herself as a trade unionist on official documents, Reginald entered her final occupation on the death certificate as 'independent means, daughter of Henry Gore-Booth, Baronet.'[27] The fact that Gore-Booth had been diagnosed with cancer of the colon eighteen months previously meant that there was no need for a post-mortem.

Eva's younger brother and sister, Mordaunt and Mabel, appear to be the only members of the immediate Gore-Booth family who attended the funeral. Her mother, Lady Georgina, stayed at home in Sligo as she was too ill for the journey to London. She outlived her daughter by only a few months, dying the following January. She sent a wreath of sweet pea flowers which was signed simply 'Gaga,' a pet name used by Eva and Constance for their mother.

The funeral service was held on 3 July 1926 at St John's Church, Hampstead. The church was a short walk from Eva and Esther's house. The coffin was carried from the house to the church and after the service it was carried to the churchyard across the road for burial.[28] Eva and Esther had chosen the hymns, 'Holy, holy, holy! Lord God almighty' and 'Jesu, lover of my soul,' to be sung at the service.[29] After the funeral service Mordaunt wrote to his mother describing his concern for Esther. 'The poor thing is quite broken up. She and her brother have been quite admirable all through. The sadness of it really made it worse for them but for Eva it was better.'[30]

Notes

1 EGB, *CE*, p. 604.
2 EGB, 'A Sketch in Florence,' *The Flame*, 2:3 (July–August 1921), 37–8.
3 Ibid, p. 37.
4 PRONI, Lissadell Papers, Mic 590, Reel 8, L/6/2:1–118, manuscript 'On Bloodstained Wings.'
5 Letter from EGB to Margaret Wroe, Villa Angelia, Santa Maria Maggiore, 1920. EGB, *CE*, p. 80.
6 On 14 March 1921, six Irish men were hanged in Mountjoy Prison. Those executed included four of Barry's friends, Thomas Bryan, Patrick Doyle, Frank Flood and Bernard Ryan, who were sentenced to death for attacking an RIC patrol in Drumcondra, Dublin.
7 PRONI, Mic 590, Reel 8, L/5, typescript of lectures given to the League of Peace and Freedom.
8 'Automatic Pistol: Limerick Man Charged with Possession,' *Freemans Journal* (25 June 1921), p. 6.
9 EGB and Clare Annesley, 'Irish Peace and Executions,' *MG* (1 July 1921), p. 4.
10 This case is not to be confused with Captain Patrick Casey who was executed by firing squad on 2 May 1921 in Cork. Casey was arrested in Mitchelstown after a British military patrol was ambushed; he was executed just over twenty-four hours later. For further details see: A.D. McDonnell, *The Life of Sir Denis Henry: Catholic Unionist* (Belfast: Ulster Historical Foundation, 2000).
11 Victor Bailey, 'The Shadow of the Gallows: The Death Penalty and the British Labour Government, 1945–51,' *Law and History Review*, 18:2 (Summer 2000), 305–49.
12 EGB, 'The Victim's Friends,' *Service*, 6:2 (April 1923), 10.
13 *Labour Party Conference Report, 1923* (London: Labour Party, 1923), p. 250.
14 W.B. Yeats, 'In Memory of Eva Gore-Booth and Con Markiewicz,' [sic] *The Winding Stair and Other Poems* (London: Macmillan & Co, 1933), p. 197.
15 EGB, *The Shepherd of Eternity and Other Poems* (London: Longmans Green & Co, 1925).
16 Ibid, p. 16.
17 'The Woman Juror's New Sphere,' *MG* (12 January 1921), p. 7.
18 Ibid.
19 PRONI, Lissadell Papers, MIC 590, Reel 7:35, letter from EGB, 21 April 1925.
20 A picture of speakers at animal week in Dublin, including Gore-Booth's friend Henry Nevinson, appeared in the *Irish Times* (29 May 1925), p. 9.
21 EGB, 'The Cry of the Dumb,' *The Inner Kingdom* (London: Longmans, 1926), pp. 75–6.

22 Letter from EGB to T.P. Conwil-Evans, Hampstead, October 1925, EGB, *CE*, p. 89.
23 Ibid, pp. 60–5.
24 For example: Reginald Roper, *Movement and Thought* (London: Blackie & Son, 1938) and *Physical Exercises for Men* (London: Blackie & Son, 1937).
25 EGB, *CE*, p. 48.
26 Roper, (ed.), *Prison Letters*, p. 311.
27 General Register Office, Hampstead district, DYC 199106, EGB death certificate, 1 July 1926.
28 PRONI, Mic 590, Reel 10, L/9:83, letter from Mordaunt Gore-Booth to his mother Georgina Gore-Booth, 3 July 1926.
29 PRONI, Mic 590, Reel 7, L/3:47–8, funeral leaflet, 3 July 1926.
30 Ibid.

Afterword

'The one thing we can do to honour her is to make her work known and help her to immortality.'[1]

Eva Gore-Booth's obituary appeared in many prestigious newspapers in Ireland, England and America, reflecting the global significance of her political and literary work. The fact that her medical condition had not been public knowledge led many people to speculate that she died suddenly. Evelyn Underhill announced in *The Times* that Gore-Booth's death occurred 'after a short illness.'[2] In her column, Underhill emphasised that Gore-Booth 'will be mourned by many people of very different types.'[3] Indeed, the diversity of her obituary notices animates how she was remembered in various countries for very different reasons. In Ireland she was recalled mainly for her literature. The *Irish Times* lamented that 'by her death Ireland loses a charming poet and essayist, whose work held no mean place in the Anglo-Irish literary movement of the new century.'[4]

In America, it appears that Gore-Booth's connection with the Irish nationalist movement was of most interest to readers. The *New York Times* highlighted the fact that Gore-Booth was the 'sister of Countess Markievicz, Irish Republican.'[5] In contrast newspapers in England praised her social reform work, especially her trade union activity. As well as an obituary notice, the *Manchester Guardian* devoted a half column of 'our London correspondence' to Gore-Booth's memory.[6] The opening section praised her highly successful trade union work, noting how she organised 'barmaids and women attendants in hotels at a time when there was a strong crusade against them on alleged moral grounds, and an attempt made to turn them out of their employment. Miss Gore-Booth addressed meetings of barmaids in many parts, and succeeded in arousing a strong feeling of comradeship among this most individualistic class of workers. The movement to deprive them of their employment was defeated.'[7] The article continued with a detailed account of other successful campaigns led by her:

> Another attempt to interfere with women workers was also checkmated by Miss Gore-Booth when efforts were made to prohibit women gymnasts and other circus performers from appearing in public. On that occasion she interviewed the Home Secretary, Sir Herbert Samuel, with considerable effect. Few people know that it was chiefly due to her that the flower sellers in London were allowed to retain their pitches when the Home Office attempted to improve them out of the streets. It was the keynote of her efforts that women who worked had the same right to their employment as men who worked, and she approached her labour for the suffrage not, as many did, for the side that women had their special activities and responsibilities as women, but that women workers should have the same rights and freedom as men workers.[8]

The London correspondent also stresses that 'Mrs. Pankhurst's decision to leave her millinery business and give her whole energies to the women's suffrage cause,' could be attributed to Eva Gore-Booth.[9]

While Eva's loss was felt in the literary world and among social reformers, her loss was felt most profoundly by those in her personal life. Constance never recovered from her sister's death. She wrote to Esther describing how she longed 'to sit in the room where she [Eva] lived and worked again.'[10] She travelled to London in September 1926 and stayed with Esther hoping to feel close to her departed sister. Markievicz's arrival in London coincided with the release of an article on Gore-Booth written by R.M. Fox and printed in the *Millgate Monthly* magazine.[11] Fox, a historian, and husband of Irish author Patricia Lynch, was a close friend of Gore-Booth's. He had visited her shortly before her death and was moved to write an article in celebration of her life. Fox provides perhaps the clearest explanation as to why Eva and Constance had such a close sisterly bond, even though their life goals appeared so very different. He explained that 'the gap dividing the sisters is much smaller than many realise, though they seem at opposite poles. Both were rebels against all that they regarded as mean and unworthy. Their passionate, selfless sincerity drove them in different directions. One came out of the smoke and flame and handed her revolver to the commanding officer when the rebels surrendered; the other was a militant pacifist.'[12] Fox later dedicated a chapter on Gore-Booth and one on Markievicz in his anthology *Rebel Irishwomen*.[13]

Recognising the importance of honouring Eva's memory, Constance wrote to Esther stressing that 'the one thing we can do to honour her is to make her work known and help her to immortality here in this world through the ideals she lived for.'[14] With this in mind Roper embarked on what would become a lengthy task to publish the remainder of Gore-Booth's work. Esther showed her devotion to Eva even after her death. She gathered manuscripts of plays, notebooks of poetry and books containing lecture notes. Within months Roper oversaw publication of the final poems written by Gore-Booth. The volume of mainly religious poetry, *The House of Three Windows*, was published by Longmans.[15] This volume was closely followed by publication of a compilation of Gore-Booth's short prose essays, *The Inner Kingdom*, which included transcripts of her final talks given to the Theosophical Society branches in Hampstead and Tunbridge Wells.[16]

Constance Markievicz returned to Dublin during the winter of 1926. She was still devastated by the loss of Eva, although her pain was somewhat eased from knowing that she had been loved and cared for by Esther. Recognising the intensity of Eva and Esther's deep emotional bond, she wrote to her cousin, Esther 'is wonderful, and the more one knows her, the more one loves her, and I feel so glad Eva and she were together and so thankful that her love was with Eva to the end.'[17]

Gore-Booth's will went to probate on 21 January 1927, she left £4,262 12s. According to her wishes, Roper received her entire estate and was appointed as literary executor. In that capacity, Roper continued to publish Gore-Booth's literature. In 1927 she oversaw publication of *The World's Pilgrim*. This extraordinary volume consists of a series of imaginary conversations between various religious and philosophical characters such as Buddha, Pythagoras, Francis of Assisi and Lazarus.[18] The loss of Eva continued to have an effect on Constance, whose own health deteriorated during 1927. In June of that year she fractured her arm in two places while cranking her car. In July she became ill during a Fianna Fáil party meeting and was brought to Sir Patrick Dun's hospital in Dublin. Markievicz insisted on entering a public ward. She was operated on for appendicitis but her health deteriorated further over the coming days.

Constance had developed complications, she now had peritonitis. Fearing for the worst, hospital staff called for her friends. Esther Roper was instantly contacted in London. She travelled to Dublin on the next boat. Esther maintained a vigil by Constance's bed with the rest of her friends including Kathleen Lynn, Helena Moloney and Maria Perolz. Constance's estranged husband Casimir and her stepson, Stanislas, arrived from Warsaw. Roper was back at home in Hampstead when she heard that Constance had died on 15 July 1927; she instantly returned to Dublin for the funeral. Constance had outlived her sister by only one year. A Catholic bible was found by her bedside, it was inscribed in her own hand 'to Mother and Eva 1927 – They are not dead, they do not sleep. They have awakened from the dream of life.'[19]

After Markievicz's funeral, Esther returned to London and began arranging a memorial in honour of Eva. She commissioned a stained glass window from Sarah Purser's workshop in Dublin, An Túr Gloine (the tower of glass). This seemed most appropriate as Purser had remained a close personal friend of Eva and Constance since she had painted their portrait as children in Lissadell. The mosaic and stained-glass artist, Ethel Rhind, worked from Purser's studio. Esther commissioned Rhind to design and make the window. Rhind was a distant relative of Eva's and in 1907 she had installed a stained-glass window, 'Harmony and Fortitude,' in the Lissadell estate church in Sligo. Now she designed a religious themed window with the inscription 'I have sought the hidden beauty in all things,' the first line from Gore-Booth's poem, 'The hidden beauty.' A portrait of Gore-Booth's face was incorporated into one of the images of the design. The window was installed in the Round House, Every Street, Ancoats, in the building where Gore-Booth held her poetry classes for the University Settlement, Manchester.

The window was unveiled at a special ceremony on 11 June 1928. Roper delivered a speech at the unveiling, a transcript of which was published along with a picture of the stained-glass window, as a Manchester University Settlement Paper.[20] In her speech Esther described how Eva, 'studied and wrote, travelled and met many interesting people, but in spite of it all, I do not think she was very happy. She seems to have been haunted by the thought of the suffering of the world and to have had a curious feeling of responsibility for its inequalities and injustices.'[21]

Roper continued working on Gore-Booth's publications and in

1929 she published a complete edition of her literature. This was an immense task, the exhaustive work culminated in a large compilation totalling 654 pages. The volume contained a complete edition of Gore-Booth's published and previously unpublished poems as well as three of her plays. Esther also included remarkable personal material. She contacted a number of Gore-Booth's friends and colleagues and asked them for their recollections. She wrote a biographical introduction of Gore-Booth, including her memories and those of her friends. She also included a section of letters written by Gore-Booth to three of her friends, Clare Annesley, Margaret Wroe and T.P. Conwil-Evans. The volume comprised previously unpublished material by Gore-Booth, such as her only autobiographical piece, 'The Inner Life of a Child.' The final publication, *Poems of Eva Gore-Booth: Complete Edition*, constitutes a wonderful memorial to Gore-Booth's life and literature.

While she was working on this edition, Roper also taught European history. She began teaching at Pinehurst School, which was run by her friend Helen Neild. Gore-Booth had written a play for Neild to perform in 1907 and she later dedicated the publication of *The Sorrowful Princess* to her. While she was working on Gore-Booth's publications, Roper became quite ill. In April 1928, Neild included a note in the *Pinehurst Newsletter*, notifying students that influenza caught Miss Roper and 'she very nearly slipped away from us and is still only frail.'[22]

Roper was not deterred and she published Gore-Booth's play *The Buried Life of Deirdre* in 1930. In the introduction she notes that Gore-Booth wrote this play between the years 1908–1912 and began to illustrate each scene herself with ink drawings during the winter of 1916–17 (see Figure 16 for an example illustrated page by Gore-Booth). According to Roper, Gore-Booth intended to illustrate the entire play before sending it for publication. Originally the play was entitled 'The death of Deirdre' and it is safe to assume that the publishers saw this as too harsh a title for publication. Longmans included copies of the twelve handwritten pages of text which Gore-Booth had illustrated, in their printed edition. There was a limited edition print of 256 copies of the play produced. Gore-Booth wrote a dedication in 1918 to E.G.R. (Esther Gertrude Roper).

When it was published Roper sent Sarah Purser a copy and asked her to approach Yeats about producing it at the Abbey Theatre in Dublin. The Irish Free State established since 1922 recognised the

16 Handwritten, illustrated page from *The Buried Life of Deidre* by Eva Gore-Booth

importance of the Irish cultural movement. The Abbey was now a state subsidised national theatre. It would be an honour for an Irish playwright to have their work performed there. Yeats, as a founder of the theatre held considerable decision making powers regarding performances. He responded to Purser harshly that the play was 'quite unsuitable for the Abbey. I suggest that you read the play your self. Backed with your powerful commendation I have no doubt "The Gate" would give it every attention.'[23] Yeats may well have recalled the disastrous first attempt to produce Gore-Booth's play *Unseen Kings* at the Abbey. Her Celtic revival plays often included complex dramatic effects which caused production concerns. The Abbey Theatre prided itself on a naturalistic approach to dramatic productions. In contrast, the Dublin Gate Theatre Studio, founded in 1927 by Hilton Edwards and his partner Micheál MacLiammóir adopted an imaginative style for the stage set and costumes for their productions. The current Gate Theatre was established in 1930, the year that the *Buried Life of Deirdre* was published.

Purser sent Roper Yeats' letter and wrote to her almost bemused by his response, 'I don't know what Yeats means by my "powerful commendation."' She explained that it was most unlikely that the Gate would produce this play, the fact that they were a new venture meant that they 'are very hard up & can't risk a failure.'[24] Instead Purser promised to speak with Lennox Robinson, the manager of the Abbey, directly. Although Markievicz's biographer, Anne Marreco, maintains that the Independent Dramatic Company performed *The Buried Life of Deirdre* in December 1911 she does not identify the theatre and there is no record that the play was ever performed.[25]

Roper's final publication in 1934 was a complete edited volume of Markievicz's prison letters to Gore-Booth. The volume is a unique publication and includes a biographical sketch of Markievicz, as well as copies of official documentation relating to her arrest and court-martial after the Easter Rising. The letters begin in 1916 and include letters sent from Mountjoy, Aylesbury, Holloway and Cork prisons as well as from the North Dublin Internment Camp and unofficial letters smuggled from prisons or sent during her time on the run. There was an abundance of letters between the sisters but unfortunately the letters sent from Gore-Booth to Markievicz were accidentally destroyed. Markievicz treasured her letters above all else, when she was in prison she carried them about her person wrapped in a handkerchief. Before she died, Constance bequeathed the letters to Esther but before she got possession of them they were destroyed. Esther published the book as a mark of respect to Constance but she also used it as a space to once again showcase Eva's literature. A section of the book is dedicated to her poems of Easter week and includes Gore-Booth's emotional account of Dublin in the aftermath of the Easter Rising. Receipts from the publishers, Longmans, confirm that Esther self financed the publication.[26]

By the time that *Prison Letters* was published in 1934 Roper's health was weak. When finally illness overcame her, her brother moved in with her, as did her friend from the Manchester trade union days, Beatrice Collins. Esther Roper died of heart failure on 28 April 1938, in her and Eva's home in Hampstead. The women had arranged to be buried together. Eva and Esther now lie in a single plot at St John's churchyard (see Figure 17). As in life, they are together in death.

Notes

1 Letter from Markievicz to Roper in Roper, (ed.), *Prison Letters*, p. 314.
2 Evelyn Underhill, 'Miss Eva Gore-Booth,' *The Times* (7 July 1926), p. 11.
3 Ibid.
4 'Miss Eva Gore-Booth,' *The Irish Times* (1 July 1926), p. 6.
5 'Eva Gore-Booth,' *The New York Times* (2 July 1926), p. 19.
6 'Death of Miss Eva Gore-Booth,' *MG* (1 July 1926), p. 5.
7 'Our London correspondence: Miss Eva Gore-Booth,' *MG* (1 July 1926), p. 8.
8 Ibid.
9 Ibid.
10 Letter from Markievicz to Roper, (ed.), *Prison Letters*, p. 313.
11 R.M. Fox, 'Eva Gore-Booth: Poet, Pacifist, and Lover of Humanity,' *Millgate Monthly*, 11:252 (September 1926), 706–10.
12 Ibid, p. 708.
13 R.M. Fox, *Rebel Irishwomen* (1935; Dublin: Progress House Pub Ltd, 1967).
14 Roper, (ed.), *Prison Letters*, p. 314.
15 EGB, *The House of Three Windows* (London: Longmans Green & Co, 1926).
16 EGB, *The Inner Kingdom* (London: Longmans, 1926).
17 Letter from Markievicz to Mrs. L'Estrange in Roper, (ed.), *Prison Letters*, p. 315.
18 EGB, *The World's Pilgrim* (London: Longmans, 1927).
19 As cited in Anne Haverty, *Constance Markievicz*, p. 229.

20 Pictures of the Round House after 1928 clearly show Gore-Booth's memorial window at the front of the building (see figure 5). In 1963 the University Settlement moved out of the Round House, which was by then in need of extensive repairs. In 1986 the council demolished the building. The current whereabouts of the stained-glass building are unknown. On a visit to Manchester in 2010 the author met with Manchester Settlement Trustee, Derek Clarke, to ascertain the current whereabouts of the stained-glass window. After extensive enquiries Clarke was unable to locate the window and it now seems most likely to have been accidentally destroyed or it was unsalvageable due to vandalism.

21 Esther Roper, *Eva Gore-Booth: An Address given at the Unveiling of a Window Placed in her Memory in the Round House* (Manchester: Manchester University Settlement Papers. No. 1, 1928), p. 2.

22 Helen Neild, *Pinehurst Newsletter* (26 April 1928).

23 Richard Haworth, private collection, letter from W.B. Yeats to Sarah Purser, undated. A copy of this letter was very kindly given to the author by the owner, Richard Haworth, grandson of Elizabeth MacGowan (Mrs Alfred Haworth), who organised the Ancoats Elizabethan Society with Gore-Booth at Manchester University Settlement. Richard Haworth is brother to Giles Haworth, who supplied a manuscript of the play *Fiametta* by Gore-Booth.

24 Richard Haworth, private collection, letter from Sarah Purser to Esther Roper, 22 December 1930.

25 Anne Marreco, *The Rebel Countess: The Life and Times of Constance Markievicz* (Philadelphia: Chilton Books, 1967), p. 137.

26 PRONI, Mic 590, Reel 10, L/16:13/14/26, receipt from Longmans Green & Co to Roper; £100, 21 March 1934; £50, 3 April 1934.

17 Joint grave of Eva Gore-Booth and Esther Roper at St John's Churchyard in Hampstead

Archival sources

Bodleian Library, University of Oxford, UK: The John Johnson collection, an archive of printed ephemera.
British Library, London, UK: Rare books and manuscripts.
Fawcett Library, London Metropolitan University, UK: Teresa Billington-Greig papers; feminism serials and organisations collection.
Glasgow Women's Library, Scotland, UK: Periodical archive, *Urania*.
John Rylands Library, Manchester, UK: Katharine Tynan collection; *Manchester Guardian* archives; suffrage collection.
Lancashire Public Record Office, UK: Papers of Selina Jane Cooper of Nelson.
Lissadell Estate, Sligo, Ireland: Lissadell Collection.
London School of Economics & Political Science, UK: Archives and periodicals library, *Urania*.
Manchester Archives and Local Studies Central Library, UK: Fawcett manuscripts; photographic archive.
McMaster University, Canada: Bertrand Russell archives.
National Archives of Ireland, Dublin: Online census records of Ireland 1901 & 1911.
National Archives, Kew, UK: Census records of England 1861–1901; Home Office registered papers; Colonial Office Record Series, Dublin Castle Special Branch Files.
National Library of Ireland, Dublin: Hanna Sheehy-Skeffington papers; Patricia Lynch and Richard Fox papers; Constance Markievicz papers; Easter 1916 papers; ephemera; periodical and newspaper collections.
Parliamentary Archives, Houses of Westminster, UK: David Lloyd George papers.
Pennsylvania State University Libraries, USA: Rare Books and

Manuscripts, Eva Gore-Booth collection.

People's History Museum, Manchester, UK: Labour history archives.

Public Records Office Northern Ireland, Belfast: The Lissadell papers; Annesley papers.

Sligo County Library, Ireland: Gore-Booth family collection; photographic archive.

St John's Churchyard, Hampstead, London, UK: Grave and headstone records.

Trinity College, Dublin, Ireland: Record of manuscripts for sale by Peter Eaton, London, 1969.

University College Dublin, Ireland: Special collections, Eva Gore-Booth collection.

University of Birmingham, UK: Church Missionary Society archive.

University of Manchester Archives, UK: University of Manchester publication records; University Settlement papers.

University of Notre Dame, Indiana, USA: Rare books and periodicals.

University of Reading, Berkshire, UK: Longmans Green & Company archive.

Working Class Movement Library Archives, Manchester: Annual reports of the Women's Trade Union Council; Women's Trade and Labour Council Records; No-Conscription Fellowship papers.

Major publications by Eva Gore-Booth

Poetry

Poems, London: Longmans Green & Co, 1898.
The One and the Many, London: Longmans Green & Co, 1904.
New Songs: A Lyric Selection made by AE from poems by Eva Gore-Booth and others. Dublin: O'Donoghue & Co, 1904.
The Egyptian Pillar, Tower Press Booklets, Series 2, No. 3, Dublin: Maunsel, 1907.
The Agate Lamp, London: Longmans Green & Co, 1912.
The Perilous Light, London: Erskine MacDonald, 1915.
Broken Glory, Dublin: Maunsel, 1917.
The Shepherd of Eternity, London: Longmans Green & Co, 1925.
The House of Three Windows, London: Longmans Green & Co, 1926.
Poems of Eva Gore-Booth: Complete Edition, Esther Roper (ed.), London: Longmans Green & Co, 1929.

Plays

Unseen Kings, London: Longmans Green & Co, 1904.
The Three Resurrections and the Triumph of Maeve, London: Longmans Green & Co, 1905.
The Sorrowful Princess, London: Longmans Green & Co, 1907.
The Death of Fionavar from the Triumph of Maeve, London: Erskine Macdonald, 1916.
The Sword of Justice, London: Longmans Green & Co, 1918.
The Buried Life of Deirdre, London: Longmans Green & Co, 1930.
The Plays of Eva Gore-Booth, Frederick S. Lapisardi (ed.), California:

Mellen Research University Press, 1991.

Fiametta: A Previously Unpublished Play by Eva Gore-Booth, Sonja Tiernan (ed.), New York: Edwin Mellen Press, 2010.

Prose

A Psychological and Poetic Approach to the Study of Christ in the Fourth Gospel, London: Longmans Green & Co, 1923.

The Inner Kingdom, London: Longmans Green & Co, 1926.

The World's Pilgrim, London: Longmans Green & Co, 1927.

Pamphlets and booklets

Women Workers and Parliamentary Representation, Manchester: Lancashire and Cheshire Women Textile and other Workers' Representation Committee, *c* 1905.

Women's Wages and the Franchise and Certain Legislative Proposals, Manchester: Manchester, Salford and District Women's Trade and Labour Council, 1906.

Women's Right to Work, Manchester: William Morris Press, 1906.

Is the Case Urgent? Manchester: National Industrial and Professional Women's Suffrage Society, *c* 1910.

Whence come Wars? London: Women's Printing Society, 1914. (A speech delivered to the National Industrial and Professional Women's Suffrage Society on 12 December 1914).

Religious Aspects of Non-Resistance, Bishopsgate: Headley Brothers Printers, 1915. (A paper read at the conference upon the pacifist philosophy of life, Caxton Hall, London, 8 and 9 July 1915).

The Tribunal, London: National Labour Press, *c* 1916.

Rhythms of Art, League of Peace and Freedom Pamphlet, London: The Pelican Press, 1917.

Political articles

'The Place of Peace,' *New Ireland Review*, XI, May 1899, p. 176.

'Fair Pay for Women,' *The Women's Tribune*, 1906.

'Women and Politics: A reply,' *Nineteenth Century*, March 1907, pp. 472–6.

'The Women's Suffrage Movement among Trade Unionists,' in Brougham Villiers (ed.), *The Case for Women's Suffrage*, London:

T. Fisher Unwin, 1907, pp. 50–65.

'Women's Suffrage and the French Revolution,' *Academy*, 14 September 1907, p. 909.

'Women's Suffrage and the French Revolution,' *Academy*, 28 September 1907, p. 957.

'Women and the Suffrage: A reply to Lady Lovat and Mrs. Humphry Ward,' *Nineteenth Century and After*, September 1908, pp. 495–506. (Reprinted as a pamphlet by the National Industrial and Professional Women's Suffrage Society).

'Women and the Nation: the workers III – "no trades for women,"' *The Englishwoman*, 5:2, 1909, pp. 507–17.

'An Equitable Adjustment,' *The Common Cause*, 30 September 1909, p. 432.

'Running a Suffrage Candidate,' *The Common Cause*, 25 November 1909, p. 432.

'Women's Wages and the Law of Supply and Demand,' *Nineteenth Century and After*, August 1914, pp. 384–93.

'Women and Trade Unionism,' *Nation*, 31 July 1915, p. 573.

'The Sinn Fein Rebellion,' *The Socialist Review*, August–September 1916, pp. 226–33.

'For God and Kathleen Ni Houlihan,' *The Catholic Bulletin*, VIII, 1918, pp. 230–4.

Literary contribution to periodicals

'To May,' *Longman's Magazine*, 26:154, Aug 1895, pp. 380–3.

'Fingerposts,' *The Yellow Book*, X, Jul 1896, pp. 214–17.

'The Place of Peace,' *New Ireland Review*, X1, May 1899, p. 176.

'Dialogue – Ass and Snake,' *Longman's Magazine*, 35:205, Nov 1899, pp. 36–9.

'A Heretic's Pilgrimage,' *New Ireland Review*, 12:4, Dec 1899, p. 214.

'The Queens Flight,' *Longman's Magazine*, 35:208, Feb 1900, p. 350.

'A Monk's Lament for Maeve,' *Longman's Magazine*, 38:228, Oct 1901, p. 558.

'Harper's Song of Seasons,' *Living Age*, 237:320, 2 May 1903.

'Maeve of the Battles,' *Longman's Magazine*, 42:249, Jul 1903, p. 235.

'Lament for Fionavar,' *Longman's Magazine*, 43:255, Jan 1904, p. 242.

'Roads of Cloonagh,' *Living Age*, 242:128, 9 Jul 1904.

'Reincarnation,' *Living Age*, 242:448, 13 Aug 1904.
'Maeve of the Battles,' *Living Age*, 238:704, 12 Sept 1904.
'Nera's Song,' *Longman's Magazine*, 45:268, Feb 1905, p. 242.
'Beyond,' *Dial*, 40:330, 16 May 1906.
'Poverty,' *Dial*, 40:329, 16 May 1906.
'Little Waves of Breffny,' *Current Literature*, 50:559, May 1911.
'Romance of Maeve,' *Literary Digest*,' 46:600, 15 Mar 1913.
'Walls,' *Literary Digest*,' 46:600, 15 Mar 1913.
'Reading given before the Irish Literary Society on Jan 20th by Miss Eva Gore-Booth,' *The Irish Book Lover*, VI, Feb 1915, p. 111.
'Little Waves of Breffny,' *Literary Digest*, 53:420, 19 Aug 1916.
'Little Waves of Breffny,' *Country Life*, 31:40, Dec 1916.

Contributions to religious and pacifist periodicals

'The Battle of the Stars,' *Occult Review*, 24, Aug 1916, p. 83.
'To CA,' *Occult Review*, 26, Jul 1917, p. 35.
'The Little Girl's Riddle,' *Occult Review*, 28, Aug 1918, p. 72.
'Consider the Lilies,' *Occult Review*, 29, May 1919, p. 266.
'The Two Roads,' *Herald of the Star*, 8, Nov 1919, pp. 514–19.
'The Sense of Something Wrong,' *Herald of the Star*, l9, Mar 1920, p. 110.
'The Messengers,' *The Flame*, 1:1, Mar 1920, p. 7.
'The Sense of Something Wrong,' *Herald of the Star*, 9:3, Mar 1920, pp. 110–16.
'The Just and the Unjust,' *The Venturer*, 1:7, Apr 1920, pp. 249–54.
'The Messengers II,' *The Flame*, 1:3, May 1920, p. 31.
'Evolution,' *The Flame*, 1:5, Jul 1920, pp. 53–4.
'The Shepherd of Eternity,' *Occult Review*, 32, Aug 1920, p. 81.
'Santa Maria Maggiore,' *Occult Review*, 34, Jul 1921, p. 8.
'A Sketch in Florence,' *The Flame*, 2:3, Jul–Aug 1921, pp. 37–8.
'The Victim's Friends,' *Service*, 6:2, Apr 1923, pp. 9–10.
'The Well where the World ends,' *Occult Review*, 41, Mar 1925, p. 148.
'Art and Peace,' *Service*, 4:1, Jan 1926, pp. 8–11.
'The Love that is God in the First Epistle of St. John,' *Friends' Quarterly*, Oct 1950, pp. 209–19.

Index

Note: page numbers in *italic* refer to illustrations